QUICKSILVER WAR

WILLIAM HARRIS

Quicksilver War

Syria, Iraq and the Spiral of Conflict

OXFORD
UNIVERSITY PRESS

OXFORD

UNIVERSITY PRESS

Oxford University Press is a department of the
University of Oxford. It furthers the University's objective
of excellence in research, scholarship, and education
by publishing worldwide.

Oxford   New York
Auckland   Cape Town   Dar es Salaam   Hong Kong   Karachi
Kuala Lumpur   Madrid   Melbourne   Mexico City   Nairobi
New Delhi   Shanghai   Taipei   Toronto

With offices in
Argentina   Austria   Brazil   Chile   Czech Republic   France   Greece
Guatemala   Hungary   Italy   Japan   Poland   Portugal   Singapore
South Korea   Switzerland   Thailand   Turkey   Ukraine   Vietnam

Oxford is a registered trade mark of Oxford University Press
in the UK and certain other countries.

Published in the United States of America by
Oxford University Press
198 Madison Avenue, New York, NY 10016

Library of Congress Cataloging-in-Publication Data is available
William Harris.
Quicksilver War: Syria, Iraq and the Spiral of Conflict.
ISBN: 9780190874872

Printed in the USA on acid-free paper

To the memory of my aunt, Barbara Elizabeth Harris, former science librarian of the University of Canterbury, Christchurch, New Zealand. Barbara was always quietly supportive.

And to Afife, Chris, Adam, and Hadi.

CONTENTS

CONTENTS

LIST OF MAPS

ABBREVIATIONS

AKP	Adalet ve Kalkınma Partisi/Justice and Development Party (Turkey)
CIA	Central Intelligence Agency
EU	European Union
FSA	Free Syrian Army
IRG	Islamic Revolutionary Guard (Iran)
ISI	Islamic State in Iraq
ISIS	Islamic State in Iraq and Syria (/al-Sham)
ISSG	International Syrian Support Group
KDP	Kurdistan Democratic Party
KNC	Kurdish National Council
KRG	Kurdistan Regional Government
LCC	Local Coordinating Committee (Syria)
MİT	Milli İstihbarat Teşkilatı/National Intelligence Organization (Turkey)
NATO	North Atlantic Treaty Organization
NCC	National Coordination Committee (Syria)
NDF	National Defence Forces (NDF)
PKK	Partiya Karkerên Kurdistanê/Kurdistan Workers' Party (Turkey)
PMF	Popular Mobilization Forces (Iraq)
PUK	Patriotic Union of Kurdistan
PYD	Partiya Yekîtiya Demokrat/Democratic Union Party (Syria)
SDF	Syrian Democratic Forces
SNC	Syrian National Council

TIMELINE

SOHR	Syrian Observatory for Human Rights
SOMO	State Oil Marketing Organization (Iraq)
SRF	Syrian Revolutionaries' Front
TOW	(Tube-launched, optically tracked, wire-guided) American anti-tank missile
UNSC	United Nations Security Council
YPG	Yekîneyên Parastina Gel/Peoples' Protection Units (Syria)

TIMELINE FOR CRISES AND WAR
IN SYRIA AND IRAQ, 2011–2017

2011

Syria

6–20 March: Arrests, protests, clashes in Dera'a inaugurate Syria's slide.

18 March: 'Friday of Dignity' protests across Syria against Dera'a crackdown.

30 March: Bashar al-Assad's 'if battle is imposed ... welcome to it' speech.

30 May: First open resort of protesters to weapons against regime live fire.

March–June: Regime releases batches of Sunni Islamist and jihadist prisoners.

July–August: Shift to Sunni insurgency, Jisr al-Shughur clashes, FSA emerges.

September: Turkey and West back regime change.

November: Rebels take Baba Amr suburb in Homs.

Iraq

Through the year, rising Sunni Arab discontent with marginalization under Nouri al-Maliki's Shi'a Arab-dominated government. Abu Bakr al-Baghdadi's jihadist ISI pursues recovery. Iraqi Sunni Arabs encouraged by Syrian Sunni uprising.

TIMELINE

December: Sunni vice-president al-Hashimi flees after murder charges.

2012

Syria

January: Jabhat al-Nusra jihadists appear as offshoot of Iraqi ISI.
February: Regime uses heavy weapons to break Baba Amr resistance.
              Sectarian divide hardens, Sunni rebels vs. Alawite core of regime.
May: Houla massacre of Sunni villagers.
June: First Geneva conference proposes regime transition.
July–August: Major rebel advances in Damascus, Aleppo, and rural north.
Rest of year: Regime leaves north-east to Kurds, resorts to air power.
              Iran organizes new NDF militia to boost regime.
December: Saudi-organized Croatian weapons given to rebels.

Iraq

ISI slowly escalates murder campaign against police and security forces, subverts tribes in Sunni Arab provinces. Strengthened by new resource base in Syria, and Iraqi Sunni anger at Syrian regime repression. Beginning of Iraqi Shi'a militia movement to Syria to back Bashar al-Assad.

December: Raid on home of Sunni finance minister provokes wave of protests.

2013

Syria

Winter 2012/13: Regime achieves stalemate in Damascus, Aleppo.
March: Rebels take first provincial capital—al-Raqqa.
April: Nusra jihadists break with ISI.
                Baghdadi turns ISI into new jihadist ISIS—rebels his first target.
May–June: Lebanese Hezbollah helps regime to take al-Qusayr.

August: Sarin gas attack against Damascus rebel suburbs.
September: Massacre of Alawites in Latakia hills by rebels.
August–October: ISIS assaults rebels from al-Raqqa to Idlib.
November: Islamist rebels form Islamic Front to face ISIS.
                          Non-Islamist rebels form SRF.

Iraq

After months of Sunni protests, Iraqi army attacks agitators in Hawija in April. Thereafter, violence across Sunni Arab provinces becomes an insurgency. ISIS aspires to be focus of Sunni Arab rebel campaign to carve out territory for itself.

July: ISIS jihadists arrange jailbreak by 1,000 prisoners.

2014

Syria

January–February: Farcical Geneva II rebel–regime 'peace talks'.
January–March: Rebels and Nusra expel ISIS from north-west Syria.
May: Regime recovers Homs old city.
May: ISIS takes upper hand over rebels in Deir al-Zor province.

Iraq

January: ISIS and tribal allies seize Falluja and raid elsewhere in al-Anbar.
April: ISIS–Iraqi army stalemate in al-Anbar province.

Syria–Iraq

June–July: ISIS takes most of Sunni Arab Iraq and eastern Syria. Iraqi army temporarily shattered.
                 ISIS leader Baghdadi declares 'caliphate'.
August: ISIS massacres Iraqi Yazidis, pushes towards KRG.
                 USA compelled to launch bombing, containment of ISIS.
                 Haydar al-Abadi becomes Iraqi prime minister.

September: USA bombs ISIS in Syria after ISIS beheads US hostages. KRG holds lines beyond KRG, including Kirkuk, Mosul dam.

ISIS attacks PYD Kurds in Kobani, northern Syria.

October: Nusra subdues SRF factions in north-west Syria. PMF repels ISIS south of Baghdad. US air power supports Kobani Kurds against ISIS.

December: Iraqi army fails against ISIS in Baiji refinery. Kurds expel ISIS from Sinjar hills.

2015

Syria–Iraq

February:	Hezbollah–Syrian regime Quneitra offensive fails.
March:	Syrian rebels advance in Dera'a, capture Busra al-Sham.
	Turkey, Saudi Arabia back Islamist–Nusra–FSA alliance.
	Alliance takes Idlib town from Syrian regime.
	PYD Kurds push ISIS out of whole Kobani area.
	Iraqi army–PMF combine expels ISIS from Tikrit.
April:	Syrian rebels take Jisr al-Shughur.
May:	ISIS takes Ramadi in Iraq, Palmyra in Syria.
May–June:	Rebels expand Idlib acquisitions.
June:	PYD Kurds achieve territorial continuity in north-east Syria.
July:	Assad admits incapacity to hold all lines against rebels.
September:	Russia begins bombing rebels to resuscitate regime.
Oct. 2015–Jan. 2016:	Russia, Iran enable limited regime advances.
October:	Iraqi army, PMF remove ISIS from Baiji
November:	KRG expels ISIS from Sinjar.
	Turkey downs Russian plane near Syrian border.
	Turkish–Russian relations slide.

December:	UNSC resolution 2254 for Russia–US backed Syria peace plan.

2016

Syria–Iraq

January–February:	Iraqi army without PMF recovers Ramadi.
February:	Syrian regime, Shi'a militias cut rebel Aleppo from north.
	PYD Kurds extend Afrin canton eastwards.
	Russian-sponsored 'cessation of hostilities' in Syria.
March:	Russia announces force draw-down in Syria.
April:	Russia and the Syrian regime resume bombing in Aleppo.
April–December:	Syrian regime advances in Damascus suburbs.
May–July:	Iraqi army without PMF recovers Falluja.
May–August:	PYD Kurds take Manbij from ISIS.
	PYD (as partially Arab SDF) consolidates partnership with USA.
	PYD aims to complete Turkish border continuity to Afrin.
June:	Turkey repairs relations with Russia.
July–August:	Syrian regime imposes east Aleppo siege, rebels break siege.
Aug. 2016–Feb. 2017:	Turkish advance to al-Bab in northern Syria.
September:	Syrian regime reimposes east Aleppo siege.
October:	Iraqi army, PMF, KRG begin campaign to remove ISIS from Mosul.
November:	Iraqi parliament legitimizes Shi'a PMF as an official army force.
Oct.–Dec.:	Regime, Russia and militias assault east Aleppo, force capitulation.
Nov. 2016–Mar. 2017:	PYD Kurds backed by USA advance towards ISIS-held al-Raqqa.
December:	Evacuation of Syrian rebels and civilians from east Aleppo to Idlib.

> Turkey, Russia look to reconcile their interests in western Syria.

2017

Syria–Iraq

January: Russia, Turkey and Iran sponsor Syrian regime–rebel military talks.
Iraqi army takes eastern Mosul from ISIS.

January–April: Syrian regime cuts across Turkey south of al-Bab.

March–May: PYD Kurds and SDF Arabs approach al-Raqqa via Tabqa dam.

February–July: Iraqi army roots ISIS out of western Mosul.

April: First US bombing of Syrian regime after gas attack against rebels.

May: Russia, Turkey and Iran negotiate de-escalation zones in western Syria.

May onwards: Competition to fill ISIS space in eastern Syria. US-supported PYD Kurds and SDF Arabs enter ISIS-held al-Raqqa.

Syrian regime starts push towards ISIS-held Deir al-Zor.

Regime encroaches on PYD–SDF, and US reacts by downing regime plane.

US and Russia cooperate on regime–rebel de-escalation in south Syria.

US opposes regime–Iran bid for command of Syria–Iraq border.

NOTE ON TRANSLITERATION

This book adopts a stripped-down version of the system used in the *International Journal of Middle East Studies* for representing Arabic words in Latin script. There are no diacritical marks, except apostrophes signifying ayn and hamza in the middle of words. At the ends of words, any 'yy' doubling is reduced to a single 'y'. Some names of prominent personalities are in forms common in the Western media, for example Abadi instead of al-Abadi and Assad instead of al-Asad. In these cases, the definite article 'al-,' which features in many Arab family names, is dropped when using stand-alone surnames or assumed names. I have also adopted common media renderings for such well-known terms as al-Qaeda and Lebanese Hezbollah. The collective word Shi'a stands for this community and its members in all circumstances, whether as noun or adjective.

ACKNOWLEDGEMENTS

Many people have helped with this book. First, I thank Michael Dwyer and Jon de Peyer, publisher and executive editor of Hurst & Company for their steadfast support and commitment. Hurst production director Daisy Leitch displayed epic care and patience in coping with my stream of corrections and making sure of a great product, together with the typesetters Prerana Patel and Sathi Patel. I am similarly indebted to Mary Starkey for her outstanding work as copy-editor, and her assiduous pinpointing of textual flaws. Sebastian Ballard transformed my rough sketching into an excellent set of maps. Robin Briggs created a superb index that effectively services a complex Middle Eastern story. I acknowledge the constructive advice of two anonymous referees; I have done my best to accommodate their recommendations.

I would like to give special mention to Fouad Ajami, a brave leader in Middle Eastern studies whose passing in 2015 was a huge loss. Fouad encouraged my work.

At the University of Otago, I am grateful to Janine Hayward, head of the Politics Department, for her backing, Kate Davis, Sharon Pine, and Shelley Morgan for their help as departmental administrators, and colleagues for an always congenial environment. Conversations with Eduardo Aboultaif, Leon Goldsmith, Mouhannad and Ahmad Taha, and Nigel Parsons (Massey University) assisted with fine-tuning the book.

At Middle East Technical University (METU or ODTÜ) in Ankara, I thank Meliha Altunışık, Özlem Tür, and Murat Tınas for their kind help and hospitality. Jonathan Curr and Taha Macpherson were most welcoming at the New Zealand embassy in Turkey, and William and

ACKNOWLEDGEMENTS

Kathy Hale were wonderful hosts in Istanbul. I am grateful to Stephanie Brancaforte, Glenn Johnson, and Steve Gordon for their really helpful input. Also in Turkey, I am much indebted to Turks and Syrians who would probably wish to remain anonymous.

Lisa Martin, Aziz Weysi, Pushtiwan Ahmad, Markus Bickel, and Detlev Mehlis opened doors for me to have a memorable experience of Kurdistan-Iraq, at a critical time in late 2014. In Irbil (Hawler), I am also obligated to Falah Mustafa, Dlawer Ala'aldeen, and Angus MacKee for giving their time to talk with me.

I thank Markus Wiener for the opportunity to trial thoughts on Syrian developments, 2011–2014, in the 2015 edition of *The Levant: A Fractured Mosaic*.

In the end, the book would have gone nowhere without the support of my wife Afife and our sons Chris, Adam, and Hadi. The cost has been the hours I have stolen for the work and writing, especially as it is not the first time.

Dunedin, October 2017

INTRODUCTION

In mid-November 2014, a Kurdish Peshmerga commander invited me to join his small convoy headed for the precariously perched military outposts on the front with the Islamic State in Iraq and Syria (ISIS) at and around the Mosul dam in northern Iraq. Once there I was able to get as far as a hilltop outlier on the western side of the Tigris river. In those days, ISIS probed the front at night. The 12 mile (20 kilometre) access route from Kurdistan Regional Government (KRG) territory was entirely exposed to the 'caliphate' in the direction of Mosul city. Our evening return in the dark proceeded at best possible speed on a dilapidated road; the atmosphere was tense, with no one saying a word. We were acutely aware that ISIS had updated capability thanks to its seizure of much of the Iraqi army's American equipment.

In the overall setting of the Syria–Iraq conflict zone this little corner illustrated both the kaleidoscopic character of contestation across the Fertile Crescent and how far matters had divaricated in the three and a half years after the street uprising in Syria in the spring of 2011. On the one hand, there was a clear line from Dera'a in 2011 to the Mosul dam in 2014. Bashar al-Assad's firestorm galvanized Islamist fanatics in northern and eastern Syria, the almost defunct Islamic State in Iraq (ISI) reached across the border to take advantage of a new Syrian base, and foreign jihadist recruits flowed into Syria via a lenient Turkey at a steadily rising rate. ISI became ISIS, which took advantage of the man-power and resources that its expanding presence in eastern Syria added to its Iraqi capacity in order to surge to Mosul and challenge the KRG Kurds. Of course, the contestants on this spin-off front were new and

1

different compared with the original collision in Syria between the Assad regime and substantially secular but largely Sunni Arab street protesters. The decisive feature that connected the 2011 regime–opposition scene in Syria to the 2014 Kurdish–ISIS scene in Iraq was the double boost ISI/ISIS received from Syria's implosion and the porous Syrian–Turkish border. This feature integrated two scenes widely separated in time, space, and character into a constantly reconfiguring and mutating Quicksilver War.

Contours of the Quicksilver War

What of the big picture? In 2011, the Syria of President Bashar al-Assad and its eastern neighbour, the new Iraq patronized by the Americans after their demolition of Saddam Hussein's apparatus in 2003, both entered trajectories towards implosion. The circumstances were independent, but the trajectories intersected and the two countries became a common arena of violence by 2014. In the Syrian case, mismanagement, repression, and complacent arrogance on the part of the ruling clique provided a setting receptive to emanations from the overthrow of the Tunisian and Egyptian autocrats in early 2011. In Iraq, a tight parliamentary election in March 2010 led the executive prime minister, Nouri al-Maliki, to turn decisively to his majority Shi'a Arab co-religionists to reboot his leadership after a forced deal with rivals in December 2010. Maliki had no intention of honouring the deal; instead, he reinforced his personal authority over the government and the new Iraqi military primarily at the expense of Sunni Arabs. The latter had only just been detached from the jihadist religious extremism that had accompanied the American occupation after 2003.

A renewed Shi'a–Sunni breakdown in Iraq became confirmed by December 2011, when the United States withdrew its last troops and Maliki's administration had Sunni vice-president Tariq al-Hashimi charged with murder a day later. Whereas in Syria a street upheaval in the dusty southern town of Dera'a in mid-March escalated into wider turbulence within days, in Iraq there was a more gradual deterioration through 2011, driven from within the corridors of power before it later overtook the Sunni Arab street.

The purpose of this book is to interpret the ongoing crises across Syria and Iraq from their onset in 2011 through their coalescence by

2

2014 to the complex scenery of geopolitical fracturing and foreign entanglement in 2017. The two modern countries make up the bulk of the so-called Fertile Crescent, a term the American archaeologist James Breasted proposed in 1916.[1] The Fertile Crescent refers to the arc of modestly watered lands fringing the Syrian desert, reaching from the Mediterranean coast across the north Syrian plain to the Tigris–Euphrates river system. It expresses the shared physical environment and cultural diversity of the two countries. Assertion and negation of diversity have been a substantial part of the story of the crises and warfare since 2011. The Fertile Crescent embraces Syria and Iraq in an overarching geography that has also become an overarching war zone.

The book title *Quicksilver War* refers to a shape-shifting pattern of interlinked conflicts across Syria and Iraq, encompassing multiple parties, theatres, interventions, and phases. The overall conflagration has constantly evolved in terms of balances of advantage, the prominence of this or that front or theatre, and the impact of outside powers. Actual warfare began when elements in the Syrian opposition, spearheaded by army deserters, took up weapons against the relentless regime military crackdown against street protestors in mid- to late 2011. In Iraq, the initial manifestation was sporadic Sunni Arab insurgent activity against the security forces in west central Iraq in 2012, which at first had no connection to events in Syria.

Syria and Iraq began to come together when Iraqi Shi'a militias crossed to Damascus to reinforce a briefly tottering Syrian regime in late 2012, and Iraqi Sunni jihadists entered Syria to take advantage of newly available spaces in 2012–13. After June 2014, the ISIS jihadists established their bellicose 'caliphate' occupying eastern Syria and western Iraq. For a while, it raided in all directions. In 2015–16, after ISIS peaked, Iraqi Shi'a warlords increased their contribution to propping up the Syrian regime in western Syria, with a crucial role in the final regime–Russian offensive in Aleppo in late 2016. Their Iranian patrons of course had strategic aspirations across both Iraq and Syria, coexisting uneasily with Russia in Syria and with the US reappearance in Iraq. With all the criss-crossing, Syria and Iraq could be considered, for a time at least, an integrated war zone.

Analysis of Syria and Iraq together, however, does not mean that they have been equal sources and stages of events. From the triggering of the crisis in Dera'a in Syria in March 2011, the primary dynamic played out in Syria. The life-and-death struggle between the Syrian regime and those whose main purpose was to displace it led and dwarfed everything else. The ISIS that we have did indeed originate in Iraq, but its particular scale, reach, and character has derived from the bonanza of resources, new territory, and access to recruits that simply would not have existed without Bashar al-Assad's military firestorm across Syria in 2011–14. Without the Syrian crisis alongside it, Iraq may well have muddled through Nouri al-Maliki's sectarian provocations. Bashar al-Assad, impresario of the firestorm, carries heavy responsibility not only for the physical wrecking of Syria but for derivative damage much further afield.

Short of the World Wars, there are few modern precedents for the Quicksilver War across Syria and Iraq, involving so many participants and shifting fortunes, and with such diverse international involvements. Two comparisons come to mind. First, the succession of wars in the former Yugoslavia between 1990 and 1999, from Slovenia to Croatia–Serbia to Bosnia to Kosovo, was easily equivalent in its twists, turns, and intricate phasing. The Yugoslav wars, however, lacked the multi-sided foreign interference that has characterized the Syria–Iraq arena. Russia could not and did not wish to exert itself for Serbia as it did twenty years later for Assad. Second, within the Middle East, the fifteen-year war period in Lebanon between 1975 and 1990 had similar complexity to Syria–Iraq, but on a lesser geographical scale. Some features of the Lebanese crisis might prove indicative for the future, specifically in Syria. Lebanon showed that an apparent victory or settlement might turn out to be nothing more than another phase in a conflict that has more dark chapters ahead. In 1983, many felt that Lebanon was on the way to stabilized government and reconstruction, but in late 1983 and 1984 it all fell apart again. Then, when Hafiz al-Assad's Syria finally registered its advantage in 1990, after another six years of various conflicts, some of the leading characters at the end of the story could not even have been imagined at the outset in 1975: Hezbollah and General (now President) Michel Aoun, for example.

Comparison and commonalities with other cases assist understanding but, as with any particular case, the Syria–Iraq war arena also stands apart, including from Lebanon's war. Syria and Iraq share a unique modern legacy that Lebanon was lucky enough to avoid: Ba'athist Arabism brutalized their politics and warped their cosmopolitan societies into the early twenty-first century. Ba'athism, meaning Arab 'resurrection', was a heady cocktail of European-style nationalist chauvinism and socialist zeal mixed together by two Syrian students at the Sorbonne in Paris in the early 1930s. Under Saddam Hussein in Iraq and the Assads in Syria, Ba'athism became the ideological justification for secular Arab nationalist tyranny in their two countries. It fostered a culture of absolutism and intolerance that also provided a hothouse environment for Islamist religious extremism. Ba'athist Syria and Iraq produced paranoid mafioso security machines that repressed non-Arab identities and manipulated Islamic movements and sectarian sentiment. Both targeted their substantial Kurdish populations with ferocious Arabization.

Saddam Hussein, who had never shown a trace of religious commitment, cynically turned to militant Sunni Islam as a prop for his regime in the 1990s. The future ISIS 'caliph', Abu Bakr al-Baghdadi (really Ibrahim Awwad al-Badri from the northern Iraqi town of Samarra), took a Ph.D. from the Saddam University for Islamic Studies.[2] For his part, Bashar al-Assad of Syria patronized murderous Sunni jihadists as tools against his Arab neighbours—against Lebanon, Jordan, and the US-promoted new Iraq. In the late twentieth century, Lebanon had plenty of misfortunes with communal jealousies and external intrusions, but not the monstrous additional load of totalitarian Ba'athism.

Like other complex, multi-player regional conflicts, the Quicksilver War of Syria and Iraq since 2011 provides insight into the agency of personalities in pivotal positions, the implications of stressed ethnosectarian identities, and the interplay of states, both with one another and with a range of semi- and sub-state actors. This book explores these topics. It weighs structure and agency in the crisis, following the hypothesis that although Syria and Iraq have been conditioned by their histories we would have nothing resembling the Quicksilver War without Bashar al-Assad of Syria. It examines the inflammation of Sunni–Shi'a, Sunni–Alawite, and Arab–Kurdish divides. It surveys the geopolitics of the wartime fragmentation of Syria and Iraq. Among the jostling post-2011 entities, the Syrian and Iraqi regimes have operated rump states; the Kurdistan Regional Government (KRG) in Iraq has been termed a 'quasi-state';[3] the ISIS 'caliphate', contracting through 2017, might be labelled a pseudo-state; and the Syrian Kurdish cantons and assorted Syrian Sunni Arab opposition bailiwicks are sub-states. Apart from the regimes and KRG, all have come out of wartime circumstances, and it remains to be seen what will survive the war period.

The book also provides an opportunity to refer to concepts of 'proxy war' and 'failed state'. These terms have been thrown about carelessly in relation respectively to the so-called Syrian civil war and the modern Syrian and Iraqi states. In popular understanding, 'proxy war' implies that local combatants are principally agents of external sponsors. It is true that local parties can service Russian president Vladimir Putin in resuscitating Russia as a global power, or the Iranian theocrats in their version of Persian imperialism, or the USA in rolling back jihadist terrorism. The local parties, however, equally look to manipulate erstwhile patrons and play among competing foreigners in servicing their own agendas of domination, survival, and geopolitical revisionism. The Syrian regime views Russia and Iran through this lens, and Turkey's mildly Sunni Islamic oriented government miscalculated in conceiving in 2012–13 that jihadist tigers might converge against the Syrian regime. Western adoption of the 'proxy' concept has not helped serious comprehension of the arena.[4] In addition, obscuring the power of local agency through terming the crisis a 'proxy war' risks devaluing the criminal responsibility of local agents.

As for 'failed states', if this means effective regime collapse then it has not happened to Syria and Iraq. The regimes and their state machinery have continued in substantial territories, including the capitals, and in mid-2017 would be better described as resurgent states. The Syrian security agency (*mukhabarat*) 'deep state' persists. At least up to 2014, it conducted its curious interactions with jihadists far more adroitly than Turkey managed in the same years. Indeed, in the Kafkaesque modern Middle East, where state success means successful repression, state terrorism, and mafia-style predation, Bashar al-Assad looks healthily viable in mid-2017.

Moving to the scale of events, the Quicksilver War has been the leading regional and international conflict of the early twenty-first century. In Syria, there were at least 350,000 deaths from violence between March 2011 and late 2016,[5] to which one can add 100,000 in Iraq in the same period, overwhelmingly after the ISIS shock in June 2014.[6] This is double the toll in Iraq between US entry in 2003 and departure in 2011, triple the toll in Bosnia in the 1990s, and triple the toll in the entire history of Arab–Israeli hostilities. In Syria, the direct war deaths are moving towards or even beyond 2 per cent of the whole population, and the proportion is obviously much higher for young adult males. In addition, out of a 2011 population of about 22 million, around 5 million Syrians fled the country as refugees up to late 2016 and at least 6 million were internally displaced. This alone is unprecedented since the demographic upheaval in the Indian subcontinent in 1947. For Iraq, one might add 1.5 million people who fled majority Sunni Arab central and northern provinces to Kurdish-controlled territory during the ISIS offensive in mid-2014.

Beyond such numbers, it is worth briefly outlining the Middle Eastern and global repercussions of the prostration and at least temporary fracturing of two major Arab states. Syria and Iraq together occupy a salient location at the core of the great continental landmass of Eurasia and Africa—the 'world island' of Halford Mackinder's early twentieth-century geopolitics.[7] They sit amid four hypersensitive regional powers—Turkey, Iran, Saudi Arabia, and Israel—each of which is intimately concerned with what happens and what others are doing in this large intervening space. As for the great powers, the West worries about the future of Iraq's oil reservoir, among the five largest in the world, and about spillover of refugees and jihadist terror—particularly from Syria. Russia has sustained the Syrian regime to compel the USA and the rest of the West to concede to Russian influence in the eastern Mediterranean. For Moscow, this is the near south and continuation of a 'great game' dating back to the nineteenth century and competition between the Tsarist and British empires.

Overall, Syria and Iraq presented a quadruple international challenge, especially after mid-2014: competing geopolitical interests among regional and global players; sectarian rupture between Sunnis and Shi'a, both within and beyond Syria and Iraq; rampant Sunni Islamic jihadist fury against enemies 'near' and 'far'; and a humanitarian catastrophe. In mid-2014, the ISIS jihadists seized the centre of the war zone and top billing in the world media, although this did not give them real top significance in the war. Their ersatz 'caliphate' based in al-Raqqa (Syria) and Mosul (Iraq) threatened the Iraqi regime, the Kurds of Syria and Iraq, and anyone else who got in their way, by mid-2014 intermittently including the Syrian regime as well as Syrian rebels. They massacred non-Sunnis and 'apostate' Sunnis, and beheaded American and British hostages. The reluctant Obama administration mobilized a dozen Western and Arab countries in a limited US-led bombing campaign to contain ISIS. Meantime, Iran pursued strategic ambitions across Iraq and Syria to Lebanon and the Mediterranean, provoking widespread Sunni Arab hostility. Iran's Russian ally, looking to retain options across the Sunni Arab world, tried to steer clear of this Iranian project.

As for the humanitarian challenge, in 2015 the stream of Syrian refugees heading towards Western Europe swelled into a flood. A million or so Syrians with the means to pay smugglers could no longer tolerate wasting their lives in Jordan, Lebanon, or Turkey, or in holding out fatuous hopes for a new Syria. Facing refugees, ISIS jihadist infiltration, and mobilization of some European Muslim citizens by the new terrorist entity, the Germans, French, and others suddenly had to be nice to Turkey, which held the European front line. Some Europeans feared incorporating Turkey into the European Union, and had stalled the supplicant 'candidate member' at the gates. Now they wanted Turkey to hold back Syrians and Iraqis, to block transit of Europeans turned rogue, and generally to serve as EU border guards. Turkey thereby acquired levers, and President Recep Tayyip Erdoğan did not hesitate to flaunt them. The Quicksilver War impact on Europe and Turkish–European relations well illustrated its international reverberations.

Chapter progression

It is not my intention to give a comprehensive, blow-by-blow account of developments across the Fertile Crescent since March 2011. After a broad, integrated overview of the war zone, I select particular dimensions for deeper study: the Kurdish situation and Turkish embroilment.

Chapter 1 discusses the overall trajectory up to mid-2014, including the internal dynamic towards war in Syria, external interventions, sectarian and jihadist trends, and the explosive fusion of Syrian and

8

Iraqi affairs in 2014. I argue several propositions. First, Syrian president Bashar al-Assad bears substantial responsibility for the crisis in Syria, its conversion into warfare, and the fertile setting offered for *takfiri* jihadism. Second, external powers extended the mess that they gravitated into, but they would not have had serious traction without Assad's role—their part was derivative. Third, the Syrian rebels threw away their chances through fratricide. Nonetheless, they exhibited sustained resilience, indicating that they really did have serious backing among Syrian Sunni Arabs. Fourth, the opportunity for Sunni jihadist inflation in eastern Syria was crucial to the June 2014 ISIS coup in Iraq.

Chapter 2 surveys the evolution of the intertwined Syrian and Iraqi crises after June 2014. It suggests the crystallization of two interacting war theatres: western Syria, where the Syrian regime faced assorted rebels; and eastern Syria combined with western Iraq, where the new ISIS pseudo-state confronted everyone. The chapter interprets increasingly radical external interventions. After mid-2014, the USA led a coalition in an aerial offensive against ISIS in Iraq and Syria. In 2015, Turkey and Saudi Arabia accelerated arms deliveries and other support to rebels in western Syria, provoking new Iranian infusions of foreign militiamen to stiffen the regime and a direct Russian aerial offensive against the rebels. I end with the crowded landscape of 2017, with Turkey, Russia, and Iran collaborating, competing, and trying to steer western Syria, while ISIS falls apart in Iraq and eastern Syria.

Chapter 3 takes up the Kurdish situation in the north of the war zone. War came to the Kurds of Syria simply as a consequence of being in Syria, and to the Kurds of Iraq borne by the ISIS tornado out of eastern Syria and Sunni Arab Iraq, exposing the divergence between the Kurds of Syria and Iraq. I explore the assets and deficiencies of the Kurds of the two countries in war-zone circumstances. Many of them looked to the fluidity around them as an opportunity for consolidating both self-rule and territory.

Chapter 4 dissects Turkey's role as a regional power abutting the battlefield, a situation different from those of the USA, Russia, Saudi Arabia, and Iran. Turkey has had to cope with a spillover of refugees and violence as well as trying to influence the course of events. My review concentrates on the latter, exploring Turkey's pursuit of regime change in Syria, treatment of border issues with jihadists and Syrian

Kurds, and promotion of preferences in northern Iraq. Between 2011 and 2017, Turkey certainly registered itself in the war zone, but fell short of matching ends to means. Policy and results through the whole period reflected the capricious agency of Prime Minister, then President, Recep Tayyip Erdoğan, as channelled by realities in the war zone and within Turkey. Policy under the pious conservative Justice and Development Party/Adalet ve Kalkınma Partisi (AKP) government of Turkey has had an Ottoman-style Sunni Islamic flavour, implying outlooks regarding Syria and Iraq different from Kemalist, secularist outlooks. The working out of policy strikingly echoes Byzantine circumstances on the same frontier.

A brief epilogue attempts to look ahead from the configuration of the war zone in mid-2017. Are Syria and Iraq returning to separate tracks? What will be the balance in the middle ground—eastern Syria? What looks to be emerging from the interplay of Russia, the USA, Iran, and Turkey?

Sources

My leading single documentary reference for following developments in Syria and Iraq has been consultation of a range of mainstream Arabic newspapers on a regular basis since early 2011. As is obvious from the notes to chapters, my principal recourse has been to the international London-based Arabic dailies *al-Hayat* and *al-Sharq al-Awsat*. Both are Saudi owned, which I have always kept in mind, but both are also sensitive about credibility as newspapers 'of record'. In addition, I have found the leading Lebanese dailies *al-Nahar* and *al-Safir* useful from time to time. In terms of simple reporting of events, there is little to choose among these publications. For Turkey, I have put considerable effort into acquiring a reading knowledge of Turkish sufficient to follow developments in Turkish news outlets. My leading sources here have been the Turkish-language independent centrist daily *Cumhuriyet*, which has had trouble with the AKP government, and the English-language *Hürriyet Daily News*.

Apart from the Arabic and Turkish press, I have also gone through a large accumulation of human rights reports (Amnesty International, Human Rights Watch, UN Human Rights Council, and Siege Watch, for example); international media commentaries; and think-tank papers (the Carnegie Middle East Center, the Institute for the Study of War, and the Rubin Center, for example). I have generally not gone to the more partisan Syrian internet and social media sites for the book, although the Arabic-language Syrian opposition site All4Syria has—ironically—been useful for following the profligate fratricide among opposition factions.

I have been fortunate in opportunities to talk with Turkish officials in Ankara and on the Syrian border, and with KRG officials and Peshmerga officers on visits to northern Iraq. As indicated, I was able to go to the Kurdish front line while in Iraq in late 2014. I have not been able to do the same in Syria; from my experience of war in Lebanon I know the value of direct observation.

Expanding secondary literature, especially on the Syrian crisis, has, of course, affected my treatment of the war zone. First, combined with the documentary sources noted above, it has provided a backdrop of information on the course of events that has helped me to evolve my own understanding. Second, it has nudged me towards a relatively concise summary approach to phases and to players and their performances, and to an emphasis on post-June 2014 developments. For 2014–17, I believe that Syria and Iraq should be considered together, and not just regarding ISIS; to date, the emerging literature has not really done this. In short, my book is an attempt both at a generally accessible synthesis and at striking out in a new direction.

My bibliography has the full references for the excellent new literature that I have come across, mainly books but including internet pieces and some salient academic journal articles. For penetrating accounts of the Syrian road from Ba'athist despotism to Hobbes's 'state of nature', see the books of Abboud, Ajami, Wieland, and Yassin-Kassab and al-Shami. For encyclopaedic coverage of the disintegration of the Syrian opposition and the increasing hold of jihadism, see Lister. For analysis of the Syrian ruling clique and the fortunes of the regime's Alawite constituency, read Goldsmith, the Kerr–Larkin collection, and Lesch. For foreign involvements in Syria consult Phillips. Iraq is much less surveyed for these years: books on ISIS by Gerges, McCants, Weiss and Hassan, and Stern and Berger address the Syria–Iraq interface while focusing on the largest and nastiest jihadist entity. Allsopp and

Gunter provide perceptive analysis of the Syrian Kurdish situation. As regards analysis available on the internet check, for example, Al-Tamimi, Khaddour, Lund, and Spyer. In the journal article literature, see Demirtaş-Bagdonis's biting critique of AKP Turkey's projection of grandeur, Stansfield's thoughtful overview of Iraq in 2014, and the clinical realism of both Natali's analysis of the KRG and Leenders' dissection of 'how the Syrian regime outsmarted its enemies'.

1

THE WAR ZONE TAKES SHAPE, 2011–2014

In any typology of wars, the Quicksilver War metastasizing across the Fertile Crescent from 2011 onwards would certainly register as a fluid and complex hybrid. It emerged out of a street uprising that became a civil war in Syria that then mutated into a wider dual-theatre regional conflict filling the whole space between Mediterranean Syria and Iraqi Kurdistan. It has featured a menagerie of players at state, proto-state, and sub-state levels; it has combined irregular, siege, and conventional hostilities; and it has manifested potent religious and group-identity drivers. The war has showcased a bizarre collection of confrontations: the Syrian regime against rebel factions; rebels against one another; jihadists against almost everyone else; Sunnis against Shi'a; and Kurds against Arabs and Turks. These contests have been intertwined, but also semi-autonomous. The resolution of any of them does not imply the termination of the others.

One can suggest a number of historical and modern regional conflicts with similarly complex attributes: the wars for Italy, 1494–1559; the revolt of the Netherlands against Spain, 1565–1609; the Thirty Years War, 1618–48; the 1848–9 uprisings in Austria and Hungary against the Habsburg monarchy; and, as noted in the introduction, the late twentieth-century wars for Lebanon and the former Yugoslavia.[1] A mixture of state and non-state participants has not been unusual, and religious and ethnic sentiments have often featured. What was notable

13

about the Syria–Iraq arena up to 2017 was that through almost six years of turmoil and foreign patronage of local participants, the six states involved in major hostilities (the Syrian and Iraqi regimes, Russia, Iran, the USA, and Turkey) avoided direct inter-state warfare. All rounds of fighting pitted states against non-state or sub-state parties, or were among these latter parties. However, there have been inter-state incidents: Turkey–Syrian regime on several occasions between 2012 and 2014, Turkey–Russia in 2015, and USA–Syrian regime in 2017. The story has a way to go.

Perhaps most obviously, borrowing the terminology of the wars of the Spanish and Austrian successions, the war for Syria that has also become a war for the Fertile Crescent is the war of the Ba'athist succession. The Arab nationalist 'resurrection' autocracies of the Assads and Saddam Hussein leave a long shadow over Syria and Iraq, and the former anticipates resuscitation courtesy of Russia and Iran.

Syria as epicentre

In its origins and development towards warfare in 2011–12, the Syrian crisis that began in March 2011 and enveloped Iraq by June 2014 had virtually no connection with the Iraqi crisis associated with the Anglo-American occupation of that country in 2003. Because of the chronological order and the close proximity in time it is tempting to conflate these two Middle Eastern disasters as if Iraq after March 2003 somehow created the conditions for Syria in 2011. Such conflation has no serious justification. The relevant setting for the 2011 Syrian crisis that became a war across both Syria and Iraq was above all else the domestic environment in Syria, largely insulated from the post-2003 turmoil in Iraq. Yes, external events contributed to the chain reaction that began in the neglected southern Syrian town of Dera'a in March 2011, but the so-called Arab Spring revolutions in Tunisia and Egypt provided the relevant wider context—not an Iraq that was relatively pacified in early 2011.

As the Syrian crisis intensified, the fortunes of the virulent Sunni jihadism entrenched in Iraq after 2003 came to depend on the new depth that Syria offered it. First, the Syrian regime's releases of jihadist prisoners in 2011, its escalation of violence mainly against Sunni Arab civilians, its demonization of opposition as religious fanaticism, and its détente with apocalyptic jihadists while it concentrated on destroying opponents who might get international endorsement, all fostered jihadist inflation. Second, the fragmentation of the Syrian opposition, the bitterness of Syrian Sunni Arabs about global indifference, and Arab oil-state backing of Islamist absolutists perfected Syria as a jihadist hothouse. Between the founding of Jabhat al-Nusra (the Support Front) as the Syrian franchise of al-Qaeda in January 2012 and appropriation of the Syrian city of al-Raqqa by ISIS in late 2013, the jihadist centre of gravity shifted from Iraq to Syria. Jihadists and hardline Islamists competed among themselves across Syria, constricting the rest of the Syrian opposition, while ISIS built a Syrian base that critically facilitated its blitz in Iraq in mid-2014.

Beyond jihadist affairs, Syria's primacy related to the priority attention the breakdown of the country attracted from Middle Eastern and world players. Russia and Iran determined to salvage the Syrian regime, their long-standing and principal Arab ally. For both powers, a commanding position in Syria was crucial to projection of influence into the eastern Mediterranean and into the core of the Arab world, challenging Western pre-eminence. In contrast, Turkey and Saudi Arabia championed Syria's Sunni Arab majority and its impetus towards regime change as their own self-assertion. Otherwise, Israel, Jordan, and Lebanon, like Turkey and Saudi Arabia, the immediate neighbours of Syria, all stood to have their strategic environment transformed by warfare and outcomes in Syria. Only the USA had a clearly superior interest in Iraq, a legacy of its involvement there between 2003 and 2011, and it was in a recessionary mood regarding the Middle East. For Shi'a theocratic Iran, US elevation of the Iraqi Shi'a Arab majority put Baghdad in its pocket by 2011, and the real game shifted westwards. Compared to Iraq, Syria had a lesser oil reservoir but a pivotal strategic location for a wider range of external powers.

Having introduced Syrian precedence in today's Syria–Iraq war zone, this chapter surveys the origins and dynamics of the interlocking post-2011 crises in the two countries and traces their evolution from 2011 into the catastrophe of our times by 2014.

QUICKSILVER WAR

Blaming structures: Imperialism and Ba'athism

Were Syria and Iraq artificial products of early twentieth-century European imperialism doomed to fail in blood and fury at some point in their post-colonial evolution? It is true that in the early 1920s France and Britain cobbled together the two states as conglomerates of wholes and parts of former Ottoman provinces after defeating the Ottoman Empire in the First World War. These conglomerates each encompassed various ethnic, sectarian, and tribal groups that might not cohere well, though both had substantial Arab Muslim majorities.

Both new countries were technically mandates from the new international organization, the League of Nations, granted to France and Britain to guide towards independence. This cover for domination reflected the strategic and commercial interests the Middle East held for the two powers. In Syria, France initially played on religious differentiation of Sunni Muslims, Alawite and Druze Shi'a Muslim offshoots, and Christians among the Arab population, as well as on fracturing in the emerging bourgeoisie. French behaviour as a high-handed mandatory authority, and an infusion of political ideologies from 1930s Europe, also encouraged intolerance and authoritarian attitudes of extreme left- and right-wing varieties. Nonetheless, by the late 1930s France more or less accepted Syrian Arab nationalism, and thereafter Syria's evolution became more a responsibility of domestic actors and other powers active in the Middle East.

In Iraq, Britain created an entity characterized by sectarian cleavage between Shi'a and Sunni within the Arab majority, and containing a large, geographically compact Kurdish-speaking minority uncomprehending or unenthusiastic about 'Iraq'. Britain played on the self-awarded right to rule of the elite of a Sunni Arab minority of around 20 per cent. Apart from imposing a treaty legitimizing its strategic military bases, Britain then pulled back from a technically independent Iraqi kingdom in 1932, when Iraq became a member of the League of Nations.

Any French and British responsibility for the trajectory of these countries after Syria acquired its independence in 1945 should be carefully qualified. Syria and Iraq emerged in the mid-twentieth century as functioning multi-communal entities with the potential for rich, cosmopolitan futures. Their futures were certainly not preordained at that point. The only alternative on offer after the Ottoman defeat was an overarching Arab kingdom in the Fertile Crescent and the Arabian Peninsula, contested between Hashemite princes and bourgeois Arab nationalists, and highly vulnerable to collapse into sectarian, ethnic, and city-state fragments. Whatever their self-interested manipulations, France and Britain ended up presiding over a middle-way solution, probably more viable and useful for the Arab majority than either a super-state or disintegration into mini-states. Further, too much has been made of 'artificial' boundaries; any separation of a state in Mesopotamia, centred on Baghdad, from its counterpart in the northern Levant, centred on Damascus, necessarily involved arbitrary lines in the Syrian steppe.

Structural features bequeathed by the French and British Mandatory regimes to a degree compromised the two countries after 1945, though modestly more competent management could have compensated. In Syria and Iraq, the dominant trading, land-owning, and office-holding upper bourgeoisie was tainted by its effective acceptance of the Mandatory dispensation. It was also threatened by the new, restive lower middle class emerging out of extended elementary education, spearheaded by new local military forces, and infected with the European socialist and fascist ideologies of the 1930s. Complacency, regressive social attitudes, and poor leadership through the 1950s, however, could not all be blamed on Europe. Events exhibited new momentum in new directions as fractious, conservative regimes with poorly representative parliaments in Syria and Iraq failed to stand up to the new state of Israel, failed to satisfy popular expectations, and failed to corral resentful army officers. Military coups, Cold War and nationalist pressures, and alternations between demonstrations and crackdowns provided opportunities for leftists and Arabists to mobilize followers and to infiltrate the officer corps.

In Syria and Iraq, the primary beneficiary of the turbulence of the Cold War decades from 1950 to the 1980s was the Arab nationalist and semi-socialist Ba'ath Party. Founded in Damascus in 1943 by the Syrians Michel Aflaq (Orthodox Christian) and Salah al-Din al-Bitar (Sunni Muslim), the party established a branch in Baghdad in 1951. Its main long-term advantage over Communist, Nasserite, and Syrian Social Nationalist competitors was its combination of clandestine organizational strength, indigenous inspiration, fervent Arabism, and penetration of the military. All the others were weak in one or other of these dimensions. The Ba'ath did well in general elections in Syria in 1954, and had no problem with participation in coalitions when this was useful, but it tended to authoritarianism and intolerance of political diversity. In Syria, its civilian leadership stampeded the country into a disastrous 1958 union with Egypt that fell apart in 1961. Thereafter, despite the prominence of civilians in the 1963 military-supported Ba'athist coup, the military wing of the party gained the ascendancy, confirmed in a second coup displacing civilians and non-Ba'athists in 1966. In Iraq, the 'civilians', including the gun-happy young enforcer Saddam Hussein, maintained control of party organs as the Ba'ath manipulated clever connections within the military to seize the state in the double coup of 1968. It leveraged, then subjected, its military allies, and gave sanctuary to party founder Michel Aflaq, who had fled Syria. From the late 1960s, the army-dominated Syrian party and the 'civilian'-led Iraqi Ba'ath detested each other until Bashar al-Assad made up with Saddam Hussein after 2000.

The Ba'athist triumph gifted Syria and Iraq decades of tyranny, termed 'security and stability' (al-amn wa al-istiqrar). Both countries endured clan-based autocracies wielding ideological absolutism, malignancy of a different order from the standard republican and monarchical authoritarianism of the late twentieth-century Arab world. Strongmen swiftly emerged in the Ba'athist milieu to establish family firms: Saddam Hussein in Iraq in the late 1960s, and Hafiz al-Assad in Syria in 1970. Subordination of the party, however, went together with rigorous deployment of the party apparatus and ideology to regiment society. Beyond demanding acquiescence, other Arab regimes, such as the oil principalities and the Egypt of Nasser, Sadat, and Mubarak, were not so concerned with reordering the lives and thoughts of their populations. Ba'athist Syria and Iraq imposed dogmatic Arabism and forced students, labour unions, and professional associations into a corporatist leader-worshipping framework redolent of Benito Mussolini's fascism and George Orwell's 1984.

Although the Iraqi regime had to acknowledge that Kurds existed it worked to crush them, while the Syrian regime outlawed any idea of communities based on religious sects and, like Iraq, strove to Arabize non-Arabs. Hydra-headed secret police machines monitored Syrians and Iraqis for any sign of dissent, backed by networks of informants and a terrifying array of torture chambers. Everyone knew, of course, that regime denial of sectarian identity was a sham; both Saddam and the Assads ultimately depended on family and clan loyalties in their own communal minorities: Sunni Muslims in Iraq and Shi'a-derived Alawites in Syria. The regimes resorted to bribery, divide and rule, and cultivation of hostility to Zionism and the West across the general population while they also played on minority fears of displacement in case of regime change. Iraq only exited Ba'athism and Saddam's dictatorship in 2003 through Anglo-American invasion and occupation. As for Syria, the Ba'athist regime entered its second half-century in 2016, clinging on in Damascus despite five years of the most destructive domestic conflict experienced by any modern Arab state.

In terms of any structural predisposition of early twenty-first-century Syria to implosion, the impact and continuation of the Syrian Ba'athist regime has shaped the landscape, with contributions from the life and death of its Iraqi twin. First, the systematic abuse of the Syrian people by the police state created severe tension between enforced servility and fierce resentment, paralleled by the fear and loathing of the population for the security machine. Decompression was bound to be tempestuous; yet it was inevitable sooner or later. Second, the hypocrisy of repressing sectarian identity while members of the Alawite minority wielded real power in the regime also could not be sustained indefinitely. Third, the transition from ramshackle Ba'athist socialism to inequitable crony capitalism as the economic foundation of the Syrian regime from the mid-1990s eliminated the legitimacy of Ba'athism as a safety net for the socially disadvantaged.

As for an Iraqi connection before 2011, Saddam Hussein's infusion of Sunni Islamism into secular Ba'athism in the 1990s, to resuscitate regime legitimacy in Sunni Arab central Iraq, opened the way to a poisonous interaction between Ba'athism and religious fanaticism in Syria as well as Iraq. In the regime's last years, Saddam even encouraged tertiary-level Sunni Islamic studies for Ba'athists and their families. After the Iraqi regime fell in 2003, Shi'a ascendancy, US disbandment of the army, and 'de-Ba'athification'—primarily of Sunni officials—invited Sunni rebellion. Insurgency amalgamated Ba'athist military and organizational expertise with vicious jihadism, a connection eased by Saddam's preceding hook-up of Ba'athism and religion. Syria's security machine attached itself to this development after 2003 by channelling outside jihadists into Iraq to undermine the Americans, facilitating recruitment among Syrian Sunni Arabs, and reserving jihadists for special Syrian operations, for example in Lebanon. The intertwining of Sunni jihadism with Ba'athist security machinery had little visibility in the Syrian crisis through 2011 and 2012, but the vigorous assertion of the Iraqi-derived jihadist–Ba'athist hybrid ISIS in eastern Syria after April 2013 accorded Syria's tragedy nasty extra dimensions.

Agency: Bashar's show?

It is probably justified to claim that the character and constraints of Syria's modern evolution implied instability, and that the Ba'athism of the Assads carried its own doom within it, but this does not explain the particular crisis of 2011, nor why it led to such extravagant devastation. The focus here is on the management of the state under President Bashar al-Assad after the death of Hafiz al-Assad in June 2000, and on leadership behaviour in the transition from a street protest movement to civil war.

'Agency', or the degree to which an individual can play a distinctive, determining role in history, is often not an easy matter. One point of view is that individual leaders are overwhelmingly a product of their social environment, cannot override broad political and economic tendencies, and thus are tightly limited. Leo Tolstoy, in *War and Peace*, takes such a view of Napoleon.[2] Another perspective is that history is chaotic, full of chance conjunctions, often with a variety of social, political, and economic tendencies at cross-purposes. In such a setting, the character of an individual leader is not so much predetermined, and the particular personality at the helm can make a great deal of difference. The historian Margaret MacMillan, for example, asks what would have happened in Middle Eastern geopolitics if Al Gore rather than George W. Bush had had the better of the counting of chards in Florida in 2000.[3] Even when broad forces seem set in one direction, a leader swimming against the tide can make a different history in the process of going under than someone more flexible. If he had lived longer in good health, how would Hafiz al-Assad, a ruthless but carefully calculating ruler, have handled the Syria of the early twenty-first century? Might he have avoided the sort of train wreck that his stiff-necked son has presided over?

It is the contention of this book that although Syria had a difficult modern background, the personal agency of the ruler and his immediate entourage was critical in making the country more vulnerable to breakdown and in turning events towards the most disastrous course when the crisis came. In speeches of March and June 2011, which give a disturbing insight into the psychology of the man, Bashar al-Assad could have concentrated on decisive opening-up of the political system, the requirement of the moment, rather than on vacuous preaching and unloading responsibility on phantasmagoric enemy conspiracies. In the Syrian case, the notion that structural predisposition and personal agency can be equated to necessary and sufficient causation for collapse does not really apply. The Syrian regime's performance through 2011 was so atrocious that it would have wrecked, fragmented, and radicalized any Syria, even one with a much kinder background. The regime no doubt owed its existence to Syria's particular nature and past, but the behaviour of its front man was his own responsibility.

When Bashar al-Assad succeeded his father in 2000, the West imagined a flexible young president who would relax Syria's politics, improve economic efficiency, and seek new relationships. Instead, the following decade unveiled a new ruler with a fixed view of the world and an impulsive personality moulded by a privileged upbringing. Certainly, Bashar diverged from the slow, cold chess-playing of his father, but the years increasingly revealed that this was not in a positive direction. Former Lebanese prime minister Rafiq al-Hariri commented scathingly on European and American delusions about Bashar to an Irish journalist only a month before his February 2005 assassination, probably masterminded by the Syrian regime: 'You silly Westerners. You think your society is the best in the world, and that anyone who spends three years in London becomes just like you.'[4] In the early 1990s, Bashar did postgraduate ophthalmology training in London, before the January 1994 death in a car crash of his older brother Basil suddenly put him in line for the presidency.

Bashar's outlook was that if he declared autocracy to be democracy that made it so. He spoke of a special understanding of democracy in

21

Syria. Elaborated in such gems as 'democratic thinking enforces and strengthens institutional thinking', this stripped the term of meaning.[5] Repression became less crude after 2000, but anyone who suggested that Bashar's world might not be the summit of enlightenment was running risks. As for the economy, 'reform' meant sidelining rural, provincial, and suburban Syria in favour of the bourgeoisie of Damascus and Aleppo. Regarding external relations, Bashar cemented Syria into a 'resistance' alignment with Shi'a Iran and Lebanese Shi'a Hezbollah against the West, Israel, and any Arabs who got in the way. Bashar's conduct of external relations exhibited impetuosity and paranoia that flashed warnings for the handling of a domestic crisis.

In domestic politics, in 2000–1 the new president allowed a brief 'Damascus Spring' of salon gatherings and criticism of corruption and administrative failings.[6] When criticism looked like extending to politics, the relaxation was terminated. Bolder spirits found themselves back in prison. It was popular to blame 'old guard' personalities who continued in senior positions from Hafiz al-Assad's time for this, exempting a circumscribed Bashar. The new 'Damascus Winter', however, remained in place into the 2011 crisis, long outlasting the 'old guard', who figured among its casualties.

The years 2005 and 2006, when the regime was under siege from the United Nations inquiry into the Hariri murder in Beirut, marked a decisive downturn for both bourgeois critics and the surviving confidants of Hafiz al-Assad. In October 2005 and May 2006, dismayed by indications of regime responsibility for political murders in Lebanon, more than two hundred Syrian dissidents signed the 'Damascus' and 'Damascus–Beirut' declarations calling for pluralist politics in Syria and Syrian acceptance of Lebanon's independence.[7] Many were detained. Christian activist Michel Kilo received a three-year sentence, and Sunni businessman Riyadh Seif was condemned to five years in 2008 for seeking to 'overthrow the government'. In June 2005, Vice-President Abd al-Halim Khaddam, Hafiz al-Assad's long-serving foreign minister and a close friend of Rafiq al-Hariri, left the country for exile in France, accusing Bashar of Hariri's murder. The October 2005 'suicide' of interior minister Ghazi Kana'an, Hafiz al-Assad's intelligence chief in Lebanon, removed a prominent Alawite and warned others. In May 2007, a presidential 'election' with no other candidates accorded Bashar al-Assad 97.6 per cent approval for a new seven-year term.

Unrelieved autocracy went ahead together with dramatically stretched income inequality. Syria as the vanguard of Ba'athist Arab nationalism and champion against Western imperialism soldiered on, but Ba'athist semi-socialism bit the dust. The Ba'athist state of the early twenty-first century incubated a new upper class from the social and communal margins of post-Ottoman Syria that, with old high bourgeoisie remnants, dominated society. For Bashar, his family and friends in this elite—Alawite security chiefs combining with Sunni and Christian entrepreneurs—would profit from state concessions, leading the middle bourgeoisie to make a new Syria. Bashar's own marriage into a leading Sunni family of Homs symbolized the upper-level cross-sectarian networking. The president himself lived modestly, though he had claim on massive resources and his extended family pursued enrichment with no restraint. The leading example of the latter was his cousin Rami Makhlouf, who cornered Syria's cell-phone and duty-free businesses and took a rake-off from a large part of the private sector.[8] Supposedly, trickle-down effects from this predatory capitalism would ultimately improve the lot of the masses.

From the mid-2000s, rural, provincial, and suburban Syria, peripheries cultivated by Hafiz al-Assad as he sought to extend regime support in the 1970s, suffered neglect as Bashar's state economized on Syria's free education system and on subsidized food and fuel. Free-trade arrangements with Turkey and China benefited importers and distributers but devastated artisans and small textile producers in the Damascus suburbs and countryside, away from bourgeois city districts.[9] Growth was limited anyway because unease about arbitrary security agency interventions and Alawite suspicion of Sunnis propelled Sunni businessmen into preferring fast profits from property and trading to long-term investments.[10] Stagnation in the 'peripheries', home to most Syrians, mainly affected the Sunni Arab majority, but also many Alawite villagers in the coastal hills who did not belong to favoured clans.

After 2007, a crippling multi-year drought across the eastern steppe lands from Dera'a on the Jordanian border to Deir al-Zor and al-Hasakeh in the centre and north worsened the situation.[11] Perhaps half a million destitute farmers and labourers, especially from the northeast, flowed into already depressed provincial towns and big city outskirts by 2009.[12] This added extra mass to social discontent, although it was supplementary rather than critical. Syrian society was already fundamentally destabilized, provoked by economic injustice, suppression of political participation, and secret-police cruelty. Further, Francesca De Châtel argues convincingly that the impact of drought was an expression of 'resource mismanagement and over-exploitation' as well as 'the abrupt cancellation of state subsidies', fingering the real culprit—not drought itself but the incompetence of a callous, corrupt state machine.[13] In 2011, it was this machine and its masters, not climate change, that opened fire on the street uprising.

The regime's domestic policies fed directly into the 2011 breakdown; bully-boy conduct of external relations previewed the Bashar who guided Syria from street clashes into outright civil war. Bashar's treatment of Lebanon's veteran prime minister Rafiq al-Hariri headed a long list of signs of disturbing personality traits. In December 2003, he summoned Hariri to Damascus to abuse him for allegedly colluding with the USA against Syria, an episode that reportedly stressed Hariri so much that he headed for a hospital afterwards.[14] In August 2004, Bashar again summoned Hariri to tongue-lash him for being reluctant to agree to an extra three years for Lebanese president Émile Lahoud. According to Hariri, Bashar threatened to break Lebanon over the heads of Hariri, Lebanese Druze leader Walid Junblatt, and French president Jacques Chirac if he didn't get his way.[15] In February 2005, UN special envoy Terje Rød-Larsen told Hariri that his life was in danger after Bashar told the envoy that Hariri was 'playing dirty roles against Syria'.[16] Four days later Hariri was assassinated. In April 2007, in a meeting with UN secretary-general Ban Ki-Moon, Bashar predicted war in Lebanon and Sunni–Shi'a sectarian conflict 'from the Mediterranean to the Caspian Sea' if the UN established a special tribunal to bring those responsible for Hariri's assassination to justice.[17]

Syria's president regularly resorted to abuse and mockery. In May 2001, he used a welcoming speech for Pope John Paul II to attack the Jews.[18] In August 2006, he turned a speech into a tirade,[19] insulting the leaders of Saudi Arabia, Egypt, and Jordan as 'half-men' (*ansaf rijal*) for not backing Hezbollah's unilateralist July 2006 war against Israel. He also threatened the Lebanese government, defining the dominant March 14 coalition as an 'Israeli product' (*muntaj isra'ili*) and forecasting that 'its fall' was 'not far away'. In February 2010, he scorned Obama administration attempts to 'engage' him. At a Damascus summit meeting with Iranian president Mahmoud Ahmadinejad and Hezbollah leader Hasan Nasrallah, he publicly sneered at US secretary of state Hillary Clinton's offer of better relations with Washington if he pulled away from his 'resistance' colleagues.[20] In Bashar's world, the superpower was easy game. France had looked to reconcile with him as soon as Nicolas Sarkozy succeeded Jacques Chirac as president in May 2007, and President Obama would similarly adjust to Assad rules, no concessions required.

The major sphere in which Bashar's activities beyond Syria after 2000 affected the 2011 domestic equation was cultivation of Sunni jihadists to destabilize neighbouring countries. Bashar feared that Syria would be targeted next after the March 2003 Anglo-American invasion of Iraq, and he determined to keep the USA busy. The Syrian regime's main interest was to buttress the Iraqi Sunni Arab insurgency that spread through central Iraq in 2003–4. Syrian intelligence agencies channelled Arab jihadists across Syria to fight in Iraq. This handily diverted the attention of Syrian religious activists to an external cause, exported nuisances to be killed off by the Americans, and facilitated Syrian intelligence connections with jihadists and Sunnis in Iraq. In Aleppo, the regime allowed a Salafist preacher, Abu al-Qa'qa', to excoriate the Americans and promote jihadism, arousing the suspicion of many Syrians.[21] Bashar restricted the jihadists in 2005–7, when he was under American heat, but returned to pressuring the new Iraqi regime thereafter, as US attention slackened. Weiss and Hassan report credible indications of Syrian military intelligence hosting meetings of al-Qaeda in Iraq with Iraqi Ba'athists in al-Zabadani to plot August 2009 bombings in Baghdad.[22]

Jihadists could and would make trouble for their handlers, but the Syrian regime acquired invaluable data and possibilities for penetration through intimate interactions with Iraqi and Syrian Sunni extremists. Abu Mus'ab al-Zarqawi's al-Qaeda in Iraq and its successor from 2006, the Islamic State in Iraq (ISI), were obviously of great interest. Bizarrely, it seems that the Americans supplied the Syrian regime with the most renowned jihadist ideologue: Mustafa Sittmaryam Nasar, better known as Abu Mus'ab al-Suri.[23] The CIA rendered Nasar to Syria, possibly in 2007, when the USA concluded that Bashar had turned a new page against jihadists and the Syrian secret police could be useful wardens. Ba'athist Syria has kept a stock of jihadists in prisons for trading and information, and as time bombs for release into crisis environments. Another example was Shakir al-Abssi, who colluded with Syrian intelligence to foment the Fath al-Islam jihadist uprising in the Nahr al-Barid Palestinian refugee camp in Lebanon in 2007.[24] This severely strained the Lebanese army and government.

In sum, the Assads had multiple means for steering jihadism when hostilities developed in Syria from mid-2011: manipulation of prisoner releases; infiltration through previous patronage of the jihadist flow into Iraq; access to and salary payment of state employees whom ISIS commandeered in eastern Syria in 2013–14; and contacts with the Iraqi Ba'athist networks that also provided Islamic State with military expertise.

From protests to war in Syria, March 2011–March 2012

From the ruler's perspective, Ba'athist Syria was in good shape in early 2011. In his 'resistance' alignment with Iran and Hezbollah he marched with history and represented all true Syrians and Arabs. The people embraced the 'security and stability' that came from the ruling clique doing 'democratic' decision taking on their behalf. Mutterings from ungrateful intellectuals and a bit of belt-tightening out on the edge of nowhere, on the fringes of Damascus and in the provincial towns, were hardly worth notice. Trickle-down economics would work its magic in some hazy future. Bashar had the Obama administration on its knees, and the Hariri assassination affair had receded into irrelevance. If not, Hezbollah was always there to tip the table over.

We know something of the self-assurance of the Syrian leader from his rambling interview with the *Wall Street Journal* in late January 2011, at the moment of crisis for Tunisia and Egypt.[25] Syria was 'stable' despite more difficult circumstances because, unlike Zine al-Abidine Ben Ali and Husni Mubarak, Bashar was 'very closely linked to the beliefs of the people'. Being united with their leader in a 'cause', Syrians would 'not go into an uprising'. As for 'reform', after a decade in power Bashar could only offer musings about 'local administration' and 'civil society', and it might still take years to open up municipalities: 'I do not think it is about time ... people are patient in our region.'

At first the downfall of the Tunisian and Egyptian rulers seemed to have little resonance in Syria, with minor demonstrations in Damascus in early 2011 promptly defused. Parameters changed, however, in mid-March, after Bashar's cousin Atef Najib, security boss in the southern border province of Dera'a, detained fifteen teenagers for spray-painting revolutionary graffiti, for example the Tunisian slogan *al-sha'b yurid isqat al-nizam* ('the people want the fall of the regime'). Najib was the son of Bashar's mother's sister, Fatima Makhlouf, and known for his foul temper.[26] He presided over the torture of the children, including fingernail extraction, and insulted their parents. On 15 March, angry crowds protested in Dera'a town and the regime responded with live fire; within a week the death roll spiralled into the dozens.

A wave of fury swept across Syria, with unprecedented demonstrations in provincial cities and the Damascus suburbs demanding justice and reform. Events in Tunis and Cairo had not been quite enough to propel into action the depressed peripheries where more than half of Syria lived; the fuse required a local spark. Dera'a was the trigger that brought swelling thousands of people onto the streets, and enabled them to find the courage to defy the security machine. Early on, there were sometimes shootings against security forces from within crowds, but it was unclear whether these were from protesters or from planted regime provocateurs.

Bashar could probably have defused the situation in late March by travelling to Dera'a and apologizing to the families, deploying the excuse of rogue officialdom. This, however, would have required public penalties against his cousin. Neither Bashar's temperament nor the Assad–Makhlouf–Shalish inner family circle would allow such a step. Bashar and others close to him also very probably believed that apologies or concessions would show weakness, and carry an unacceptable risk of putting the regime on a slippery slope to dissolution. Unsurprisingly, therefore, the president went on the offensive against the inflating protests in deploying lethal force against Friday street processions and in propagating a clever regime narrative of victimhood at the hands of terrorists and fanatics.

As the ruling clique's front man, Bashar laid down the gauntlet in his 30 March speech to the People's Assembly.[27] He derided the 'new fashion that they call revolutions', asserting that 'Syria is facing a great conspiracy whose tentacles extend to nearby and far-away countries'. People were deluded by the 'sedition' of an undefined 'they' who used 'incitement', 'intimidation', 'weapons', and 'killing'. Bashar piously noted: 'The Holy Quran says, "sedition is worse than killing"', legitimizing the killing of protestors. He proclaimed that 'if the battle is imposed on us today, then welcome to it' (*ahlan wa sahlan biha*).[28] This was a little much for regime translators, who reduced 'welcome to it' to 'so be it' in the official English rendering. At that time, the only push to impose battle was the regime's shooting down of protestors.

Faced with regime absolutism, opposition demands morphed from reform to regime change by April; ironically, absolutism could stimulate the same consequences as might be feared from concession. Opposition activists, however, managed to maintain a creditable record of non-violence through about ten weeks of attempted violent suppression. During this period, the regime not only intensified its shoot-to-kill approach, but also implemented mass detentions, abuse, and torture, recorded in the June 2011 Human Rights Watch report *We've Never Seen Such Horror*.[29] The fate of a thirteen-year-old Dera'a boy, Hamza al-Khatib, who disappeared into the regime gulag in late April and whose carved-up body was returned to his parents in late May, became a metaphor.

In March, May, and June 2011, the regime released prisoners, most notably Islamist militants held in the formidable Sednaya jail. As Charles Lister indicates in his fine account of Syrian jihadism,[30] the militants could be relied on to splinter the Sunni Arabs who were the great majority of demonstrators, and to pull many towards radical Sunni Islamic visions of Syria's future. The regime wanted a reality to underpin its narrative that it faced a terrorist opponent inconceivable as an alternative government. Indeed, beneficiaries of the 2011 'amnesties' later became the top leaders in Salafist militias—most prominently, Hassan Abboud of Ahrar al-Sham in the north-west and Zahran Alloush of Jaysh al-Islam in the Damascus countryside. Regime violence appeared calculated to steer the street crowds towards ugly revenge and repudiation of fragile secularist activism. The first open resort of protesters to weapons was on 30 May in the towns of Rastan and Talbisa,[31] north of Homs, and thereafter there was a gradual descent into armed clashes.

Bashar al-Assad outlined the regime's fully developed narrative of victimhood, laced with demonization of the protestors, in his 20 June speech at Damascus University.[32] He refined his earlier message that street opposition was 'sedition', emerging out of 'snake pits', reflecting 'conspiracies' that are like 'germs, multiplying every moment everywhere'. Those who challenged the regime could be divided into two categories. The majority comprised 'outlaws' and individuals wanted by the law. Bashar professed surprise at their number—'more than 64,400 people ... equalling more than five military divisions'. Even 'more dangerous' were 'those who have [Sunni] extremist and *takfiri* ideology'. According to Bashar, 'this kind of ideology lurks in dark corners in order to emerge when an opportunity presents itself'. Of course, the leading dark corners were the deliberately cultivated jihadist colonies in the regime's prisons, and Bashar himself had just given *takfiris* (those who accuse other Muslims of being unbelievers) their opportunity by sending them from detention onto the streets.

Through the speech, Bashar painted the opposition with the colours of the regime's own campaign. In the same breath as branding adversaries as *takfiri*, he accused the opposition of 'invoking detestable sectarian discourse'. He portrayed early June incidents in Jisr al-Shughur in Idlib province, where security forces suffered casualties in controversial circumstances, as 'atrocious massacres' committed by insurgents with 'sophisticated weapons'. Near Ma'arrat al-Nu'man, meanwhile, people tried to protect a patrol and 'paid the price by being tortured and having their bones broken'. Bashar's account presented a saintly regime devoted to the public good, a Syrian 'majority' that only wanted to show their 'love' for the leader, and a small criminal, fanatical minority of foreign-inspired malcontents. The president went on to tick off lifting the forty-eight-year-old emergency law, a new law on political parties, constitutional adjustment, and the old stalwarts of an anti-corruption campaign and 'dialogue'. Given that the law retained all necessary backing for repression and that the regime operated without regard for law, it was all purely cosmetic. Even Russia's Vladimir Putin later affirmed that Bashar offered nothing and provoked rebellion.[33]

July–August 2011 marked a decisive shift from protests and protest suppression towards warfare. Mass demonstrations peaked in mid-July, with crowds of one million plus on two Fridays in Hama and Deir al-Zor, considered together. Thereafter the regime escalated use of armour and elite infantry in a successful bid to make such large gatherings impossible. For their part, the opposition local coordinating committees (LCCs) declared 8 July the Friday of 'no dialogue', expressing their conviction that the regime could not be reformed. The American and French ambassadors attended the mass protest in Hama the same day, to acclamation from a vast crowd that drew inappropriate conclusions about Western commitment. In late July, army officer defectors announced the creation of a 'Free Syrian Army' (FSA) as an umbrella for multiplying local insurgent bands, almost entirely Sunni Arab but initially denying sectarian or Islamist orientation. The denials were untenable; from the beginning, the FSA could not properly coordinate forces across Syria, or counter rising religious militancy.

Through August, other features of the future emerged. Saudi Arabia and Turkey declared their exasperation, and committed themselves to the opposition, but as yet without serious material input. Turkey assisted the establishment in Istanbul of the Syrian National Council (SNC) of exiled politicians. The SNC was fractious and unbalanced from its first moments: Turkey favoured the Muslim Brotherhood, injecting an Islamist bias, whereas Kurds and Turkmen resented Arab domination. While SNC worthies planned their new Syria in their hotel rooms, the jihadist Islamic State in Iraq (ISI), equipped from 2010 with an energetic new leader—Abu Bakr al-Baghdadi (or Ibrahim al-Badri)—was rejuvenating in Sunni Arab parts of Iraq, and saw opportunity in the Syrian chaos. In August 2011, al-Baghdadi commissioned an ambitious Syrian associate, Abu Muhammad al-Jawlani, to organize a branch of ISI in Syria.

After the Syrian army forced insurgents and civilians to flee Jisr al-Shughur into Turkey in June 2011, armed clashes graded into more sustained hostilities from late September onwards. Initial hotspots included Rastan and Talbisa north of Homs; the countryside in Hama and Idlib provinces, especially Jabal al-Zawiya; al-Zabadani between Damascus and the Lebanese border; and the Dera'a countryside.[34] Into early 2012, the regime was able to gain the initiative in these areas, cornering and killing a large group of rebels in Jabal al-Zawiya in December 2011, and retaking al-Zabadani town in February 2012. FSA fighters from the Farouq Brigades, however, took control of the large Sunni suburb of Baba Amr in Homs from November 2011. Escalating urban firefights followed, with regime shelling, insurgent capture of other Sunni neighbourhoods, and sectarian killings of both Sunnis and Alawites. In February 2012, Baba Amr became a prototype for many suburbs in Damascus and Aleppo when the regime cut it off and laid siege to it with heavy artillery. The siege lasted three weeks, until the FSA withdrew amid an army advance on 1 March. Many hundreds of civilians died under regime bombardment; on 22 February alone, when an American journalist and a French photographer were killed, reports indicated about eighty deaths.[35]

Regime success only guaranteed a deepening of the crisis, with Assad convinced of the viability and necessity of the security solution to 'terrorism' and the embittered rebels equally convinced that regime ruthlessness would bring outside intervention. After all, the latter could already cite calls for Assad to 'step aside' as having 'lost legitimacy' from US president Barack Obama and European leaders, and a majority vote in the League of Arab States to declare Syria's seat 'vacant'. The positive verbiage stoked Syrian opposition expectations, and the West, unwilling to supply any serious content to it, failed to calculate the consequences of disappointing these expectations. One warning sign flashed on 23 January 2012, when Jawlani's ISI jihadists formally launched their Syrian branch, Jabhat al-Nusra, with an internet publicity video. First and foremost, they targeted Assad, but they also demanded hardline Sunni Islamic law for Syria and attacked the West.[36] They initially indulged in sporadic bombings that killed civilians, which caused rebels and activists to disown them, but they also took on board Abu Mus'ab al-Suri's recommendation for flexibility in cultivating popular support. Amid Syrian rebel disillusion they would become formidable.

Baba Amr marked the transition to war. Up to mid-2012, the rebels acquired their weaponry from captured regime stocks, defecting officers and soldiers, the black market, and smuggling across the Lebanese and Iraqi borders.[37] As yet foreign states had little direct involvement. Similarly, technical and organizational expertise came from regular army defectors, and to a lesser extent from jihadists. Foreign advisers and fighters were still insignificant.

The war began as an indigenous struggle for mastery of the Syrian state, with existential commitment to either regime preservation or regime change. It did not begin nor has it really become a proxy war on behalf of foreigners. Of course, some of the parties, most notably the regime and rebels in western Syria, have had shared interests with outside powers and have become dependent on those powers for armaments or direct military intervention. Nonetheless, their basic drives remained distinct from and sometimes inconvenient to those of their aspirant patrons. The jihadists have not been openly supported by any states, although some may see advantage in their temporary perpetuation. Overall, if in 2017 all the external meddlers pulled back from Syria and Iraq without sponsoring any genuine conciliation, hostilities would continue. The outsiders would then find themselves drawn back into the mess.

Given these observations, how were external connections developing by the opening phase of the war in early 2012?[38] First, Russia made it clear that it would not allow the West and the Arabian Peninsula states to mobilize the UN Security Council for Libya-style 'responsibility to protect', and assuredly not as a Trojan Horse for regime change. Together with Iran's determination to facilitate Bashar's perpetuation through material and financial aid, this inflated the Syrian president's confidence that he could push the margins on the application of lethal force.

Second, Arabian Peninsula countries and individual Salafist financiers in those countries were putting in place their uncoordinated, divisive flows of money to the FSA and emerging Islamist and jihadist factions in the Syrian rebellion. Turkey provided a platform for transfers into Syria, but proper activation could only come after Syrian rebels took official border crossings. Meantime, Turkey floated the idea of a buffer and/or security zone (*tampon bölge ya da güvenlik bölgesi*) on the Syrian side of the border as early as September 2011,[39] with endorsement from Prime Minister Erdoğan in March 2012.[40]

Third, the USA and the EU inaugurated policies of sanctions and severing of relations with the Syrian regime, also toying with limited legitimization of 'moderate' exiles and FSA factions. The sanctions might be irritating, but Russia and Iran plainly did not have to worry about any substantive Western challenge to their partner in Damascus.

Syria decomposes, April 2012–September 2013

The war was pure quicksilver through its first eighteen months. In 2012, the momentum was generally with the rebellion as it seized territory in the main metropolitan areas of Aleppo and Damascus and considerably extended its rural holdings, including along the Turkish border north and west of Aleppo. In 2013, the pendulum swung back to the regime, which stabilized its affairs in Damascus and secured its connection between the capital and the Alawite coast through the Homs region. Along the way, the rebellion and the regime assumed new features and shapes, both becoming more nakedly sectarian. The balance in the armed opposition shifted dramatically to the advantage of hardline Sunni Islamists and jihadists, with a rising inflow of foreign religious zealots. The regime fell back on religious minorities, particularly Alawites and Christians, and more secularized bourgeois Sunnis who had common interests with it—probably 30–40 per cent of the country. The sectarian shift was clearer in the regime military forces, with desertions of Sunnis offset by the formation of the mainly Alawite paramilitary National Defence Forces (NDF), backed by foreign Shi'a militias from Lebanon and Iraq. In parallel, major new belligerents appeared, with the Syrian Kurdish Democratic Union Party (PYD) carving out 'cantons' in the north from July 2012, and the Iraqi jihadist ISI reinventing itself as the Islamic State in Iraq and Syria (ISIS) from April 2013.

Syria's religious minorities were not by any means united behind the Assads. Many Christians initially supported the repudiation of autocracy, but the rise of the jihadists, financed from the oil states, repelled them. The Christian sects are important because they total about 10 per cent of Syrians, close to the Alawite proportion.[41] Compared with Sunni Arabs, a much smaller fraction fled the country, while they had far fewer casualties than Alawites. If anything, Alawites have been more conflicted than Christians, because they were trapped from the outset into carrying the main load for Bashar al-Assad. Druze (3 per cent), Isma'ilis (1 per cent), and Twelver Shi'a (1 per cent) represent a second tier in demographic weight, but found themselves strategically significant as warfare developed.

Druze and Isma'ilis have mostly disdained the regime. Druze concentrate in al-Suwayda province on the Jordanian border, with an outlier on the Turkish border west of Aleppo. As the majority in al-Suwayda, next to the regime–rebel contest around Dera'a, they have been important since 2011. They resisted regime conscription and simply sought survival; they were also cool towards rebels. Assad had their territory without their sympathy. The main Isma'ili Shi'a population is in Salamiya, east of Homs, with others in a coastal mountain pocket (Masyaf) amid Alawites. Salamiya saw demonstrations supporting the uprising in 2011.[42] The town became critical to the regime when it provided access to Aleppo after rebels closed the main highway north of Hama in late 2012. Thereafter, Salamiya was constricted between Assad's security machine and jihadists in the nearby countryside. The jihadist Jabhat al-Nusra alienated Isma'ilis and Druze. In January 2013, it took responsibility for a bombing in Salamiya that killed many civilians.[43] In June 2015, it massacred twenty Druze in a village on the Turkish border.[44] As for Twelver Shi'a, they backed the regime, linking with Lebanese Hezbollah and Iranian advisers. Some Shi'a villages later became sensitive locations, whether within rebel-held Idlib province or between rebel eastern Aleppo and the Turkish border.

The spring months of 2012 after the fall of Baba Amr witnessed the culmination of the shift of gravity in the opposition, from continuing civilian protests alongside armed action to the eclipse of civilian initiative in favour of insurrection. Regime escalation, now to include helicopter gunships, was decisive; the regime evidently wanted freedom to deploy its military superiority in a showdown on its terms. In May 2012, this took the form of a sectarian massacre of more than one hundred Sunni Arabs in Houla in the Homs countryside. A UN Human Rights Commission report later found 'the highest levels of the armed and security forces' culpable.[45] In early June, in his first public address for a year, Bashar al-Assad summed up the regime's treatment plan for Syria and its people: 'When the surgeon enters the operating theatre and … extracts and amputates, what do we say to him? You fix on his [hands] being bloody or do we salute him for saving the patient?'[46]

Bashar's apparatus, however, tottered in the summer of 2012, as the opposition burst out of its peripheral confines. This was the more credible of two occasions when it seemed as if the regime might crack—the other being in mid-2015. Rebels assumed command of parts of the Damascus countryside and suburbs, backed from a stronghold in Douma and the East Ghouta, so that by July they could contemplate encroachment into the inner regime and bourgeois citadels. On 19 July, rebels took A'zaz north of Aleppo and the Bab al-Hawa border crossing to Antakya in Turkey. In late July, armed groups from the northern countryside penetrated the Sunni quarters of eastern Aleppo, largely the poorer segment of the city. On 31 July, the town of al-Bab to the immediate north-east fell to rebels; when added to eastern Aleppo the opposition now commanded positions threatening the Aleppo airport and the military–industrial complex at al-Safira. Rebels also advanced in rural Dera'a province alongside the Israeli-occupied Golan Heights and maintained their redoubts in Homs and al-Qusayr straddling the main highway from Damascus to the coast.

Strain became perceptible within Syria's opaque ruling clique. On 18 July, Bashar's brother-in-law Assef Shawkat died, together with the defence and interior ministers and other senior commanders, in a mysterious explosion in the security headquarters in Damascus. Whether it was an FSA attack or a clearing-out of compromise-inclined persons within the ruling clique,[47] it did not look good. As for high-level defections, in early July Manaf Tlass, from perhaps the most important Sunni family in regime circles and a brigadier-general close to Bashar, decamped to Turkey. In early August, he was followed by the regime prime minister, Riyad Hijab, who termed the regime 'terrorist' and fled to Jordan. These were merely the most eye-catching in a flood of Sunni Arab desertions.

How, then, did Assad make it through the 2012 emergency?[48] First, defections were virtually entirely Sunni and hardly touched the Alawite elite army units, the air force, or the security services. Second, the regime pulled back troops from eastern Syria, keeping main bases as a presence but otherwise leaving large expanses to the Kurds, rebels, and jihadists. Third, Iran intervened decisively. Iranian advisers and Lebanese Hezbollah laboured to create the new 90,000-man paramilitary NDF, tapping a mixed reservoir of Alawite militias and other manpower from minorities and loyalist Sunni clans. By mid-2013 the NDF had made up for the hollowing out of regular army units. Iran also oversaw inflows of thousands of Hezbollah and Iraqi Shi'a fighters as well as pumping money into the regime, helping to back up military and civil servant salaries. Iran took the lead over the Russians, who covered military hardware and the international arena. Fourth, Alawites remained loyal to the regime, reflecting their deep fear of the Islamists and jihadists in the Sunni interior. The coast, where most of Syria's 2.5 million Alawites live and are the majority, was thereby secured. Given that Bashar had ignored his community and its religious shaykhs before 2011, while he circulated among the Sunni upper class, this was an interesting situation. Many Alawites fumed, but they were without options. Fifth, the regime retained its trump cards of airpower and firepower, it operated on interior lines in its core territories, and, for the moment at least, it had a cohesive central command compared with its fractured enemies.

The major problem was that the instruments of survival mortgaged the future. The umbilical relationship with a hegemonic Iran and foreign Shi'a militias could not be compatible with any serious reconciliation with most Syrian Sunni Arabs. Reliance on district-focused paramilitaries patronized by Iran and Hezbollah opened the way to decentralized military authority compromising regime cohesion. The NDF was also the end of the regime's Syrian manpower reserves, and its ultimate inadequacy would make the regime even more beholden to non-Syrian Shi'a.

Rebel gains continued, from the shocks administered in Damascus and Aleppo in July 2012 to the first capture of a provincial capital, the city of al-Raqqa, in March 2013 (Map 1). Along the way, coalitions of rebel groups took towns such as Ma'arrat al-Nu'man and Saraqib on the Homs–Aleppo highway, constricting regime access to the north; important army and air bases such as Taftanaz near Idlib, with copious weaponry; and the main hydro dams on the Euphrates. Starting with eastern Aleppo in late July, the regime responded with bombing by fixed-wing aircraft as well as helicopters, adding Scud ballistic missile strikes against Aleppo and the north from December. For its part, the FSA component of the opposition received its first major shipments of foreign weaponry at the end of 2012, acquired by Saudi Arabia from Croatia and transferred with Western approval via Jordan and Turkey.[49] The items included recoilless guns and rocket and grenade launchers.

As for numbers of fighters, by late 2012 combined rebel strength totalled at least 75,000, almost entirely Sunni Arab Syrians apart from about 3,000 foreigners.[50] Thereafter recruitment within Syria grew towards 100,000, a level sustained through subsequent years. It reflected the imperative for sustenance through militia pay, but also real mass Sunni Arab backing of regime change.

More broadly, what were the circumstances of the opposition and its expanded territories by early 2013? If anything, the survival and prolongation of the rebellion is more remarkable than the resilience of the regime. After all, the opposition had to manage largely without the firepower and steadfast allies that Bashar al-Assad could muster. An argument can also be made that Sunni Muslim allies of the rebels—the oil-state Arabs and Turkey—compromised the cause. They all supported Islamists, although the Saudi government viewed anything touched by the Muslim Brotherhood as a challenge to its own Islamic credentials. Also, Saudi Arabia had been bitten enough by al-Qaeda, a poisonous outgrowth of its own Wahhabi Sunni Islam, to tread carefully with militant Islamists in Syria. Islamist commitment and exploits, however, influenced Qatar, Turkey, and private Qatari and Kuwaiti financiers. Salafists, Brotherhood derivatives, and even jihadists appropriated considerable foreign aid. Secular and modestly religious FSA factions also pocketed aid, but still lost recruits to the Islamists, and the Syrian regime gained extra public relations ammunition for painting the whole armed opposition as *takfiri* terrorists.

Rebel fragmentation reflected Syrian internal conditions as well as competing foreign sponsors, and this was not necessarily prejudicial to military operations. The armed uprising was geographically splintered, developing in separate areas across Syria, so it was inevitably multi-headed. This gave it redundancy and meant that it could not be easily decapitated. Also, rebels could light fires in different places to stretch the regime. Rebel groups proved able to come together for increasingly sophisticated combined operations, at first against the regime and later against both the regime and ISIS. More injurious than the existence of scores of groups per se was the steady shift in the opposition balance towards Salafists and jihadists,[51] which by 2013 led to turf warfare among the more religiously inclined as well as between the more and less religiously inclined. Also, the constant violent splintering

Map 1: Syria, late 2012–early 2013

and recombining of factions with private squabbles and racketeering interests demoralized the opposition popular base.

De facto administration under the rebels differed greatly from place to place and time to time, although it was all decrepit and arbitrary. The LCC activists who facilitated the 2011 protests became involved in rudimentary service provision in combination with armed groups and ad hoc civil society associations.[52] Islamists and the Jabhat al-Nusra jihadists set up Islamic judicial bodies that in places—Aleppo, for example—competed with secular counterparts. Jabhat al-Nusra was flexible about collaboration, and flaunted a commitment against economic exploitation, notably over flour supplies in Aleppo in late 2012, which deepened its popular reach.[53] Intensifying aerial bombardment and territorial discontinuity, in addition to warlord predation and incompatible ideologies and agendas among factions, together precluded any serious attempt at governance. The circumstances made it fatuous to anticipate any concrete role for the SNC or its successor exile assemblage from late 2012, the National Coalition of Syrian Revolutionary and Opposition Forces. Disconnection between the external and internal oppositions was inevitable, regardless of Western patronage and National Coalition interventions.

When considering wartime economic interactions across Syria it is best to set aside maps of zones of control or influence. Lines have been porous, and food, civilian goods, and military supplies have crossed them with pay-offs here and there. Smuggling within Syria is rife. For example, the Rastan pocket and surrounds north of Homs has supposedly been enclosed by the regime since 2013—in other words, for four years. Yet somehow ammunition and other goods have made it in. Similarly, a smuggling route from the south-east has fed into the rebel East Ghouta pocket near Damascus. In both cases there has been sufficient local farmland for at least partial food self-sufficiency. Refugee outflows since 2012 have meant that civilian populations in rebel enclaves probably declined to around half pre-war levels by 2014. Otherwise, there have been understandings between the sides for electricity, gas, and fuel transfers.

Despite rebel successes towards al-Raqqa and in the Idlib countryside, the regime managed to force a stalemate in Damascus and Aleppo by early 2013, and to isolate the opposition in Homs. Iraqi Shi'a militia and the new NDF were increasingly available to help secure inner Damascus. The regime could look ahead to a slow grind to wear down the opposition in suburbs close to the centre such as Jobar and Barzeh or, like Hajar al-Aswad and Daraya, positioned between the centre and outer military facilities. In 2013, the strategy of blockading and starving suburbs into dictated truce arrangements began. In Aleppo, the regime stabilized its hold on the wealthier west. The opposition became contained in the eastern suburbs, with communications north to the Turkish border vulnerable to interruption. In late 2012, deliberate aerial bombing of hospitals and queues at bakeries in the north[54] indicated the regime's determination to strike civilian facilities in order to drive out populations and destroy the civilian milieu in which rebel activity operated.

Regime offensive operations from April 2013 concentrated on clearing rebels from the pivotal Homs gap connecting the coast with the interior. The great crusader castle of Krak des Chevaliers that overlooks the gap indicates its enduring strategic salience. Here the regime had a common interest with Lebanon's Hezbollah, which wanted the adjacent Lebanese border cleared of anyone who might impinge on the Hezbollah and Shi'a stronghold in the northern Beqa'a Valley. Hezbollah thus took the lead role in the regime's assault on the rebel-held town of al-Qusayr, through which rebels in central Syria had a supply line from Lebanese Sunnis and the nearby Beqa'a Sunni town of Aarsal. Al-Qusayr also fringed the main highway between Damascus and Homs. Backed by intensive artillery and aerial strikes, Hezbollah and regime regular troops compelled the rebels, including their reinforcements from northern Syria, to give up the town in early June 2013. The regime then swivelled to Homs itself, where it took the inner suburb of al-Khalidiya in July, leaving surviving rebels bottled up in the old city.

Paralleling the Qusayr affair, which sharpened Sunni–Shi'a animosity across the eastern Arab world, an upheaval among Sunni jihadists altered the geopolitics of the Syrian war. These dramas intensified interplay between Syria and Iraq on both the sectarian and jihadist levels. ISI, Jabhat al-Nusra's parent, rapidly inflating in Sunni Arab provinces of Iraq, conceived integrating jihadists in Iraq and Syria under its command. The ISI leader Baghdadi's chief military advisor, the ex-Ba'athist Iraqi army officer Haji Bakr, crossed to Syria in late 2012 to assess affairs there, including Jabhat al-Nusra.[55] Baghdadi's priority was combining western Iraq and eastern Syria in a 'caliphate' that would make war against infidels and apostates—land would be taken from the Syrian rebels before bothering the Syrian regime.

Jabhat al-Nusra's Jawlani, in contrast, prioritized getting rid of Assad and anchoring jihad in pragmatic collaboration with non-jihadist Sunnis. In late 2012 and early 2013, Jabhat al-Nusra built power and reputation across Syria. It gained major new revenue from oilfields it took in eastern Syria in late 2012, assumed a leading position in Aleppo and north-west Syria through its service and relief activities, and led in inter-factional battlefield coordination. It was not about to be bossed around. In early April 2013, Baghdadi demanded that it submit to absorption in his new Islamic State of Iraq and Syria (ISIS). Jawlani refused, and extracted endorsement from al-Qaeda chief Ayman al-Zawahiri, who was uncomfortable with Baghdadi's ambition and fanaticism. Both the Jabhat al-Nusra flaunting of its al-Qaeda affiliation and the jihadist divorce sent shock waves through Syria.

Baghdadi had the edge in resources, and his fervent global jihadist vision had greater appeal than the narrower focus of Jawlani, particularly to foreigners. At first, he stripped away followers from Jabhat al-Nusra, especially in al-Raqqa and eastern Syria. Among others, he incorporated Chechens from the jihadist Jaysh al-Muhajirin wa al-Ansar, notably the dynamic young Georgian Tarkhan Batirashvili (Abu Omar al-Shishani), who by August 2013 was the ISIS military commander in northern Syria. In its first months in Syria, ISIS wore a fair face, in the manner of Sauron in Tolkien's *Silmarillion*, as it insinuated itself into rebel-held lands and among local people. It even contributed a suicide-bomber vehicle assault to the combined rebel operation that overran Minnigh air base north of Aleppo in August. Nonetheless, ISIS had no interest other than the incorporation or elimination of partners. Jabhat al-Nusra weathered the initial challenge, and a reckoning loomed across rebel Syria. Assad could enjoy the show.

As Syria decomposed through 2012 and 2013, neither regime nor opposition was focused on anything other than the demise of the other. A gathering of external powers in Geneva in June 2012 proposed a cease-fire, humanitarian relief, and a transitional authority. The content of the latter was entirely disputed. The Syrian opposition and its backers required Assad to go in advance of the transition; Russia envisaged Assad and the regime as the leading element of the transition. As for Bashar himself, Lakhdar Brahimi, international mediator between 2012 and 2014, remarked: 'It seems to me that Assad has never doubted for a single day that he would win through, and has never for a single day thought about concessions.'[56]

Indeed, all parties—regime, rebels, and jihadists—fancied their prospects of coming out on top in a military solution. By early 2013, the only available military instrument not yet deployed was chemical weaponry. US president Barack Obama declared in August 2012 that poison gas would be a 'red line'—the one contingency that would bring direct US intervention. There is no concrete evidence that anyone other than the regime possessed weapon-ready chemicals in 2013; it had a large military stock of sarin nerve gas as well as other agents. Almost two years after Obama's empty pronouncement that Assad should go, the regime had no reason to take him seriously. In mid-2013, minor gas releases did not elicit any reaction of note. Although the regime had passed through its 2012 crisis and had the military advantage, forcing rebels back in Damascus was tough and decent infantry was precious. Temptation existed. Whatever the case, on 21 August 2013, rockets released large quantities of sarin into rebel areas of Damascus, in the Obama administration's estimation killing around 1,400 inhabitants.[57] No one other than the regime had a credible conjunction of motive, gas, and delivery systems. Fanciful claims that the opposition killed its own people to precipitate intervention require extraordinary evidence; instead, the balance of indicators points strongly to the regime.

The USA had no doubts, and geared up to punish Bashar al-Assad for resorting to weapons of mass destruction. The alarmed Russians, prompted by none other than US secretary of state John Kerry, pounced on the idea that Assad could escape by chemical disarmament. Obama himself preferred an exit to implementing his red lines, while Kerry added farce to backtracking by proclaiming how deliberately inconsequential any military strike would be.[58] Far from taking a hit, Assad was able to exude virtue and indispensability as overseeing reduction of his illicit chemical stocks. Here Obama and Kerry surrendered not just to Russia but also to Assad's Iranian friends, whom the US president was desperate not to upset during negotiations over their nuclear programme. The bewildering succession of red lines, military posturing, and headlong retreat, with Obama ducking for cover behind Congress and the British parliament, could only tell both Assad and the jihadists that the Obama White House was feckless and a push-over.

Syria and Iraq: towards a joint war zone, 2013–2014

Iraq in 2011 had the appearance of a country heading in a different direction from neighbouring Syria's trajectory towards breakdown. Whereas Iraq's chaos between 2003 and about 2008 had little impact on Syria's affairs, the 'Arab Spring' that triggered upheaval in Syria in 2011 had little impact on Iraq. By 2011, Iraq did seem to be coming out of the death and destruction that both Saddam Hussein and the United States had gifted it, and was operating a rough pluralism in which Shi'a Arabs, Sunni Arabs, and Kurds were all participating. Sunni Arabs broadly seemed to be adjusting to their minority status, after having been the community of power up to 2003. Kurds seemed to have a decent acknowledgement of their national distinction in a new federal structure.

Appearances, however, masked unpromising realities. The link-up in 2007–8 of boosted US forces in Baghdad and western Iraq with Sunni Arab tribes tired of turbulence—the 'surge' and the Sahwa (Sunni awakening) movement—severely reduced the Sunni jihadists who had sowed mayhem after 2003, but left them the capacity for resurgence. ISI no longer could claim territory, but it retained potent networks in such Sunni Arab towns as Ramadi, Falluja, and Samarra—and above all in the major northern city of Mosul. From May 2010, its new leader Abu Bakr al-Baghdadi made a new military structure of disaffected and highly experienced Ba'athist officers headed by his assistant and former Iraqi intelligence colonel, Haji Bakr. Baghdadi seized the chance to begin carving out a new domain in Syria from late 2011.

Meantime, through 2010–11 a steady US troop drawdown to nothing steadily lessened US influence on the American-created and Shi'a-dominated new Iraqi federal government. In these years, Nouri al-Maliki, US-backed prime minister from the Shi'a Da'awa (Islamic Call) Party since 2006, turned from previous pragmatism to sectarianism. Despite being narrowly defeated in the March 2010 general elections, he remained head of government by wearing down rivals in eight months of stonewalling and making phoney promises to transfer the defence and interior ministries. Finally securing sufficient acquiescence in November 2010 to continue in his post, he exploited his prime ministerial role as head of the armed forces to establish personal chains of command bypassing the formal hierarchy. Through 2011 and 2012, he sidelined Sunnis, favoured Shi'a, reduced finance for the Sunni Sahwa tribal levies that had faced down the jihadists, and promoted new de-Ba'athication.[59] In the perception of Sunni Arab Iraqis, Maliki's inferred sectarianism burst into the open with the December 2011

43

murder and terrorism charges against Sunni vice-president Tariq al-Hashimi, who fled the country.

Sunni anger simmered into 2012, stimulated further by Iranian-assisted entrenchment of Shi'a militias in Baghdad and southern Iraq and Maliki's support for Syria's Bashar al-Assad. Maliki's position on Syria was curious, given that his own government had charged Bashar's regime with facilitating massive jihadist bombings against public buildings in Baghdad in late 2009.[60] It came out of Maliki's cultivation of Syrian regime, Hezbollah, and Iranian links during twenty-three years as a guest of the Syrian and Iranian regimes (1980–2 and 1990–2003 in Damascus, and 1982–90 in Tehran). It expressed the prime minister's worries about the implications for Iraq of any Sunni Islamist takeover in Damascus.[61] It also reflected consolidation of the already ubiquitous Iranian influence over Shi'a political blocs and Iraqi state institutions with departure of the last US forces in December 2011.

Thereafter, the Obama administration's studied lack of interest in Iraq left Baghdad to Tehran. This apparent indifference went together with the bequeathing of local US weapons stocks to the fragile new Iraqi army. What if the sectarian warfare and anarchy of 2006–7 resurfaced and such weapons 'fell into the wrong hands'? In contrast to US caution regarding the Syrian opposition, the question did not seem to arise regarding Iraq. It was not as if there weren't obvious warning signs in Iraq's quickening new slide. On 19 December 2012, a security force raid on the home of the Sunni finance minister precipitated a Sunni Arab descent to the streets in al-Anbar province and the north in sustained fierce denunciation of Maliki.

As turbulence intensified in Iraq, spillover between Iraq and Syria in both directions was inevitable. Many Iraqi Shi'a already felt themselves in the camp of Assad and Iran, while Sunni Arab western Iraq and Iraqi Kurdistan both graded into the Sunni Arabs and Kurds of Syria. By early 2013, Iraqi-linked jihadists had the initiative among Syrian Sunni Arabs. Similarly, Shi'a–Alawite convergence and Kurdish assertion were sharpening across the two countries.

As observed above, Syria's war originated within Syria and was the primary engine propelling both countries into the abyss. Much of the growth of Iraqi Sunni jihadists and Shi'a militias alike came from the attractions of Sunni and Shi'a causes in the Syrian warfare of 2012–13.

The jihadist ISI could look to carve out its bastion in eastern Syria from which men and material could enter Iraq. Shi'a militias could wield the rallying cry of Shi'a holy places in danger, especially the shrine of Sayyida Zeinab in Damascus, as a recruiting tool in Iraq. In late 2012, the Abu al-Fadl al-Abbas Brigade was formed for this purpose, and joined by several other new and existing paramilitaries—Asa'ib Ahl al-Haqq (a splinter from Muqtada al-Sadr's Mahdi army) and contingents from the Badr Brigades and Kata'ib Hizballah. By late 2013, several thousand such militiamen were widely engaged against Syrian Sunni Arab fighters. As they expanded and gained experience under Iranian direction, these contingents could move back and forth between Iraq and Syria, swaying the balance across both countries.

Although sectarian and ethnic differentiation appeared similar in Iraq and Syria, the post-2011 situations diverged in important respects. Sunni Arabs were the main source of challenge to both regimes, but in Iraq they were a minority of 20 per cent that had just been demoted from centrality in the state, while in Syria they were a majority of 60 per cent that had been under minority rule for almost half a century. In Iraq, a Lebanese-style ethno-sectarian carve-up of the regime among Shi'a Arabs, Sunni Arabs, and Kurds had prevailed since 2003; in Syria, formal rejection of any such carve-up persisted even years into the war. In Iraq, Sunni Arab rancour about their recent loss and desperation about their minority predicament made them potentially very dangerous. Nonetheless, they could not be an existential threat to the new ascendancy of a Shi'a population almost three times their size, especially given their uneasy relations with the Kurds. In Syria, the very fact of a Sunni Arab majority and numbers five times those of Alawites made Sunni Arabs an existential threat as soon as the conflict acquired a sectarian dimension. At the same time, Syrian Sunni Arab political naivety and openness to extravagant religious radicalism made them vulnerable.

Tribal and clan affairs illustrate Sunni Arab circumstances. In Iraq, American detachment of western Iraqi tribes from the nihilist jihadism of 2007–8 opened the chance for Sunni–Shi'a rapprochement. Maliki's sectarian tactics through 2011 helped the jihadists to recover. Tribal affairs were convoluted: factionalism and personal jealousies within and among the tribes gave opportunities for Maliki as much as for ISI. For

QUICKSILVER WAR

example, Maliki maintained influence in the Jubbour tribe around Tikrit and had the Albu Assaf shaykh Ali Hatem of al-Anbar province on his State of Law list for the 2010 elections, though Ali Hatem thereafter opposed him.[62] Generally the tribes had no time for fanatic jihadist interpretations of *shari'a*, and could have been largely won over by a sensitive Shi'a-headed government in Baghdad. In the circumstances of 2012–13, however, sectarian inflammation and money carried the day. Iranian-backed Shi'a militias grew provocatively while the government cut back salaries for the Sahwa groups, and ISI had new resources of cash and weapons with which it could entice Sunni tribes.[63] In Syria, Assad's regime paid more attention to Sunni tribal shaykhs than did the new leaders in Iraq, but regime incompetence and arrogance in mismanaging agriculture through the drought also fuelled bitterness in eastern Syria. In the end, the regime preserved significant penetration but the tribes largely swung to rebellion and were then subverted by al-Nusra and ISIS.

Iraq's descent into new hostilities after the relative stabilization of 2008–11 proved more subtle and gradual than the regime-driven military firestorm in Syria. It began with scattered incidents from early 2012, for example ISI killings of police in Shi'a areas and al-Anbar province in February–March, and a jailbreak in Tikrit in September. ISI also targeted tribal Sahwa chiefs at the same time as Maliki deserted them. The pace quickened from December 2012, when the humiliation of the finance minister brought months of Sunni street protests, an Iraqi Sunni echo of the Syrian events of 2011. These manifestations eased ISI resurgence in the Sunni provinces and likely ISI interactions with Ba'athist and Salafist Sunnis, for example ex-Ba'athists in the Naqshbandi religious order.

Events crossed a threshold on 19 April 2013 when agitators clashed with Iraqi troops in Hawija, in the Sunni Arab west of Kirkuk province. The army then assaulted a demonstrator campsite in Hawija: forty-two died, among them three soldiers. Clashes between the army and gunmen followed across the whole Sunni Arab expanse of northern and central Iraq. Jihadists, Salafists, and Ba'athists all mobilized to face the authorities, who even resorted to bombing from helicopters in Sulayman Bek, south of Hawija. Sunni–Shi'a sectarian killings, car bombings, and murders of Sahwa personnel escalated. The Iraq Body

Count estimate of monthly civilian deaths from violence went above a thousand in July 2013, for the first time since April 2008, and stayed there.[64] Also in July, the jihadists issued a major statement of intent to anyone who might be paying attention when they organized a jailbreak of a thousand largely jihadist detainees from the Abu Ghrayb and al-Hout prisons near Baghdad.[65]

In late 2013, this state of affairs did not really ring alarm bells in an Iraq inured to insurgencies. Compared to Syria, the geographical scope was more limited, largely restricted to Sunni Arab and mixed Sunni–Shi'a areas amounting to a third of the country. Armed clashes were still intermittent rather than incessant. The media were distracted with other topics, particularly divisions among Shi'a, for example Muqtada al-Sadr's opposition to Maliki's third term in power, and disputes between Baghdad and the Kurds.[66] The continuation of the Sunni protest assemblies and encampments, termed *al-hirak al-sha'abi* ('the popular momentum'), masked the more significant dynamic of resurgent jihadist subversion of tribes and steerage of a Sunni coalition interested in armed rebellion. Also in late 2013, ISI had only just reiterated its ambitions in Syria by renaming itself ISIS; it had immediate business consolidating a position there that could later help sway Iraq. Despite the persistence of the elevated death toll, for the moment there was a strategic pause in Iraq.

In Syria, Assad held the advantage in late 2013. The sarin episode told him and everyone else, once and for all, that the regime and its allies did not have to worry about any direct Western intervention. At the same time, ISIS besieged the opposition, seizing the initiative in al-Raqqa in August and spreading out across opposition territory as far west as the Idlib countryside. ISIS moved into al-Bab north-east of Aleppo, and in October it threw the Asifat al-Shamal FSA faction out of A'zaz, south of the Bab al-Salameh border crossing to Turkey. ISIS and the Syrian regime carefully steered clear of one another: the opposition held what ISIS wanted, including manpower, and the ISIS depredations eased regime offensives against the rebels. Meantime, in September 2013, the opposition's reputation took a severe hit when Human Rights Watch reported a massacre of 190 Alawites, including fifty-seven women and eighteen children, by Jabhat al-Nusra and several rebel factions in the Latakia hills[67]—the first such large-scale sectarian atrocity from the opposition side. In February 2014, Jund al-

Aqsa, an offshoot of Jabhat al-Nusra, killed sixty civilians and soldiers in the Alawite village of Ma'an, north of Hama.[68]

Syria's Salafist and jihadist rebels, particularly Ahrar al-Sham and Jabhat al-Nusra respectively, found confronting ISIS unavoidable by November 2013. In parallel, the opposition faced a determined regime attack around Aleppo, driving rebel factions away from al-Safira and the airport and threatening supplies from Turkey. As a result, the non-jihadist Islamist factions formed their first general alignment, the Islamic Front, spearheaded by Ahrar al-Sham (Idlib and Aleppo), Jaysh al-Islam (Damascus), Liwa al-Tawhid (Aleppo), and Suqur al-Sham (Idlib and Aleppo). This, however, did not end their frictions with the non-Islamist FSA factions. The latter made their own alignment, the Syrian Revolutionaries' Front (SRF), more effectively to stand up to the regime, ISIS, and what was by 2013 the Islamist majority in the armed opposition. Its initiator, Jamal Ma'arouf, headed one of the oldest rebel groups, the Syrian Martyrs' Brigade of Jabal al-Zawiya. Another smaller assemblage of ex-FSA groups in rural Aleppo, Jaysh al-Mujahidin, notably featuring the Nur al-Din Zanki Brigade, appeared in January 2014.[69] Together these three loose alignments could mobilize perhaps 80,000 fighters across Syria, the majority being from the Islamic Front.[70] Their problem was that they could only bring a fraction of this to bear on ISIS, and many were reluctant.

The military assault against ISIS of what the latter derisively termed the (Syrian) Sahwas began in early January 2014 with attacks on ISIS facilities across the Idlib and Aleppo countryside. At first the SRF of the old FSA led the way, with Salafist participation. ISIS abuse and ferocity soon pulled in both Ahrar al-Sham and Jabhat al-Nusra. It all coincided with termination of the hiatus in Iraq, with a dramatic flare-up between the Iraqi regime and an alignment of ISIS and Sunni tribal groups across western Iraq. These parallel hostilities in Syria and Iraq were a dry run for later ISIS multi-front actions.

After what the Iraqi government viewed as provocations against security forces in December 2013, the latter arrested Sunni Member of Parliament Ahmad al-Alwani at his home in Ramadi on 28 December. The next day they demolished the Sunni protest camp in Ramadi, sparking clashes between the army and gunmen from clans of the Dulaym tribal confederacy, the largest in al-Anbar province. The army pulled back, and gunmen took over much of the cities of Falluja and Ramadi in the first days of January 2014. ISIS piggybacked on tribal groups to move in and claim leadership of the upheaval. By mid-January, ISIS established itself in parts of towns along the Euphrates from al-Qa'im near the Syrian border through Haditha, Hit, Ramadi, Khalidiya, Saqlawiya, and Falluja to Abu Ghrayb on the outskirts of Baghdad.

The new Iraqi army, literally still under construction, could only react in a piecemeal fashion, relying on firepower and remaining loyal Sahwa tribes, for example the Albu Risha and Albu Bali of the Dulaym confederacy.[71] ISIS launched diversionary actions towards the Shi'a areas south of Baghdad and in the mixed Diyala province, stretching the security forces and provoking advances by Shi'a militias, which further alarmed Sunnis. It took the army until mid-March to restore a shaky supremacy in Ramadi, the Anbar provincial capital. ISIS tightened its grip on Falluja, where the inflamed Sunni militancy prevalent since US devastation of the city in 2004 enabled the jihadists both to preserve their cooperation with the insurgent tribes and to enforce stringent Islamic law. Falluja gave ISIS a territorial anchor in Iraq, a strategic position on the western approaches to Baghdad, and a base for intensified raiding and intimidation up and down the Euphrates.

Considering Iraq and Syria together, how might we assess ISIS performance in its opening double conflict in early 2014? Putting aside the barbarism and nihilism of the ersatz 'caliphate' project, ISIS showed serious military capability. The Syrian opposition had expelled it from its 2013 extensions into north-west Syria by March 2014, including in A'zaz and rebel-held parts of Aleppo, but this represented a pyrrhic victory. First, ISIS retired in reasonable order to the eastern Aleppo countryside, from where it presented a continuing menace. Second, the opposition lost at least a couple of thousand fighters killed,[72] a real dent in its manpower advantage over the Syrian regime, especially with the inflow of Lebanese and Iraqi Shi'a to the regime side. The rebels also leaked fighters to the attractions of ISIS absolutism and salaries.

The basis of the ISIS financial advantage at this early stage is unclear. Its clandestine and criminal networks in Iraq's Sunni Arab towns would have automatically given the organization a head start over the Syrian rebels even if the latter had been less fragmented. Levitt points to ISIS involvement in real-estate transactions in Mosul while the city was still under Iraqi government control, for example.[73] Otherwise, like the Syrian rebels, ISIS had generous donors in the oil principalities[74] and, unlike the rebels, was proof against the splintering effects of donor competition. As yet it only had a minority share in Syrian oilfields. In sum, superior organization and pooling of assets in Syria and Iraq were probably the most significant elements.

From the course of events, it seems that ISIS calculated three immediate requirements in eastern Syria. It needed a well-buffered command centre, so it wiped out Jabhat al-Nusra's residual foothold in al-Raqqa in January. It needed access for supplies and foreign recruits across the Turkish border, so it made sure of the Jarabulus border crossing and eyed Syrian Kurdish border holdings for the next phase. It needed the fertile corridor of the Euphrates into Iraq for the territorial contiguity of its prospective 'caliphate', so in late April it commenced a drive ultimately to clear Jabhat al-Nusra, the Islamic Front, and the FSA from Deir al-Zor city and the whole of the province.

ISIS proved adept at pivoting between fronts and adjusting priorities according to conditions. In February 2014, it withdrew forces from Deir al-Zor for operations in al-Raqqa and Aleppo to the west and in Iraq's al-Anbar to the east. It thereby made its 8–10,000 fighters in Syria[75] and its 6,000 in Iraq[76] count against superior numbers. One estimate claimed that two-thirds of the Syrian total was non-Syrian, with the largest numbers from Saudi Arabia, Libya, and Tunisia.[77] For their part, Chechen jihadists contributed a tough elite, battle hardened against Russia in the Caucasus; the movements of senior commander Batirashvili from eastern Aleppo to al-Anbar to Deir al-Zor illustrated this flexibility. ISIS had good communications and planning, while the very limited impact of the loss of Baghdadi's military deputy Haji Bakr north of Aleppo in February indicated command redundancy. Of course, in early 2014 ISIS was not yet disturbed by aerial bombardment. Only the Iraqi army deployed helicopters and aircraft against it in a desultory fashion, and the only impact was to shift more Sunni Arab sympathy towards ISIS. In Syria, the regime's air force left ISIS headquarters and buildings in al-Raqqa untouched.[78]

By April 2014, ISIS compelled a stalemate in Iraq's al-Anbar province. Jihadists seized Iraqi security-force weaponry and ammunition from stocks near Ramadi, and even acquired Kornet anti-tank missiles.[79] ISIS occupied the Falluja dam on the Euphrates and closed the outlets to flood lands near Falluja, bogging the Iraqi army down and incidentally sparking the accusation that the government didn't mind the flooding because it prevented Sunni voters from participating in the April 2014 general elections.[80] The situation also enabled ISIS to incorporate new cadres, raising its Iraqi numbers towards 6,000 by June; unlike in Syria these were virtually all locals.

What really gave ISIS room for manoeuvre in Iraq, however, was its allies. Support among the tribes gave it numbers beyond its own, while the Naqshbandi ex-Ba'athists had cells across the Sunni north beyond al-Anbar. The tribal umbrella gave extra security to ISIS mobility in the desert and steppe, out of which it could suddenly emerge into Iraqi towns or across the border into Syria. The problem for ISIS was that these were allies of convenience, thrown up by the errors and provocations of Maliki. They inhabited a different universe from the jihadists and were unreliable. ISIS had to use them quickly and then crack down on them. ISIS therefore had to be in a hurry.

In particular, ISIS hastened through May to make sure of Deir al-Zor, without which there was no connection between al-Raqqa in Syria and al-Anbar in Iraq. It also coveted the oil of eastern Syria, then mainly in the hands of Jabhat al-Nusra and the Syrian tribes, but strategic necessity was primary. Pivoting forces back from al-Raqqa and bringing fighters from Iraq, ISIS assembled 2–3,000 troops around Deir al-Zor city to battle perhaps 10,000 Syrian rebel opponents scattered through the province.[81] The FSA and Islamist groups facing ISIS had little confidence. They commented on superior ISIS mobility, firepower, and supply chains from east and west;[82] some speculated on a deal by which the Syrian regime did not touch ISIS in bombing runs from its Deir al-Zor air base in exchange for ISIS delivering positions it abandoned in Aleppo to the regime.[83] By early June, ISIS had taken the whole western part of Deir al-Zor province and made inroads into the city in a nasty assault that included such tricks as booby-trapping bodies;[84] but rebel holdouts remained, especially towards the border.

Deir al-Zor was a metaphor for transformation in the Quicksilver War. Between late 2013 and mid-2014, the irruption of the ISIS jihadists changed a Syrian war with a focus of regime against opposition into a Syria–Iraq war zone with a double focus: the Syrian regime and ISIS itself. As eastern Syria coalesced with western Iraq, the Syrian regime became a peripheral player in places such as Deir al-Zor. Nonetheless, the ultimate outcome in what we might term the eastern theatre of an expanded war zone, where ISIS was busy appropriating the territorial core, still depended on developments in western Syria. Either the emerging ISIS territorial entity would falter before resolution in western Syria, or whatever emerged in command of Damascus would assert itself in eastern Syria. In the meantime, ISIS dynamism and Iranian interaction with Iraqi Shi'a would affect the balance to the west. Two theatres still made a single war zone.

What then was happening in western Syria while ISIS was struggling for eastern Syria and western Iraq? On the diplomatic front, the Syrian National Coalition gained credit in the West for being mildly cooperative at the farcical January–February 2014 'Geneva II' peace talks. The regime, persuaded by Russia to attend, would only discuss 'terrorism', its label for the whole opposition. As a result, the opposition was spared parading its own insistence that Assad should have no role in a Syrian transitional administration.

On the ground, developments varied among the main sectors. In rural north-west Syria, the consolidation of both Islamists and FSA factions to face ISIS and their victory against it at horrendous cost did bring some benefits. The USA relaxed constraints on the Turks and Saudis shipping in lethal American-sourced equipment, and anti-tank missiles began appearing.[85] From March 2014, having expelled ISIS, the now better-coordinated factions in Idlib probed towards the coast along the Turkish border (see chapter 4) and rounded out holdings north of Hama.

In Aleppo and the centre, the regime advanced in early 2014, and the opposition paid an immediate price for the hit to its resources from the fight with ISIS. There was ebb and flow in Aleppo, but overall the rebels proved unable to remove the threat of encirclement. Along the Lebanese border, the regime and Hezbollah achieved a major success in the Qalamoun hills by April, with Islamist rebels largely cleared out. Homs old city finally fell to the regime in May 2014, while humanitarian conditions in blockaded rebel Damascus suburbs beyond the East Ghouta redoubt became more precarious. In mid-2014, the regime had a solid hold over lands connecting Damascus to the coast.

To the south, in Dera'a and Quneitra provinces bordering Jordan and the Israeli-occupied Golan Heights, the evolution was similar to the rural north-west. Here the FSA and milder Islamists were much stronger than in Idlib province, and received favourable attention and supplies through a US–Jordanian–Saudi 'operations room' in Amman. This helped the rebels to advance in the countryside, and to sustain gains into the medium term. Even with Jabhat al-Nusra added, the Israelis did not want Iran and Hezbollah to displace them.

It is interesting to set the slow-moving grind in the cities and complicated hilly terrain of the western theatre against events in the more spacious environment to the east. ISIS made its decisive lunge to carve a caliphate out of Iraq and Syria in less than a month of lightning assaults in June–July 2014. For the breakthrough shock in northern Iraq, it deployed a motorized strike force of no more than a couple of thousand men. ISIS inaugurated its blitz on 4 June by killing the top government Sahwa ally in Ramadi, Muhammad Abu Risha. Prime Minister Maliki commented sagely that ISIS elements 'have become pursued like rats and don't have the capacity to fight the sons of the tribes and the army'[86]—a glimpse of how aware the government was of the real state of play. On 4–5 June, ISIS struck the town of Samarra in what may have been a diversion to confuse the Iraqi regime, giving the impression that the target was the Shi'a Askari shrine.

Simultaneously, another mobile strike force plunged into Mosul, coordinating with sympathetic cells among the residents. ISIS evidently had good intelligence on the poor preparedness of the 30,000 Iraqi soldiers in the vicinity, and their alienation from the local population. After a few days of disorienting clashes, army morale collapsed and the troops, mainly Shi'a in a Sunni city, fled on 10 June. The jihadists looted more than $400 million from the banks and a vast haul of weaponry, immediately transferring much of their booty to Syria to finish the Deir al-Zor campaign by assault and bribery. At the same time, by way of gratitude for jihadist ease of movement in and out of Turkey, ISIS took care to seize the Turkish consulate in Mosul and kidnap all forty-nine Turkish staff (see chapter 4). While doing all this, ISIS also sent a column south from Mosul on 11 June to take the Baiji oil refinery and Tikrit, menacing Baghdad from the north while a second force stood on the western approaches to the capital from Falluja.

Important questions arise for which we can only give tentative responses without more data from within the ISIS military command. Was the blitz in Sunni Arab northern Iraq, followed by the clearance of rivals from Sunni Arab eastern Syria, pre-planned, or was it a set of improvisations after a surprise crumpling of the Iraqi security forces? The swift sequencing points to advance preparation of the campaign, with accurate forecasting of the impact and results. What were the roles and relative weights of ISIS jihadists based in Iraq, ISIS Iraqi allies, and ISIS contingents from Syria in the 4–11 June breakthrough in northern Iraq? Again, the sequencing suggests shrewd pivoting between the two countries. Did elite foreign fighters based in Syria join the mobile columns and the shock squad of suicide bombers breaking into Mosul? If so, was their pre-programmed purpose to shift captured weaponry to eastern Syria? It seems clear that the fall of Mosul and the disintegration of the Iraqi army psychologically overawed Jabhat al-Nusra units and Syrian tribes in Deir al-Zor, making it easier for ISIS to cobble together Syrian and Iraqi provinces and take over Syrian oilfields by mid-July 2014.

Everyone knew the ISIS mission to manufacture a new entity spanning the Syria–Iraq border, but there was no sign of Iraqi government awareness of unfolding disaster even when ISIS charged into Mosul. Maliki's initial reaction was simply to advance the date of a 'national unity conference' for al-Anbar province. Iraqi 'security experts' defined the ISIS move as 'an attempt to show force and to lessen the pressure' the Iraqi army was applying in Ramadi and Falluja.[87] No one registered the imminence of Baghdadi's 'caliphate', except perhaps the KRG Kurds.[88] In Baghdad, there was a total intelligence as well as military failure; Iraq headed into the abyss in denial.

2

WAR IN SYRIA AND IRAQ, 2014–2017

In its June 2014 blitz, ISIS secured predominance in contiguous areas of western Iraq and eastern Syria amounting to above a third of the combined territory of the two countries (Map 2). When it set out on its coup in early June it only controlled modest, discontinuous portions of this expanse. After the blitz, it occupied the geographical centre of the overall war zone, and pursued hostilities with all other local parties either within or around its perimeter. Starting with Syrian opposition factions and the Iraqi regime, it lost little time in assaulting the Kurds of Iraq and Syria as well as Syrian regime outposts within its new domain. Along the desert margins of western Syria, ISIS engaged the regime in a bizarre mixture of warfare and continued détente, some-times simultaneously, while also sparring with the rebels over turf.

As for the contest within western Syria from 2014 onwards, ISIS and other jihadists continued to prove a disaster for the Syrian Sunni Arab rebels and a gift that kept on giving for the Syrian regime. In the wider world, ISIS furnished fodder for Syrian regime propaganda painting all its opponents as 'terrorists' or their camp followers. While ISIS fascinated the global media with its cruelty in Iraq and Syria and terror attacks in Europe, Bashar al-Assad's apparatus got on with its larger-scale killing away from the limelight. Even when ISIS was at its peak, rough counting of Syrian civilian deaths for December 2014 had the regime leading ISIS 85 per cent to 5 per cent in responsibility.[1]

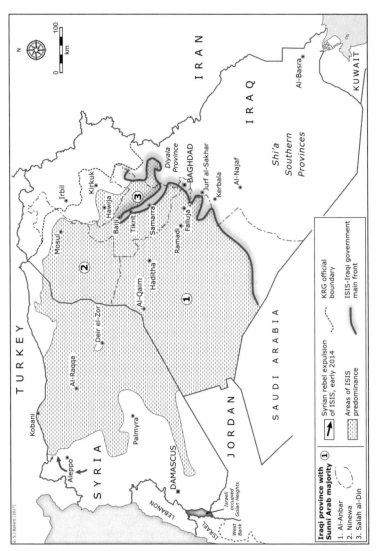

Map 2: Iraq and ISIS, late 2014

Aside from servicing Assad's public relations, ISIS and surrogates in western Syria—in the Yarmouk Valley near Dera'a, in rural Damascus, and east of Aleppo—kept up bothering the rebels while the latter fought the regime.

Most significantly for events in western Syria and for the integration of the Syria–Iraq war zone, the ISIS offensive and barbarities of summer 2014 in Iraq and Syria cemented Russian and Iranian justification for their salvaging of the Syrian regime. ISIS provided perfect cover for the dramatic Russian aerial bombardment against the Syrian rebels from October 2015 onwards, and for the accompanying stepped-up Iranian-coordinated infusion of foreign Shi'a militias into western Syria. Russia and Iran were not just leading the world in fighting 'terrorism', but only they had any legal rights as external powers in Syria. Russian deputy foreign minister Oleg Syromolotov struck a virtuous pose in a February 2016 interview: 'In fighting terrorists in Syria at the invitation of the legitimate Syrian government, Russia attacks not only ISIS targets but also … other terrorist groups, including Jabhat al-Nusra.'[2] According to Syromolotov, 'it is impossible to talk about the legitimacy of antiterrorist efforts in Syria by any one state except Russia and Iran'. In fact, Russia, while constantly citing ISIS, concentrated on bombing all the Syrian regime's more immediate adversaries, targeting ISIS only intermittently. As for Iran, the rise of ISIS enabled the Islamic revolutionary regime to pose with Assad as protectors of Syria's minorities, while the ISIS coup in Iraq bound fearful, enraged Iraqi Shi'a more tightly to Tehran. In serious respects, ISIS, if only for a time, suited the strategic interests of Russia, Iran, and Assad.

By June 2014, the dream of a pluralist new Syria with freedom and equality for all its people promoted by idealist activists during the 2011 street protests had become a distant nostalgia. The Syrian regime and the jihadists and Salafists were solidly entrenched as the leading options, and they all represented despotic rule. After 2014, the outlook for Sunni Arabs in both Syria and Iraq was grim. In Syria, demographic truncation of the Sunni Arab majority was well under way, strategic areas of western Syria, particularly around Homs, Damascus, and Aleppo were substantially depopulated, and by 2016 at least one-third of Sunni Arab Syrians were refugees outside Syria. At the same time, the regime war effort gobbled up young adult Alawite males. As long as the Iranians ensured a steady inflow of Lebanese, Afghani, and even Pakistani Shi'a fighters the sacrifice of his own community left Assad unfazed. In eastern Syria and Sunni Arab Iraq, ISIS at first brought a degree of order and religiosity not unwelcome to many of its local Sunni co-religionists. Within months, however, this became regimentation and terrorization. Like Assad, ISIS imported a horde of foreigners into its portion of Syria, who assisted in repressing local Sunnis. In Iraq, temporary ISIS command of Sunni Arab provinces simply guaranteed the slow re-conquest after mid-2015 that would leave these provinces wrecked and their inhabitants mostly destitute.

The toll of deaths from violence in Syria from March 2011 probably passed 200,000 some time in mid-2014, according to a careful UN-commissioned study,[3] then rose by 150,000 in the following three years. In Iraq, a parallel 'civilian' toll reached over 18,000 for the period between April 2013 and July 2014, which could be termed the initial phase of a renewed Iraqi civil war, to which a further 45,000 may be added up to the end of 2016.[4] Total deaths from violence for the joint war zone over the two-and-a-half years between mid-2014 and early 2017 approached a quarter of a million.

Regarding the composition of the death toll by mid-2014, the estimates for Syria show a heavy bias towards combatant casualties (two-thirds) compared with civilians, and towards males (85 per cent).[5] The relatively conservative SOHR count for 2011–14 also points to significantly higher losses among regime troops and militiamen (65,803) compared with among rebel fighters (46,301, including 15,422 non-Syrians, mainly jihadists).[6] The imbalance may reflect an early profligate regime use of military manpower. It also suggests Alawite losses difficult to sustain for a community of about 2.5 million. In a sensible analysis, Kyle Orton calculates a death toll of 10–11 per cent of military-age male Alawites (very roughly, 75,000 out of 700,000) between 2011 and 2015.[7] The overall picture has some similarity to the First World War in Europe—a demographic bulge in younger age groups supplying plenty of military cannon fodder and feeding high attrition of young adult males.

This chapter dissects the Quicksilver War in its expanded form across Syria and Iraq from June 2014 onwards. It begins with 2014–15 in the eastern and western theatres, featuring the fortunes of ISIS and the

Syrian regime respectively. The USA intervened directly in the war for the first time, in late 2014 launching an aerial campaign against ISIS in Iraq and Syria and working to rebuild the Iraqi security forces. In Iraq, circumstances forced the USA into uneasy interaction with Iran and Iranian-backed Iraqi Shi'a militias, themselves engaged against ISIS at the same time as they disparaged the USA. In Syria, the USA de-emphasized removal of Assad as a priority and tried to compel Syrian rebels to focus on ISIS rather than their primary enemy: the Syrian regime.

To the west, Turkey and Saudi Arabia assisted the rebels to shake the Syrian regime by mid-2015, which provoked the first direct Russian intervention against the rebels—an aerial onslaught paralleling the US and allied effort against ISIS. Under the Russian aerial umbrella, Iran's Revolutionary Guard imported more Iraqi Shi'a and other militiamen into Syria to enable the depleted regime military to make ground attacks. In Syria, Iran's overriding objective was victory for Bashar al-Assad against any alternative that might garner international recognition. ISIS was a convenient spoiler, and the Iranians displayed no serious interest in its early removal from Syria.

The chapter surveys war-zone geopolitics through 2016–17, interpreting the interplay of local entities and external powers. Leaving Iraq largely to the USA and Iran, Russia took the lead in western Syria through 2016. Escalation through bombardment in Syria also elevated Russia in world affairs. Russia's position, however, was delicate. It needed partners for Syrian stabilization, which gave Turkey leverage. It needed ground forces for coercion, which kept Iran in play. Both countries had ambitions at odds with Russian supremacy. Turkey could play between Russia and the USA, while Iran could plot with Bashar. For its part, Russia could turn to the Syrian regime or the Syrian Kurds to check Turkey. It could stand aside from Israeli air strikes on Hezbollah, the regime, and Iranians in southern Syria. In 2017, the Quicksilver War has become multi-dimensional chess.

Countering ISIS

On 29 June 2014, ISIS announced its transfiguration into the 'caliphate', the only legitimate authority on the planet. ISIS leader Baghdadi ascended the *minbar* of the great mosque in Mosul to present himself as the caliph, or successor of the prophet Muhammad as head of the global Islamic community. In early July, Jabhat al-Nusra and FSA factions in the east of Syria's Deir al-Zor province surrendered or departed, removing the last obstacle to ISIS's fusion of eastern Syria and western Iraq into its pseudo-state.

To the outsider, ISIS military and organizational expertise in addition to initial popularity with many of the 6 million or more Sunni Arabs within its new territory seemed to give it a chance of viability. It had oilfields and the advantage of interior lines in a compact space, and was flush with new mobility and weaponry from its massive haul of booty. It simply needed to be minimally nice to its potentially handy population base and to exploit its central position to subvert neighbouring Sunni peoples and states. With its opponents tripping over one another in terms of their mutual detestation and cross-cutting interests it could probably have built some covert relationships.

Instead, because it was an absolutist millenarian cult with a divine mission to impose its reading of Sunni Islam by force, ISIS intended war with everyone it encountered, and terrorized even its own sympathizers. For ISIS, what others viewed as a lunatic commitment to ultimate destruction was a blessed project that would win through by divine favour. Beyond those who submitted to the caliph and joined the elect, the fate of humanity was either servitude or eradication.

Only the timetable of eradication might be flexible. ISIS and the Syrian regime, for example, treated each other as temporarily useful while each had more immediate targets. Each, however, had only limited tolerance for outposts of the other that became inconvenient. ISIS viewed Turkey as a body within which supporting infrastructure could be incubated, rather like alien seeding in other bodies in Ridley Scott's *Alien* movies, and delayed a terrorist assault until Turkey started a crackdown. Syrian Kurds offended ISIS by asserting ethnic identity ahead of religious identity, and by standing in the way along the Turkish border; those who didn't submit or flee were to be eliminated promptly. Religious communities ISIS condemned as blasphemous, most immediately Shi'a Muslims, Shi'a-derived Alawites, and adherents of the Yazidi faith, were to be destroyed wherever the jihadists reached them. As 'people of the book', Christians had slightly more varied options: servile status, conversion, or death depending on the whim of the moment. Virtually all prudently fled.

ISIS could only remain distinct from its jihadist competitors in the rarified universe of al-Qaeda offshoots by remaining true to its vision of the fortified caliphal state as a citadel for unrelenting war against the rest of the world. Whatever the wavering among its flock, the shadowy core leadership of Baghdadi, Salafist renegades, embittered old Ba'athists, and imported Arab, Chechen, and other militants seemed consumed by the vision. Some of them may have sensed that the extremity of their vision doomed the caliphal citadel, but the spectacular victory of 2014 obscured longer-term reality. In any case, they could not go back on repudiation of Jabhat al-Nusra's focus on 'jihadism in one country' (to paraphrase Stalin), or of Usama bin Laden's stress on global al-Qaeda action unfettered by risky territorial commitment. Their vision and their 'caliphate' were the basis for the Middle Eastern and worldwide mobilization of young Sunni Muslim recruits vital for their military enterprise. On the ground, the 'caliphate' needed continuously to add territory and resources to sustain the mobilization.[8] ISIS thereby provoked a crushing array of enemies that would eventually prevail regardless of disunity and distraction. It locked itself into a ruinous trajectory towards suicide.

ISIS was at its zenith in late 2014 and early 2015. It rounded out its territory with a series of extra gains that outweighed several setbacks, at least in the eyes of its followers. It established a rudimentary administration that for a brief period provided a degree of order and stability satisfactory to traders and others prepared to turn a blind eye to mutilation and murder. It also called forth resistance and American-led responses in Iraq and northern Syria that would end ISIS expansion by mid-2015.

Directly after the fall of Mosul, the Iraqi government and Iraqi Shi'a reeled from the ISIS massacre of up to 1,700 captured Iraqi Shi'a air force cadets at Camp Speicher near Tikrit. This galvanized Iraq's Shi'a majority, with a mass infusion of Shi'a militia into Baghdad and Shi'a areas facing ISIS south of Falluja. By late June, after a brief scare, the Shi'a move secured the capital, albeit with Iran looming in the rear. Local Shi'a demographic domination meant that Baghdad was not in serious danger, apart from the usual car bombs and perhaps an ISIS raid. Directly to the north, however, the mixed Diyala province was vulnerable. ISIS found itself blocked at Samarra and tried to cut the

Samarra–Baghdad highway from both sides while it also infiltrated Diyala. Again, the Shi'a militias tipped the balance, checking ISIS.

Through July–August 2014, ISIS conducted several operations to consolidate its new domain. Despite mixed results, the coordination across several fronts further demonstrated battlefield skill. In eastern Syria, ISIS decided that it could no longer cohabit with the Syrian regime. In late July and August, it overran a large army facility north of al-Raqqa and the important Tabqa air base. It prefaced these moves with a damaging raid on the al-Sha'er gas field east of Homs. It executed up to 400 regime troops and civilian personnel in the three locations, sending a shock wave into the Alawite coastal heartland. ISIS also attacked the regime base near al-Hasakeh, where it was repulsed, and invested the regime redoubt in Deir al-Zor city. Overall it added enough Russian arms and ammunition to its American haul from Iraq to keep itself afloat for several years.

In Iraq, ISIS took the Yazidi town of Sinjar in early August, astride communications between Mosul and al-Raqqa, and pushed its northern perimeter towards the Kurdistan region (see chapter 3). Here it provoked American aerial bombing, which assisted the Kurdish Peshmerga to recover lost territory except Sinjar. ISIS barbarity towards the Yazidis assured the USA and the Iraqi regime of solid Western military backup and UN endorsement, stacking up more enemies for the jihadists.

Simultaneously, ISIS imposed a siege on the Shi'a Turkmen town of Amerli, east of Tikrit. Western air power, Kurdish Peshmerga, and Iraqi Shi'a militias forced ISIS to withdraw, but the incident indicated its capacity to push east, threatening communications between Iraqi Kurdistan and Baghdad. This was especially the case with ISIS entrenching itself in the strategic district of Hawija,[9] from which it had excellent access both east to Kirkuk and south to Iraq's largest oil refinery at Baiji. Hawija had been a centre of Sunni Arab anger in 2013, and remained so. As is often the case, however, the picture was intricate. A little to the south, at Dhuluiya near Samarra, members of the Sunni Jubbour tribe, many of them middle class, resisted ISIS and looked to Baghdad.[10]

As for the Iraqi regime, the most urgent priority after the June 2014 disaster was leadership change. Prime Minister Maliki was responsible for events and President Jalal Talabani was physically incapacitated. Iraq could not rebound and the USA could not contribute without change.

By good chance, Talabani's tenure of the largely ceremonial presidency, a Kurdish preserve, finished in July 2014. Fouad Masoum, a flexible politician from Talabani's Patriotic Union of Kurdistan (PUK) who had religious and Communist backgrounds, won the parliamentary vote to succeed Talabani. In August, with the US pressing and Iran acquiescing, he nominated a new Shi'a prime minister.

Maliki gave way with bad grace to his urbane and Western-friendly Da'awa Party colleague Haydar al-Abadi. Iran, confident of its influence through major Shi'a parties, militias, and personalities, including the unforgiving Maliki, could bide its time. Abadi emphasized sectarian tolerance and selected a prominent Sunni Arab as defence minister. He provided the Obama administration with the window-dressing it needed in Baghdad to furnish military aid against ISIS. In an awkward dualism that characterized a number of binaries in the war zone (Russia and Turkey, Baghdad and Irbil, and the Syrian regime and Syrian Kurds) the USA and Iran interacted separately with Baghdad as they looked to different eventual scenarios.

Washington intended gradually to reconstruct, retrain, and re-equip the Iraqi army on a long timetable to have indigenous forces defeat ISIS. In descending order, this would avoid a large-scale ground commitment entailing American casualties, give legitimacy to the outcome, and compensate for complacency before the disaster. The legitimacy obviously depended on the rebuilt army and other security forces being perceived as more or less non-sectarian. The USA wanted these official forces, with significant Sunni Arab participation at all levels, to lead in liberation. It wanted Shi'a militias kept secondary and supervised. US and Iranian agendas diverged here.

From early August 2014, the USA coupled its incipient new advice and training programme with air strikes to help the KRG against the ISIS advance, strikes that were soon extended more widely in Iraq. After the ISIS beheadings of American hostages James Foley and Steven Sotloff in eastern Syria, the USA began bombing jihadists in Syria in mid-September. The third element in the American concept was the involvement of other countries in a US-led coalition, whether for training and equipping Kurds and Iraqi Arabs or for bombing ISIS. France commenced limited bombing in Iraq in mid-September, followed by crucial Sunni Arab participation in the air offensive

(Jordan, Saudi Arabia, the United Arab Emirates, and Bahrain). Britain and Australia joined the bombing in October.

For Iran, the ISIS threat opened opportunities for more leverage over Iraqi Shi'a, Baghdad, and the KRG, but also imposed more need for leverage because of the bumped-up Western presence. In June 2014, Iran wasted no time sending extra Quds Force advisers and weaponry to Shi'a militias, which they helped reorganize into a more coherent framework termed Popular Mobilization Forces (PMF or al-Hashd al-Sha'bi). In late October, the PMF led in expelling ISIS from Jurf al-Sakhar south of Baghdad, a locality from which the jihadists could potentially interrupt communications between the capital and the Shi'a provinces. Iran also dispatched arms and advisers to Diyala province, and arms to the Peshmerga, especially those affiliated with the PUK. Diyala and Kurdistan bordered Iran, so Iranian penetration there was to be expected.

Iranian strategic interest, however, extended to all of Iraq; the country as a whole, especially the Sunni Arab areas seized by ISIS, physically separated Iran from its stake in Bashar al-Assad and western Syria. Iran's deficient air power put it at a disadvantage in the depth of Iraq compared with the US-led coalition. To compensate, Iran played on the Iraqi government's need for manpower to have the new Shi'a PMF plus their Iranian advisers inserted into operations in the Sunni Arab provinces.

In late 2014 and early 2015, ISIS focused on the Syrian Kurdish town and de facto canton of Kobani, midway in the scatter of Kurdish autonomous authorities along the Syrian–Turkish border. This was at the far western end of ISIS's holdings, close to the ISIS 'capital', al-Raqqa. Chapter 3 discusses ISIS's motivations and the events in more detail. The main points are that US-led aerial bombardment tipped the balance in favour of the Syrian Kurdish Democratic Union Party (PYD), and the PYD repelled ISIS, going on to achieve continuous Syrian Kurdish control along two-thirds of the border with Turkey by mid-2015. The affair was a vivid demonstration of the aerial interdiction that a great power could apply, which no doubt registered with the Iranians and Russians regarding western Syria. It also precipitated a sharp worsening in Turkey's already troubled relations with both Syrian and Turkish Kurds. For AKP leaders, the PYD was in cahoots with the outlawed Kurdistan Workers' Party (PKK) on the Turkish side of the border. It was thus a 'terrorist' front, and its self-rule was a threatening precedent. For PYD-inclined Syrian Kurds and much of Turkish Kurdish opinion, the AKP was out of the closet as Islamists in cahoots with ISIS. These hardening narratives coloured developments in Syria in following years.

Meantime, intermittent flare-ups occurred in northern Iraq, with the Iraqi government and the KRG anxious to take initiatives. In November 2014, Iraqi forces, including Shi'a militia, took advantage of a foothold inside the Baiji oil refinery north of Tikrit to try to expel ISIS from the town and refinery. ISIS had a strong position because of a supply line to its Hawija redoubt. Unsurprisingly the premature Iraqi experiment failed; ISIS turned the tables and wiped out government gains by late December. The Kurds had better fortune with an offensive to break ISIS encirclement of the Sinjar hills in December 2014. The KRG, PYD, PKK, and a new PKK-linked Yazidi militia all had skin in the game here. Many Yazidis who stayed on in the hills after the August Peshmerga retreat under ISIS pressure felt that the PKK and PYD had come to their rescue from across the Syrian border. The large KRG Peshmerga force that broke through in December could not fully reverse such sentiments. Tension among these Kurdish factions persisted, with the PYD and PKK suspecting KRG collusion with Turkey against them.

Iraqi prime minister Abadi and his advisers chose Tikrit for the next bid to begin rolling back ISIS and to puncture its martial aura. Tikrit was a provincial capital and the first step on the return to Mosul. The main problem was the shortage of regular troops in early 2015, with the second reconstruction of the army still at an early stage. The government had no choice but to turn to the Shi'a PMF and its Iranian handlers, chief among them Quds Force commander Qasem Soleimani. The PMF provided 20,000 fighters alongside 3,000 from the army and 1,000 Sunni tribesmen,[11] against a much smaller ISIS force. ISIS mounted a strong defence in Tikrit's urban terrain through March 2015, using booby traps and snipers, and the army and PMF found themselves stalled after good progress. The Shi'a commanders wanted their own victory, and rejected any US role. In the end, they had to relent, and the government requested coalition air strikes to break ISIS in the city centre.

PMF fighters took revenge for atrocities against Shi'a by torturing, killing, and mutilating captured ISIS personnel and looting Sunni properties. The Sunni vice-president, Usama al-Nujayfi, demanded a 'cessation of abuses against Sunnis' and maverick Shi'a leader Muqtada al-Sadr called for punishment of those who resorted to 'torture and disfiguring of corpses'.[12] The government and the PMF recovered Tikrit, but the former wanted to have regular troops and federal paramilitary police as the centre of gravity in coming phases, which would slow momentum. More immediately, ISIS exploited the government focus on Tikrit to improve its position further north in the Baiji refinery.

Baiji apart, ISIS looked to be checked across Iraq and Syria in the mid-spring of 2015. Syrian Kurds, the KRG, the Iraqi government, and the PMF had pushed back, Iraqi security forces kept positions in the long-standing ISIS heartland of al-Anbar province, and ISIS and the Syrian regime continued to co-habit Deir al-Zor city. The medium-intensity US-led aerial bombardment caused gradual attrition and restricted mobility. Aerial intervention was decisive in Kobani and Tikrit, and ISIS had no answer to it. On the other hand, in the nine months since its 'big bang' appearance on the international stage, ISIS had considerably augmented military manpower, from both the inflow of foreign Muslim enthusiasts and local Sunni enrolment. It also still had its inflated arsenal largely intact. ISIS prestige, the ISIS *raison d'être* of the territorial 'caliphate', and the organization's appetite for resources all required periodic expansion. As its al-Qaeda rivals surmised, this defied reality. Still, in early 2015, ISIS retained the capacity to surprise its adversaries.

ISIS struck simultaneously at Ramadi in Iraq and Palmyra in Syria in a few days in mid-May 2015. The surviving Iraqi government presence in and near Ramadi potentially destabilized ISIS domination of al-Anbar, including its stronghold in Falluja, sandwiched between Ramadi and Baghdad. After months of skirmishing along the Euphrates, ISIS mounted a 'shock and awe' assault on government positions in Ramadi using suicide truck bombs. A sandstorm temporarily neutralized air power.[13] Iraqi soldiers hastily pulled out; ISIS thereby secured both the provincial capital and a more firmly anchored rear for its forward positions in Falluja and beyond.

ISIS interest in Palmyra (Tadmur) presumably grew out of its stand-off with the Syrian regime in Deir al-Zor. Seizing Palmyra would take away the closest jumping-off point within regime territory for relieving the regime's Deir al-Zor enclave. It would also give ISIS a good southern flank for extending into the gas fields east of Homs. In early May, ISIS first chewed off some regime holdings in Deir al-Zor and took al-Sukhna, the principal settlement between Deir al-Zor and Palmyra. It then swept across the desert towards Palmyra. Regime forces offered indifferent resistance, and ISIS overran both the town and the famous Roman-era ruins by 21 May. As in northern Iraq, ISIS intended to destroy relics it considered idolatrous or polytheistic and to make money out of trading antiquities. Its first relic for demolition in Palmyra, however, was the regime's notorious Tadmur prison, for decades one of Syria's top crime scenes for human rights abuses. Were former inmates taking revenge? Was ISIS bidding for popular favour? Was there a deal with the regime over Palmyra?

In sending several thousand fighters west to Palmyra and beyond, ISIS exploited Syrian regime distraction by rebel advances in Idlib province in the spring of 2015. The interaction of the western and eastern war theatres is clear. The more fundamental issue is what ISIS hoped to do with victories that could only have a short shelf-life. Here there was space for logic. First, ISIS positioned itself east of Damascus and Homs to be ready for any unravelling of the Syrian regime arising from the concurrent rebel campaign underwritten by the Turks and Saudis. If ISIS could entrench itself in Damascus it might manage a second wind for the 'caliphate'. Conversely, the Syrian regime and its Russian ally had the argument of a Palmyra terrorist nest to alarm the world. Second, the reputational reverberations of ISIS inflicting Ramadi- and Palmyra-style shocks might shift the domestic equation in some Sunni Arab countries. On any realistic reading of, for example, Jordan and Saudi Arabia, this had no chance—especially after the January 2015 ISIS burning to death of downed Jordanian pilot Muath al-Kasasbeh. However, such thinking within ISIS would be no more far-fetched than German hopes for the Battle of the Bulge in 1944.

Estimates of ISIS military manpower strength in early 2015 ranged from less than 30,000 to 200,000. Daveed Gartenstein-Ross in *War on the Rocks* assesses 100,000 as plausible, of which the elite elements might have been about 15,000.[14] This can be reconciled with the total of 15,000 in Syria and Iraq for June 2014 if a lot of camp followers were not then included, and on the basis of known inflation in late 2014. As Gartenstein-Ross observes, it fits with the available populations and estimates of attrition; the latter simply don't make sense for a force of 30,000. It also fits with the scale of multi-front fighting, simultaneous offensives, and garrison requirements across the 'caliphal' territory. ISIS indulged in human-wave attacks on its front with the KRG, a luxury more compatible with higher manpower levels.[15]

Even with much of its weaponry being free loot, ISIS needed a revenue inflow to maintain around 100,000 fighters. Its caliphal project also required an administrative apparatus adapted to implementing its version of divine governance. After all, the 'caliphate' was the ideological justification for ISIS warfare and the beacon for its recruits. Inevitably the instant 'Islamic state' was a confidence trick; the new set of ISIS agencies (*dawawin*, singular *diwan*) and provinces simply cannibalized the existing infrastructure of Syria and Iraq.[16] In eastern Syria, Damascus continued to pay teachers and government technicians in hydro and gas power plants,[17] while in western Iraq Baghdad paid salaries until August 2015 as if nothing had happened.[18] ISIS thus had a free ride, and made sure it creamed off a tax of up to 50 per cent as well.[19]

The new feature was infusion into the regular course of life of extremist religious edicts and ferocious punishments, including beheadings, other death penalties, and displays of corpses. One bizarre ISIS extortion tactic, which Aymenn Al-Tamimi illustrates nicely, was enforced purchase of repentance certificates by anyone previously associated with its rivals.[20] ISIS demanded, for example, that al-Raqqa teachers repent and submit to re-education, on pain of death for apostasy.[21] At Mosul University, ISIS abolished most of the humanities, which were considered blasphemous.[22] After a brief economic upsurge under laissez-faire rebels in 2013,[23] eastern Syria joined western Iraq in being ruthlessly squeezed under ISIS. Both the towns and tribes were thoroughly intimidated. Only cash cows such as transiting traders and oilfield operators found the 'caliphate' amenable. ISIS also reportedly arranged through a Greek Catholic go-between to transfer oil to the Syrian regime, helping to keep Bashar al-Assad's war machine running in western Syria.[24]

According to a February 2017 King's College London study of ISIS finances,[25] this parasitic criminal enterprise boomed into late 2015, making $2–3 billion in the year-and-a-half after its 2014 coup. Pillaging Mosul was a one-time bonanza, but ISIS quickly increased its income from oil and taxes as it imposed its writ. Coalition bombing of small oil-refining sites failed to dent the oil-trafficking business. Nor did it affect taxation. ISIS had no problem sustaining its military spending into late 2015, with pay to troops higher than in any Syrian rebel group, but conditions began to bite thereafter. Ramadi and Palmyra were poor pickings, and US-led air strikes and falling oil prices began to knock out the supports of the pseudo-state.

Lucky Assad?

Alongside the drama of ISIS, the unrelenting struggle for western Syria wound its bloody course towards a direct Russian intervention that would tie Moscow's global standing to the fate of Syria. In parallel, Tobias Schneider suggests,[26] the Syrian state and regime devolved from a more-or-less coherent mafia into a loose conglomerate of bits of administrative machinery exposed to local gang bosses. This was the state and regime that Russia promoted as 'Syria'. By 2016, the Obama administration had a similar outlook, being mainly concerned to find common ground with Vladimir Putin on defeating jihadism and neutralizing western Syria. President Obama's senior Middle East adviser, Robert Malley, spoke of a 'transition that preserves state institutions and avoids chaos'.[27] Given that the leading state institutions still functioning in a meaningful manner were Assad's security agencies, Malley appeared to mean preserving the very instruments of chaos that were the sources of much of Syria's misery.

Even before receiving his injection of oxygen from Russian aerial escalation from October 2015 onwards, Bashar al-Assad continued to enjoy advantages. His monopoly of air power, his superiority in heavy weaponry, and the absolute commitment of Russia and Iran all remained undented. Although the state apparatus was derelict, the regime's monopolization of the bits and pieces in western Syria put the population in thrall to it for jobs, permits, property registration, passports, and so forth. Kheder Khaddour details how Bashar weaponized the provision of public services.[28] In this respect, large numbers of internally displaced Sunni Arabs congregated in Latakia and inner

Damascus where they were dependent on the regime, which could claim them among its support base.

In the public relations arena, jihadist agendas and horror shows breathed life into the regime narrative of Bashar as a hero and every-one's friend against terror. Damascus worked hard on its narrative, making serious inroads in a Western world weary of the Middle East, while the opposition relied complacently on friends and its conviction of the transparent justice of its cause. It did not help that ISIS behead-ings, Jabhat al-Nusra kidnapping for revenue (acquired mainly from Qatar), and Islamist paranoia almost completely deterred Westerners from going to rebel areas and reporting on conditions from mid-2014 to 2016. Meantime, the regime smiled on a stream of foreign visitors. Bashar was far from being delusional in not ceasing 'to bet on the mili-tary solution' and believing he would ultimately 'win and recover rule over all of Syria', in the words of former UN envoy Brahimi in October 2014.[29]

In Tobias Schneider's counter-reality,[30] gradual decomposition of the Syrian regime into a patchwork of local bailiwicks was well advanced by 2015. Regime commanders were having increasing difficulty mobi-lizing troops even apart from the impact of years of attrition suffered by the Alawite community. Local strongmen were doing their own lucrative supply deals with rebels, and even with ISIS, while army and paramilitary units autonomously lived off blackmail of besieged sub-urbs. Local armed groups would not necessarily support one another against rebels, and could clash over smuggling. In such a scenario, it is easy to conclude a diminution of Bashar and the ruling clique.

Qualifications are in order. First, decomposition diminished any alternative to Assad even as it circumscribed the president himself, making him if anything more salient to the Russians as the anchor of their vaunted legitimacy in Syria. Second, a more capricious environ-ment probably tightened officer-corps allegiance to the regime. Khaddour contributes a study of dependence and loyalty in Dahiyat al-Asad (literally 'the Assad suburb') near Damascus, Syria's largest military housing complex.[31] The officers, disproportionately Alawite but including Sunnis, have been tied to the regime by individual ben-efits, a deterrent to autonomous solidarity. Third, the alignment of core regular forces, Lebanese Hezbollah, and other imported militias could still match fractious rebels, even if fractious themselves. Schneider notes the ascent of elite paramilitaries such as the Tiger Forces in Hama province, under Alawite swashbuckler Suheil al-Hassan, and the Desert Hawks in northern Latakia and the eastern desert. These moved among fronts as required. Finally, if the regime's allies enabled it to dominate western Syria, it could reconstruct the apparatus of despotism later. Equipped with Russian and Iranian backing, it would restore the fealty of local bosses. Assad probably did not lose too much sleep over warlordism on his turf.

All the same, regime circumstances were not exactly robust; the rebels in western Syria theoretically had a chance to shake the stalemate in early 2015. Further, their backers—principally Turkey and Saudi Arabia—seemed more committed than at any time previously. Fear of losing the initiative to ISIS and the Syrian Kurds across northern Syria propelled the Turkish government towards trying to tip over the whole Syrian table via their rebel friends. For its part, Saudi Arabia had energetic new leaders fiercely hostile to Iranian penetration of the Arab world. In late 2014, Turkey patronized serious convergence of rebel factions in north-west Syria at a time of real rebel receptivity. Again, ISIS activities no doubt affected perspectives. Turkey, Saudi Arabia, and Qatar cooperated (a first) on a major weapons infusion. The immediate targets were the regime-held towns in Idlib province, but the drive would only be decisive if it caused cracking within the regime. It needed to lead promptly to a thrust towards the coast.

In the event, the Idlib towns fell, but a second phase never eventuated. Turkey, Saudi Arabia, and the rebels appeared not fully to understand that they were fundamentally challenging Russia and Iran, and that time was of the essence. Saudi Arabia overextended itself in March 2015 when it embarked on a bombing spree in Yemen, where it also sniffed Iranian meddling. Saudi attention to Syria soon faded, an early win for Iran. Above all, the rebel 'army of conquest' (Jaysh al-Fath), in which the hardline Islamist Ahrar al-Sham and the jihadist Jabhat al-Nusra were the overwhelming majority, paused after its Idlib victories, giving Russia the whole summer of 2015 to prepare its own escalation. It may have been that the rebels simply lacked the confidence and wherewithal to go for broke, and limited themselves accordingly, regardless of the condition of the regime side.

Contrary to the image of Russian anxiety about a failing Assad, Russia's bombing campaign against the rebels only began on 30 September 2015, more than two months after Iranian appeals in July. Russia's build-up of capacity mainly at Hmeimim air base near Latakia, now exclusively a Russian facility, was conducted openly and was hardly a rush. President Putin clearly wanted Iran to feature as subordinate. Groundwork for, and opening of, direct intervention proceeded as Kremlin theatre. An unhurried timetable made sure that everyone registered Russia's status as a reluctant but determined great power that was the primary mover in Syria and indispensable to resolution in the Middle East. When Russia annexed the Crimea in March 2014, Barack Obama had dismissed it as a mere 'regional power' acting out of 'weakness'.[32] This remained a running sore. Syria in late 2015 was the time and place for conclusive rebuttal. As for Assad, the Russians presumably calculated the limits of the rebel surge, and decided that their Syrian associate could safely be left to wait for their move, again to register the true order of things. In any case, if necessity required, Russia would not have a problem mounting early blows.

As for the overall military trajectory in western Syria, there were fateful developments between the mid-2014 ISIS coup to the east and the end of the first phase of Russian intervention in the west in early 2016. In late 2014, the Jabhat al-Nusra jihadists, pushed out of eastern Syria by their rival ISIS, reoriented themselves exclusively to the west. Here they rose to their zenith as shock troops cleverly embedded in wider rebel force structures.[33] Together with the partially jihadist Ahrar al-Sham, they exerted intimidating superiority over what was left of Western-friendly armed factions in north-west Syria. In early and mid-2015, jihadists and radical Islamists dominated campaigns, dealing severe blows to the regime, but they failed to break the stalemate. Between October 2015 and February 2016, Russian bombing and Iranian ground reinforcement shifted the initiative to the regime, again shaking but not yet smashing the balance in western Syria.

Jabhat al-Nusra's energetic impulses in the west in reaction to the ISIS surge in the east posed a dilemma for the immediate target of those impulses: the non-jihadist rebels. The rebels could not persevere against the regime without Jabhat al-Nusra, and had already mortgaged themselves to the jihadists. However, Jabhat al-Nusra's allegiance to al-Qaeda and espousal of ultimate war against the West meant that the West could never tolerate Jabhat al-Nusra steerage of an alternative Syrian regime. In the event, Jabhat al-Nusra settled the matter to its own satisfaction in the Idlib countryside in October 2014 by branding the Western-aligned SRF and Harakat Hazm as 'corrupt', and seizing their positions in the hills of Jabal al-Zawiya.[34] SRF leader Jamal Ma'arouf fled to Turkey.

Jabhat al-Nusra firmed up a strategic command of territory centred on the main Hama to Aleppo highway between Khan Shaykhun to the south and Saraqib to the north, together with flanking upland. From here the jihadists could strike out against the regime southwards (Morek) and eastwards (Abu al-Duhur), and dominate Idlib province from its geographical core. They also secured strongpoints in the hilly terrain along the Turkish border. Meantime, Turkey promoted a rebel agglomeration of hard and soft Islamists and US-favoured factions that in theory excluded Jabhat al-Nusra but in practice cooperated with it. Turkey hosted a meeting of the seventy-two factions of the 'Revolutionary Command Council' in Gaziantep on 29 November 2014.[35]

Certainly, Jabhat al-Nusra needed the rebel alliance, particularly the hard Islamists. The other rebels gave it political cover and augmentation of troops and weaponry for the long-term fight. Beyond Idlib, Jabhat al-Nusra was often the dynamic element on the rebel side; it and its partners registered a chequered performance of ebb, flow, and static line-holding in late 2014—a mirror image of their regime enemy. In Aleppo, Jabhat al-Nusra was prominent in preventing the regime from imposing a full siege to accompany its crescendo of dumping barrel bombs out of helicopters. On the Lebanese border, it had a tactical liaison with fighters pledged to ISIS—a warning for the future—in surviving a combination of Syrian and Lebanese security forces and Hezbollah. In August 2014, they attacked Hezbollah outposts and kidnapped thirty Lebanese soldiers and police. Lebanon teetered on the brink of being dragged into the western Syrian theatre.

In Damascus, the factions fought each other as much as they confronted the regime's starvation sieges; the Islamists of Jaysh al-Islam saw off competitors in their East Ghouta enclave, while Jabhat al-Nusra infiltrated. In the far south, Jabhat al-Nusra had an important role in a campaign to broaden rebel territory in Dera'a and Quneitra provinces.

Here, however, the Western-aligned militias of the Southern Front were much stronger than the SRF in the north-west, and favoured by Jordan and Israel. In addition, in late 2014 Jabhat al-Nusra and the Southern Front faced a new ISIS affiliate, the Yarmouk Martyrs Brigade, which commanded difficult terrain wedged alongside the south of the Israeli-occupied Golan Heights.

Western Syria thus presented an intricate patchwork of fronts and territories for both the rebels and the regime. Each front had its own special features and geopolitical significance. Nonetheless, after the ISIS declaration of its 'caliphate' the rebel focus had to be on their largest contiguous holding: rural Idlib and adjoining parts of Aleppo, Hama, and Latakia provinces, comprising much of the best farmland of north-west Syria. The long-standing regime command of a corridor from Latakia to the towns in the centre of this holding constituted a continuing danger to all the rebels. At the same time, the rebels enjoyed the opportunities of easy supply routes from Turkey and possibilities to strike out towards Latakia, Hama, and Aleppo. In July 2014, the Islamic Front and Jabhat al-Nusra probed south towards the Hama military airport,[36] but a vigorous Iranian-assisted regime riposte in October led to loss of all gains and the town of Morek, potentially exposing Khan Shaykhun. The regime inserted its Tiger Forces and the episode highlighted rebel limitations. In December, Jabhat al-Nusra linked with Ahrar al-Sham and the jihadist Jund al-Aqsa to overwhelm the regime's large Wadi al-Da'if base, a threat to the large town of Ma'arrat al-Nu'man since rebel capture of the latter in October 2012. This highlighted opportunities.

After two months of preparations among Islamist rebels, including absorption of the Salafist Suqur al-Sham by Ahrar al-Sham, a new alignment termed Jaysh al-Fath (Army of Conquest) emerged in mid-March 2015.[37] It mobilized 6,000 fighters and promptly dispatched about half of these in a multi-pronged attack on regime troops in Idlib city.[38] The planning was meticulous, showing that the armed opposition had come a long way since 2012; the city fell on 29 March. Allocation of shares among the factions in a proposed fifteen-seat 'civil administration' indicated both relative weightings and the outlook under rebel rule. On the basis of one seat per 250 fighters in the storming of Idlib, Ahrar al-Sham received seven and Jabhat al-Nusra four,[39] with four for others.

Jabhat al-Nusra's investment of about 1,000 men, a third of the attackers, would have been from a reservoir of several thousand in rural Idlib, perhaps half of its total of around 10,000 in western Syria.[40] Unlike ISIS in eastern Syria, Jabhat al-Nusra was from its early days primarily Syrian Arab; at most, 30 per cent of its jihadists came from outside Syria in 2015.[41]

As regards governance, the hard Islamists and jihadists wanted a dominant role, which would make coexistence with the provincial civil society of coordinating committees, emergency services, and relief organizations delicate. Ahrar al-Sham, however, signalled that its objective was 'a stable and representative government in Damascus'[42] rather than an Islamist emirate, somewhat restraining Jabhat al-Nusra. The overriding constraint was of course Turkish regulation of external weapons supplies. Jabhat al-Nusra could seize SRF TOW anti-tank missiles, but a sustained flow depended on working relations with groups derived from the old FSA that had channels to Saudi Arabia and the USA; these were also a major component of rebel strength against the regime in the Ghab Valley and the Latakia hills.

The regime pulled its troops back to military camps in its corridor to the coast, and shifted provincial administration to Jisr al-Shughur. Unlike in eastern Syria, where it maintained bureaucratic capacity and technical staff for reassertion of 'legitimacy' after the demise of ISIS, the regime had no interest in maintaining administrative facilities that might benefit credible alternative 'legitimacy'. On the contrary, it bombed such infrastructures after losing the provincial capital.[43] The rebels in turn successfully assaulted Jisr al-Shughur in a four-day operation between 22 and 26 April. In late May, they closed the regime corridor towards Idlib by overrunning the town of Ariha and the Mastouma military camp. A couple of hundred regime soldiers held out in the Jisr al-Shughur hospital for almost a month before about half escaped south to the Ghab Valley. At the same time and into the summer, rebels extended their territory in the north Latakia hills (Jabal al-Akrad overlooking the Ghab, and Jabal Turkman adjoining the Turkish border). These had Sunni populations of Kurdish and Turkmen backgrounds, and were potentially a springboard into Alawite areas.

For whatever reason, the rebel momentum petered out through the summer. It terminated with Jaysh al-Fath capturing the Abu al-Duhur air base east of Ma'arrat al-Nu'man. The rebels had invested the base since 2012; Jabhat al-Nusra was the spearhead of the final attack, and so emerged from the succession of Idlib victories on a high note. On the one hand, the rebels were at their most effective since 2012, and in July 2015 Bashar al-Assad made an unprecedented acknowledgment that the regime could not defend all its positions. On the other hand, the regime was beaten but not routed. It held onto its side of the Ghab Valley, and the hills towards the coast. What was now clear to all was that the regime could no longer maintain itself by itself; its own air power was inadequate and the viability of its ground forces depended on Iran and the foreign Shi'a militias. The Iranians bypassed the regime in negotiating with Ahrar al-Sham for the security of the surrounded Shi'a villages of Fu'a and Kafraya north of Idlib, in exchange for Hezbollah allowing Sunni civilians and fighters to leave al-Zabadani near the Lebanese border.[44] For the first time Assad publicly commended Hezbollah for their 'important role [in Syria] and their efficient and vital discharge of duties [*ada'uhum al-fa'al wa al-naw'i*] together with the army'.[45]

In the late summer of 2015, on the eve of direct Russian intervention, the rebels were at their maximum spread in western Syria. The regime had not just fallen back from Idlib province, but had lost lands in Dera'a and Quneitra after a February 2015 offensive south of Damascus managed by Iran and Hezbollah fell flat in snowstorms. Iran had its own agenda in the south, where it aspired to a presence on Israel's Golan front. For Israel, this was the primary strategic threat, beside which Jabhat al-Nusra and ISIS barely rated as irritants. In January, an Israeli air strike near Quneitra killed an Iranian general and Hezbollah rising star Jihad Mughniya, son of assassinated party military chief Imad Mughniya. Iranian and Lebanese Shi'a precedence was also controversial within the Syrian army and regime; senior intelligence officer Rustum Ghazaleh strongly objected to subordination to Hezbollah.[46]

Elsewhere, Assad failed yet again to pinch off the rebel pocket in Aleppo, despite new infusions of foreign militiamen. Given that the regime's only supply route to Aleppo involved a circuitous secondary road east of Homs on the ISIS margins, Aleppo was at risk of being lost as long as the rebels stayed entrenched there. For both sides Aleppo, the old commercial centre of Syria, was critical in prestige as well as strategic terms. Near Damascus, Jaysh al-Islam briefly threatened the regime's main road north to Homs in a surprise mid-September thrust out of the East Ghouta.[47] Jaysh al-Islam thereby moved up on Russia's target list.

'Upon the request of the Syrian side', Russia began assembling a large 'aviation group' in northern Syria in the mid-summer of 2015.[48] The Russians dictated terms to the regime, signed on 26 August 2015. The Hmeimim air base effectively became Russian territory; the 'Syrian Arab Republic' would be solely responsible for any damages resulting from Russian 'activities'; and Russian personnel would be 'immune from Syria's civilian and administrative jurisdiction'. By late September, US sources estimated the influx of men and material at 500 Russian marines and 'dozens' of combat airplanes and attack helicopters.[49] US secretary of state John Kerry remarked that the deployment simply represented 'force protection'.[50] Open-ended, unrestricted bombing commenced a few days later. The Russians spoke of attacking ISIS; on 30 September, all missions were against rebels fighting Assad in western Syria and not a single bomb fell on the ISIS 'caliphate'.[51]

Russia maintained the narrative that it was doing the international community a service against 'terrorism'. The prominence in rebel ranks of Jabhat al-Nusra, Jund al-Aqsa, and other jihadists with past or continuing associations with al-Qaeda gave the Russian line some traction. Russia also wanted the Salafist Ahrar al-Sham designated as 'terrorist'; Saudi Arabia vigorously resisted, aware that giving way would expose more than half of the armed opposition to equivalence with ISIS. Russia's anti-terror services in Syria remained highly selective throughout its intervention, tailored to shoring up the Syrian regime's strategic position in north-west Syria, Aleppo, Damascus, and the far south. The course of events in late 2015 and early 2016 points to a Russian agenda of regime recovery but not sweeping victory, at least not too soon or too easily. Vladimir Putin knew his Assad, and would have wanted him kept on a leash. Russia's interest was to wield its intervention to play the field from a commanding position between regime and opposition and among other external powers. This did not necessarily suit its Iranian partner.

Apart from helping the regime to subject suburban Damascus, Russia's focus was northern rather than southern Syria. Putin left Israel free to take action against Hezbollah and Iran in the south. He needed Iranian-sponsored militias to ensure that regime forces in the north could take advantage of aerial bombardment, but he had no affinity with them. The Russian priorities were to bolster the regime heartland in the Alawite coastal region, to constrict the rebel stronghold in Idlib, and to intensify the softening up of rebel-held eastern Aleppo.

Inland from the coast, regime elite units stiffened with Russian advisers pushed against rebels in the north Latakia hills from October 2015. The risk of a sudden rebel raid towards the Russians at Hmeimim had to be eliminated. By the end of the year the regime had taken rebel hill holdings up to the margins of Jisr al-Shughur, and on 12 January 2016 it captured Salma, the rebel strongpoint in Jabal al-Akrad since 2012. In parallel, it tried to advance under Russian cover in the interior north of Hama, also from early October. Rebel activity here endangered Hama city and the regime positions towards the coastal mountain range. The rebels, a mixture of old Hama FSA units and incoming jihadists, mauled regime armour with TOW missiles and recovered Morek town. In early 2016, the rebels had a modest advantage on this front.

The more important balance in and around Aleppo trended towards the regime and the Russians. In villages in open country south of Aleppo the rebels, including Jabhat al-Nusra, lost ground to the army, Hezbollah, and the Iranians in late 2015, while the regime also moved east into ISIS territory. These gains helped buffer government-controlled western Aleppo. In early February 2016, the regime, Hezbollah, and Shi'a militias advanced with Russian air support to the encircled Shi'a villages of al-Zahra and Nubl north of Aleppo. They thereby cut Aleppo rebel access north to Turkey, achieving a regime strategic objective pursued since 2013. At the same time the Kurds in the Afrin canton (see chapter 3) took the opportunity to advance in the opposite direction immediately north of the regime thrust, taking rebel holdings almost as far as A'zaz, on the border. There was now only one road linking the rebel Aleppo pocket to the outside.

In early 2016, the Russians were ready for a pause. In Damascus, they struck a surgical blow on 26 December 2015 with the airstrike assassinating Zahran Alloush, the militant Islamist commander of Jaysh al-Islam in the East Ghouta. Further south, in January 2016 they assisted Assad to take Sheikh Miskin, near Dera'a and abutting the

Dera'a–Damascus highway. This buttressed the regime's persisting outpost in Dera'a town, close to the Jordanian border. With projected gains in Latakia and Aleppo also accomplished, the regime's military position was transformed by late February 2016, courtesy of Russia and Iran. From the outset of their campaign, the Russians aimed at an international masterstroke; adjusting the military equation could alternate with truces testing diplomatic progress.

Russia wanted to bring the international community round to a Syrian political track in which the regime had the clear upper hand, and Moscow would be the gatekeeper for such essentials as the fate of Bashar al-Assad. The Holy Grail was US participation in Russian-steered diplomacy and jointly coordinated bombing of 'terrorists' in western Syria. This would not just implicate the Americans in Russia's Syria project and signal Russia's return as a top-tier great power, it would also potentially associate the USA with war crimes. Russia managed to get Iran included in the International Syria Support Group (ISSG) that came out of discussions of concerned countries in Vienna in late October and mid-November 2015. The renewal of Syria peace talks, moribund since early 2014 and initially minus the Syrians, came about due to the Russian shock treatment. The USA, fresh from the July 2015 nuclear deal with Iran, relented on previous discouragement of Iranian participation. After the mid-November ISIS terror outrages in Paris, Putin asked whether French demands for Assad's departure 'had protected Paris from the terrorist attack'.[52] Only days later, French foreign minister Laurent Fabius opened the possibility of cooperation with 'Syrian regime forces', for the first time slackening French rejection of the regime since 2011.[53]

Very much on the defensive, non-jihadist Syrian rebel factions met under Saudi cover in Riyadh in mid-December. They formed a 'high commission' for negotiation and reiterated their rejection of Assad in any transition. Russia wanted at least two of the participants—Ahrar al-Sham and Jaysh al-Islam—designated 'terrorists'. Simultaneously, the ISSG supplied the text for UN Security Council (UNSC) resolution 2254, passed unanimously on 18 December.[54] Putin praised US secretary of state Kerry for his efforts in bridging gaps and noted that his own plan mostly coincided with US thinking.[55] The resolution proposed talks between the Syrian parties for a Syrian transition administration within six months and a new constitution and UN-supervised elections within eighteen months. Nothing in the text precluded Assad's perpetuation, and insistence on 'continuity of government institutions' left his security machine to overawe the transition. As for definition of 'terrorists' and action against them, the resolution gave Russia and the USA broad scope 'to eradicate the safe haven they have established over significant parts of Syria'.

Russia reluctantly accepted a political transition according to the 2012 Geneva declaration, but made it plain that 'confronting terrorism' was the top priority and that a transition could be described simply as 'political reforms'.[56] The rebel Riyadh caucus suspected the regime of looking to use the delivery of humanitarian aid as a tool to compel the rebels to forget about Geneva.[57] They also rejected insertion of the Syrian Kurdish PYD and the regime-tolerated NCC 'opposition' into negotiations. They refused to attend talks in Geneva when the regime launched its north Aleppo offensive in early February. US secretary of state Kerry criticized them in reported comments to aid workers at a Syria donor conference in London, forecasting three more months of Russian bombing that would 'decimate' the rebels.[58] He accused them of obstinacy: 'What do you want me to do? Go to war with Russia? Is that what you want?' The Kremlin was doubtless gratified.

Late February 2016 marked five months of continuous heavy engagement of Russian air power, including naval cruise missile strikes. Bashar al-Assad profited, but beyond a certain point Vladimir Putin was not interested in coddling someone he knew was unfit to lead Syria. In January 2016, he told the German tabloid *Bild* that 'President Assad has done much wrong over the course of this conflict'.[59] Otherwise the balance sheet was mixed. First, the map had shifted in some critical locations, but not greatly overall. The rebels were probably tougher than Moscow had anticipated. Second, much of the Russian ordinance was not precision guided, and civilian casualties were inevitable. In December 2015, Amnesty International detailed Russian responsibility for 'hundreds' of civilian deaths and warned of 'war crimes';[60] in January 2016 the SOHR put the toll at 1,015, including 238 children.[61] Such reports left Moscow unperturbed; nonetheless, there was reputational attrition. Third, into the future the Russians needed to show that they were actually serious about making their own dent in the ISIS 'caliphate'. In November 2015, they bombed in and around Deir al-Zor, where they were also shoring up the regime's surviving enclave within the ISIS domain.

As for geopolitics, Russia had to juggle among the other powers active in Syria and Iraq. At the outset of Russia's campaign, Russia and Iran moved to establish a joint operations room in Baghdad consisting of themselves and the Syrian and Iraqi regimes. They felt that the spread of ISIS across Syria and Iraq and the crucial role of Iraqi Shi'a militias in propping up the Syrian regime required monitoring of the whole Fertile Crescent. They were closely concerned with the operations of the US-led coalition in Iraq, which spilled into eastern Syria. Russia also had a sensitive relationship with its Iranian partner.[62] Iran could not complain, having requested Russian action, but there were differences. The Russians and Iranians were mutually suspicious, each afraid of being displaced by the other as dominant over the Syrian regime, which gave Bashar space to play off his patrons. The Russians were wary of Iranian involvement in Sunni–Shi'a sectarian confrontations and distrusted Hezbollah.[63] Russia looked for good relations with Saudi Arabia and Sunni Arab states, whereas Saudi Arabia and Iran were in confrontation. Separately, Russia had a crisis with Turkey after the Turks shot down a Russian warplane in November 2015. In such a fraught environment, Russia promoted the 27 February 2016 'cessation of hostilities', a time-out for retuning.

Flux across the Fertile Crescent, 2015–2017

While Russia prepared and implemented its intervention in Syria, the tide turned against ISIS in Iraq. After running the Iraqi and Syrian armies out of Ramadi and Palmyra, ISIS 'caliph' Baghdadi blustered about striking into Baghdad and Kerbala, while Iraqi Shi'a populist Muqtada al-Sadr warned that ISIS could do damage in these directions.[64] In reality, Baghdad and Kerbala lay beyond anything but brief disruption from ISIS suicide bombers, even at the jihadist apogee in mid-2015. That did not mean that Arab Iraq was not compromised. ISIS had rooted itself in the Sunni centre and north in a way that could only be reversed by devastating military uprooting. Meantime, Iran took advantage of Iraqi Shi'a consternation to reinforce its influence within the Shi'a Arab majority.

Through the summer of 2015, Iraqi prime minister Abadi faced constraints because of reduced oil prices, street discontent with regime corruption, and conflicting Iranian and American agendas. Baghdad presented a crisis-ridden home front that did not make the real war any easier. Abadi's response was a reform programme to combine ministries, eliminate top official posts, and reduce fiscal diversion into patronage networks. Meantime, Iranian-backed former prime minister Maliki became one of three new vice-presidents, and consolidated an alternative power base.

Abadi accused Maliki of squandering billions of dollars while prime minister.[65] At a meeting of Iraqi Shi'a political leaders, Iranian Quds Force commander Soleimani shielded Maliki and attacked Abadi, eliciting a scathing response that compelled Soleimani to walk out.[66] Abadi believed that Soleimani had no right to attend. Abadi's reform drive produced some restructuring, but mainly stalled. Angry demonstrations in Baghdad also petered out. The Shi'a split persisted, with Abadi receiving endorsement from Muqtada al-Sadr and Grand Ayatollah Ali al-Sistani against Maliki, militia leaders, and the Iranians.

Relations between the Shi'a PMF and the still-fragile official Iraqi security forces also continued to pose problems. Despite domination by three Iranian-oriented militias, the PMF reflected the broader Shi'a spectrum. Sadr had a foothold with his Saraya al-Salam (Peace Brigades), and Sistani promoted wider Shi'a participation in the dire situation of mid-2014.[67] Both rejected the Iranian-organized dispatch of thousands of militiamen to Syria to prop up Bashar al-Assad. Unlike the Iranians, both were wary of the Sunni–Shi'a sectarian rift that was deepening by the day across the Fertile Crescent.

At the same time, the very fact of broad Shi'a sympathy for the PMF meant that Abadi had to be careful in dealing with PMF interests; his reputation in his own community as well as military necessity advised enlistment of the PMF in liberating Iraqi territory from ISIS. Here he had to balance the PMF with Sunni tribal fighters and limited American patience for the Iranian role in Iraq. The Iranian-leaning PMF command threatened to fight 'foreigners'[68]—meaning Americans—in the future, while the USA did not want the PMF in al-Anbar province, even if this delayed the recapture of Ramadi for months.[69] Abadi had to cope with PMF pressure to be designated a parallel Iraqi army, both state-approved and beyond the state. The PMF rejected the notion of being a province-based national guard, correctly sensing a subterfuge to split it up.[70]

On the battlefronts, dissension in Baghdad and US concern to have capable army and elite police units with Sunni levies to offset the Shi'a PMF obscured the ISIS shift to a largely defensive posture. The aerial campaign across western Iraq and eastern Syria, intensified in late 2015 after ISIS terror attacks in Paris and Brussels and the downing of a Russian airliner by an ISIS affiliate in Egypt, ended the organization's ability to deploy convoys across long distances in open terrain.[71] Nonetheless, the Americans had a way to go in promoting new Sunni paramilitaries; in September 2015, tribal shaykhs in al-Anbar spoke of a new 'brigade of the Abbasid army' numbering a mere 1,000.[72] It was just as well that ISIS fighters in Ramadi barely approached 1,000 themselves.[73] In the summer of 2015, ISIS had the town of Haditha in al-Anbar under siege, close to Americans at the Ayn al-Asad air base. Access was by helicopter or an occasional armoured convoy.[74] For the moment, government forces were stalemated on the fringes of Ramadi, while towards Mosul and the north ISIS remained entrenched in the Baiji refinery.

Compared to KRG Peshmerga advances against ISIS along the northern Iraq front and the Syrian Kurdish rollback of ISIS around Kobani and al-Hasakeh through early 2015, Iraqi government performance did not rate so well. In September, the Syrian regime and allied militias pushed into the ISIS zone east of Aleppo, relieving the Kuwayris air base, cut off since 2013. Baghdad and the PMF needed to register their own new blow—the victory at Tikrit was fading. Most especially, the Iraqi army had to break through Baiji for liberation of Mosul and Ninewa province to be even on a timetable. In turn, the Americans had to relent on reluctance to provide air cover for the PMF. In mid-October 2015, several thousand Iraqi troops and a larger number of Shi'a militia assaulted around a thousand ISIS jihadists in Baiji. Iranian General Soleimani inevitably played a coordinating role among ground forces. It was a total success, and despite PMF prominence it indicated the return of Iraqi official security forces—under an American more than an Iranian umbrella—as a significant player.

By December 2015, the Iraqi army, federal police, counter-terrorism units, and supporting Sunni tribesmen finally recovered enough strength to make a conclusive move into Ramadi. The innovation was the complete sidelining of both the PMF and the Iranians. In the lead-up, also with US-led aerial buttressing, the KRG Peshmerga expelled ISIS from Sinjar town in mid-November and threatened 'caliphal' communications from Mosul into Syria. Iraqi forces cleared ISIS from the Anbar provincial capital by February 2016. Of course, the majority in the re-emerging Iraqi army was Shi'a, but allegiance to a rebounding national institution conferred some insulation from Iran. Overall, forces patronized by the USA had the edge over those patronized by Iran as the way opened for advances on Falluja and Mosul and thereafter the destruction of ISIS in Iraq.

In early 2016, there seemed to be incipient regime resurgence in both Syria and Iraq. In western Syria, the Assad regime looked to Russian air power and Iranian associated militias to enable it finally to crack the rebel hold on eastern Aleppo and restore Syria's second city to its hands. In Iraq, the regime in Baghdad depended on US air power and had Iranian assistance, declining in value by 2016, to head for Mosul and expel ISIS from Iraq's second city. In both cases, the target was primarily Sunni Arab and the prospective attacking forces primarily of other identities. However, although the Russians and the Syrian regime favoured viewing the two offensives as identical—a righteous legitimate camp taking on fanatic terrorists who held civilians captive as human shields—the parallels lacked any serious content.

In particular, the Syrian and Iraqi regimes were entirely dissimilar. The Assad regime remained a brutal autocracy based on denial of diversity, whether of people or opinions. In contrast, despite its gross corruption and imperfections, the Iraqi government and federal system that had superseded the Ba'athism that Syria had yet to escape, represented a rough-and-ready pluralism proven in multiple electoral contests since 2005. Of course, post-Ba'athist Iraq reflected the preferences of an occupying power: the USA. The same was true of post-1945 Germany and Japan. That did not mean that it might not fashion something positive out of a defeat of ISIS. The same could not be said of the unreconstructed tyranny, propped up by Russia and foreign sectarian militias, that would follow Syrian regime crushing of the non-ISIS rebels.

Force majeure in Aleppo

In western Syria, the 27 February 2016 truce enabled Russia to signal that it might be modestly flexible and to demonstrate that its declarations against ISIS weren't simply a smokescreen for targeting others. On 14 March, President Putin announced a drawdown of Russian aircraft in Syria on the basis of progress in the campaign. He told rather than consulted Bashar al-Assad:[75] a new message that the latter should not take Russian cover for granted. For his part, Bashar then declared that Iran had been the 'chief supporter' of his regime since 2011.[76] Putin may have intended a hint to the West that Russia, unlike its protégé in Damascus, looked ultimately to political answers. Although observers in the Bosporus noted that Russian shipping heading for Syria was more heavily laden than that returning to Russia, this curious episode may have been more than a cynical fraud. The truce also assisted Russia to register a public relations coup by providing vital air support and logistics to a ground thrust with a Shi'a militia vanguard that expelled ISIS from the Palmyra heritage site in late March. During major hostilities elsewhere, the regime and Iranians could not spare the resources. Thereafter Russia even brought in an orchestra to play amid the older ruins and newer rubble. In military terms, Palmyra could be a regime launch point towards eastern Syria as much as an ISIS threat to Damascus.

The Syrian regime, however, had its sights set on utilizing Russia's intervention to smash the rebels in Aleppo; ISIS in the Homs desert and eastwards was for a following phase. The Russians agreed that horizons would be decisively wider after a victory in Aleppo, but conceived a subsequent rebel-regime political settlement with compromises rather than Assad's fixation on a military solution. In any case, the truce did not produce the progress towards Russian–American coordination that the Russians wanted, and Russia did not discourage the regime from resuming barrel bombing and bombardment of eastern Aleppo through April and May. In June 2016, the assault escalated to bombing of hospitals and use of incendiaries, with alleged Russian involvement.

Russian air power facilitated an all-out regime bid from 25 June to besiege eastern Aleppo by cutting its remaining road access to the opposition-held west Aleppo countryside. The offensive coincided with a bizarre initiative by the Obama administration to appease the Kremlin with an agreement for the joint bombing of Jabhat al-Nusra. By this stage, Putin probably preferred to see out the last months of the vacillating Obama, and to have a fait accompli in Aleppo before the new US president took office. The Russians were unresponsive on restraining regime bombing, and indicated that any departure of Assad would be years away, depending on the solidity of a Syrian government pleasing to them.[77] The USA knew full well that shared targeting of Jabhat al-Nusra would entail collateral damage and would benefit Assad and ISIS, also propelling more rebels into jihadist ranks.[78] Russian coolness stalled the initiative, while Assad chimed in with a revelation to the Australian TV channel SBS about Western collaboration with his regime: 'They attack us politically, and then they send their officials to deal with us under the table, especially security, including your government.'[79]

Force multiplication courtesy of Russia through 2016 also assisted the regime to produce significant gains in the surrounds of Damascus. In April and May, the regime, beefed up with Hezbollah fighters, overran the southern third of the large and hitherto well-defended East Ghouta rebel stronghold. This pushed the rebels back from the vicinity of Damascus international airport and deprived the East Ghouta of significant farmland, critical for ongoing food supplies. Incredibly, confronting a reinforced enemy, the local rebels fell into factional fighting in the same weeks, with hundreds of casualties as the domineering Jaysh al-Islam clashed with Jabhat al-Nusra and the former FSA-affiliated Faylaq al-Rahman.

A reduced East Ghouta looked ahead to more perilous times as through the summer the regime turned to tidying up the West Ghouta urban fringe near the Mezze air base and air-force intelligence facilities. Here the long-running starvation sieges of the shrunken suburbs of Daraya and Mu'adhamiyat al-Sham approached a conclusion satisfactory to the regime. The terms featured busing of rebels to Idlib and dispersal of the remaining few thousand civilians, refining a model that would be applied to surrendering besieged rebel pockets from Damascus to Homs and Aleppo.[80] Daraya gave up in August 2016, followed by Mu'adhamiya in September.

Meanwhile, the regime's Russian and Iranian allies proved crucial in its achievement of the full isolation and siege of eastern Aleppo by

27 July 2016. The regime had tried and failed several times since 2013 to pinch off the northern entry to the large rebel sock-shaped pocket (Map 3); the Syrian air force and roving elite ground units had long been insufficient on their own. Russian aircraft spearheaded shattering new air strikes while Iran mobilized additional Shi'a militias, especially from southern Iraq. In August, the Iraqi Harakat al-Nujaba, part of the PMF, committed 2,000 extra fighters to Aleppo.[81] Even in such a lopsided contest the rebels outside Aleppo, flush with new equipment from Turkey and the Arabian Peninsula principalities, managed by 6 August to break open access to the pocket from the south, also cutting the regime's main supply route into western Aleppo. Russia and Iran could not tolerate such a reverse; amid vigorous bombing, the regime and militias restored the siege on 4 September. The rebels tried another assault from the south-west in October, but merely suffered losses; the Russians perhaps calculated the sapping effect.

A last abortive ceasefire lasted a few days between 12 and 19 September 2016. The USA and Russia agreed that the regime and rebels should pull back on humanitarian access corridors.[82] The USA hoped, fatuously, that Russia might be persuaded to ground the regime's aircraft. If the ceasefire held for a week, the USA would consider coordination with Russia against 'al-Qaeda'.[83] Why anyone would suppose that the regime and its allies would suffer being bound by withdrawals and restrictions, whilst on the verge of taking their prize, is a mystery. Russia played along to show its interest in diplomatic outcomes; the regime could sink everything any moment without any visible Russian hand. In the event, an American mistake in bombing the regime instead of ISIS in Deir al-Zor let Putin and Russian foreign minister Sergei Lavrov off the hook. Deliberate regime bombing of a civilian aid convoy approaching Aleppo then terminated the lull on 19 September.[84]

According to the UN, more than 300,000 people still lived in rebel eastern Aleppo at the beginning of 2016,[85] down from probably twice as many in 2011. About 111,000 registered in the January 2017 evacuation of eastern Aleppo, setting a minimum number for those who lived through the siege months of September to December 2016.[86] About 3,500 people, overwhelmingly non-combatant, reportedly died in military actions between June and December 2016.[87] Rebel shelling of course killed civilians in western Aleppo and, in

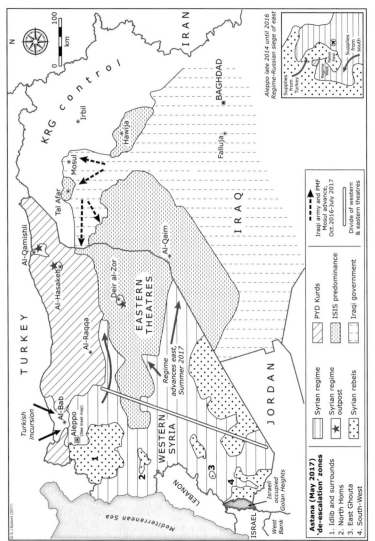

Map 3: Syria–Iraq war zone, July 2017

early 2016, in the Kurdish suburb of Shaykh Maqsud, sandwiched between the two sides. This toll, however, was a small fraction of that in the east. As for overall population displacement, most of the million or more who fled eastern Aleppo and the Aleppo countryside from 2012 onwards headed to Turkey.

Rebel forces in eastern Aleppo in late 2016 numbered 6,000–8,000, from the whole array of factions: Islamists, jihadists, and the old FSA. Jabhat al-Nusra contributed 150–200 elite warriors;[88] in late July 2016, the jihadist organization rebranded itself as Jabhat Fath al-Sham (Syrian Conquest Front) and formally separated from al-Qaeda, presumably at the belated insistence of its Qatari backers. This was a transparent manoeuvre from an extremist group responsible for sectarian massacres of Alawites, which had endorsed terrorism in Europe and made raising revenue by kidnapping foreigners and Syrians a fine art.[89]

From late September to early December 2016, Russian and Syrian aircraft conducted a cruel final softening up of eastern Aleppo. Ground forces pinched off higher and more open ground in the north of the pocket in late September. The air assault targeted hospitals and other medical facilities in a clear pattern,[90] obviously to hasten civilian morale collapse and rebel submission. More widely, there was liberal resort to cluster munitions and incendiaries. Syrian air-force helicopters repeatedly dropped chlorine-gas bombs,[91] and the regime doubtless took note of the lack of serious international reaction. In this phase, Russia removed Turkey from the equation. Turkey was compelled to trade Russia's toleration of its August 2016 ground push into northern Syria (see chapter 4), primarily aimed at forestalling Syrian Kurdish continuity along the whole border, for accepting the fall of eastern Aleppo.[92] Turkey turned to arranging contacts between Russia and Syrian armed factions in Ankara, whereupon the Russians graciously dropped their objections to participation by Ahrar al-Sham and Jaysh al-Islam.

With Turkey out of the picture and the November 2016 US elections producing president-elect Donald Trump, who declared himself ready to work with Vladimir Putin, no one in eastern Aleppo could entertain illusions. The regime's Tiger Forces and thousands of militiamen inaugurated the conclusive ground operation in late November, taking the Hanano military base and housing. Resistance began to crumble across the rebel pocket, and on 5 December Russia vetoed a potentially restraining New Zealand-initiated UNSC resolution. Rebel capitulation followed on 13 December, with the regime dictating evacuation terms. Militias did as they pleased in eastern Aleppo for a few days, while green buses ferried the 111,000 residual residents, including several thousand rebels, to rebel Idlib province. It was the largest such demographic adjustment in the western Syria theatre. Iran insisted on smaller parallel evacuations from the Shi'a villages of Fu'a and Kafraya in Idlib. It was all over by 23 December, when the regime resumed full authority over Aleppo.

Liberating Mosul

As for the eastern theatre of the Syria–Iraq war zone, advances against ISIS through 2016 were principally in Iraq. ISIS revenues were in conclusive decline with the attrition of bombing and loss of territory, but in 2016 the organization still generated not far short of $1 billion, around half of its 2015 peak.[93] Its core territory remained intact, though substantially eroded across the north by the Kurds and in the east by the Iraqi Shi'a PMF and Iraqi official forces. More time passed for it to fortify various remaining strongholds: al-Raqqa, al-Bab, Deir al-Zor, and the border town of Abu Kamal in Syria, and Falluja, Mosul, Hawija, Tal Afar, and al-Qa'im in Iraq. In late June 2016, a US–British–Jordanian bid to use a new force of Deir al-Zor and Homs tribesmen to sweep from Jordan along the Syrian side of the Syrian–Iraqi desert border into Abu Kamal foundered.[94] In December 2016, ISIS retook Palmyra from the Syrian regime, holding it until March 2017. This indicated how stretched regime, Hezbollah, and Iranian ground resources were in the last months of the Aleppo battle. In short, a hard road remained against ISIS, whether in Iraq or Syria.

In Iraq, Prime Minister Abadi's main immediate headache remained how to deploy the Shi'a PMF in battles to come in Sunni provinces. The PMF question also continued to be a measure of the prime minister's authority in Baghdad and the regime and parliament. Here his adversary Maliki linked with powerful Iranian-backed PMF administrator Abu Mahdi al-Muhandis and the hardline PMF militias of Kata'ib Hizballah, the Badr Brigades, and Asa'ib Ahl al-Haqq.[95] Abadi wanted the PMF incorporated into the Iraqi army under the prime minister as commander-in-chief, in a structure diluting autonomous militia identities. The Iranians and their clients aimed for an unfettered status resembling that of Iran's Islamic Revolutionary Guard, which would allow the IRG effectively to direct the PMF as a resource both for Iranian subordination of Iraq and Iranian reinforcement in Syria. In February 2016, Abadi formally approved the PMF becoming part of the army as 'an independent military formation' under its existing militia command.[96] On essentials, the Iranians came out best.

In a very practical sense, Iran's manipulation of the PMF connected the two theatres of the Syria–Iraq war zone. Iranian influence among a majority of the 140,000 Iraqi Shi'a enrolled into the autonomous militias threatened Iraq's own sovereignty. Concurrently, into 2016, Iran's supervision of about 8,000 PMF-derived fighters[97] in western Syria represented the largest component of Iranian military reach across the Fertile Crescent to the Mediterranean. In Iraq, it was a challenge that kept Abadi and the mercurial Muqtada al-Sadr more or less in the same camp, especially as the Abu Mahdi al-Muhandis-dominated PMF management restricted financial allocation to PMF units associated with Sadr and Sistani. The challenge also kept Abadi open to the concerns of Sunni Arab Iraqis and the KRG, easing allocations of roles in the approaching Mosul offensive. The Islamic Republic's ambitions were sometimes cathartic for those on the receiving end.

Iraqi forces could not head for Mosul before eliminating the large ISIS garrison embedded in Falluja since early 2014, only 50 miles west of Baghdad. As a dry run for Mosul, Abadi and the army command wished to use the elite counter-terrorism units otherwise known as 'the Golden Division' as the main force within the city. Al-Anbar Sunni tribal militiamen (al-hashd al-asha'iri) and the federal police would provide support. The PMF was in the vicinity, but to be limited to operations on the outskirts. The town and the ISIS opponent were both substantially bigger than was the case for Ramadi, and the decision to again largely do without the PMF imposed delay. Clearance of the eastern outskirts began in late May 2016, and the Golden Division entered Falluja from the south in early June. Progress became slow, and PMF leaders al-Muhandis, Hadi al-Amiri, and Qais al-Khaz'ali threatened to drive in from Saqlawiya to the north, which the USA prohibited.[98] There were also accusations against the PMF of 'routinely' abducting men and boys among civilians coming out of Falluja.[99] The PMF believed that many of these were jihadists, and in any case viewed Falluja Sunnis as fellow travellers with ISIS. Such attitudes made it a severe risk to permit the PMF free access.

In early July 2016, with full success in Falluja achieved, Abadi could shift to Mosul, and felt able to offer the PMF some sort of participation in the most important battle against ISIS. Given that the PMF had secured Baghdad and the approaches to Shi'a southern Iraq in 2014, they could not be denied a role near Mosul. Abadi's problem was that he was caught both between local actors and between Iran and Turkey. Neither the Kurds nor the Ninewa province Sunni Arabs welcomed Iraqi Shi'a Arabs to northern Iraq. Iran insisted on a PMF presence to add to its Kurdish connections to give it a serious hand in Mosul developments. Turkey regarded itself as a backstop for Sunni Arabs, Kurdistan Democratic Party (KDP) Kurds, and Kirkuk and Tal Afar Turkmen vis-à-vis either each other or any outside party, above all Iran and Shi'a militias. The Iran–Turkey divide in western Syria only added to suspicions.

Movement north from Baiji commenced even before the recapture of Falluja. In June, the Iraqi army advanced past the Qayara air base, where in October US and other international coalition Special Forces established an initial forward position for assisting the Iraqis. American and Iraqi mediation enabled a rough understanding of ground rules among the Iraqi government forces, the KRG Peshmerga, the Sunni militiamen of former Ninewa governor Athil al-Nujayfi, the PMF, and Turkey. Only government forces would assault Mosul. The KRG and PMF would respectively clear ISIS from eastern and western rural fringes. The KRG, Sunni militias, and Turkey would work together. Into the autumn, ISIS withdrew northwards towards Mosul, laying waste to villages and torching oil wells and the sulphur plant at al-Mishraq, reducing visibility and fouling the atmosphere.[100] The Iraqis and the supporting US-led coalition took a risk in bypassing the significant ISIS Hawija enclave, which menaced Kirkuk.

Iraqi engagement of ISIS in Mosul proceeded as a much larger-scale version of Falluja. Around 50,000 Iraqi regular and special troops outnumbered the PMF contingent, even without thousands of Peshmerga and Sunni militiamen. They confronted more than 5,000 solidly entrenched ISIS jihadists.[101] Through late October 2016, the army and Peshmerga approached the Mosul suburbs east of the Tigris River from their eastern outskirts. They took the deserted and ransacked Assyrian Christian town of Qara Qosh and other outliers. In early November, the federal forces penetrated eastern Mosul. Perhaps half of the pre-June 2014 population—well over a million people—still lived in the city. This at first led to a decision to limit aerial and artillery bombardment, which slowed the already taxing advance along booby-trapped streets.

Forcing ISIS out of the eastern neighbourhoods absorbed two-and-a-half months and cost the counter-terrorism Special Forces around 4,000 dead and injured.[102] Only in late January 2017 could the emphasis shift to the more formidable challenge of the closely packed old city and the main ISIS redoubt on the western side of the Tigris. Meantime, the PMF militias moved forward in the semi-desert west of Mosul, overrunning the Tal Afar air base and cutting the main road from Mosul to Syria west of Tal Afar town. Having interrupted ISIS communications on the last remaining exit, they paused. Turkey and the KRG Kurds were unwilling to accept them in the majority Sunni Turkmen town.

Crushing ISIS in western Mosul took from 19 February to 10 July 2017—almost five months—and involved a different mode of urban warfare. Depletion of elite units in the eastern Mosul fighting meant a bigger role for less well-trained regular and police forces, and relaxation of restraints on covering fire.[103] Liberal use of artillery and bombing largely levelled the old city. Most of the population in the west— the bulk of the 700,000 the UN estimated as displaced from Mosul by July 2017[104]—managed to get out, but civilian casualties soared as ISIS forced concentration of about 100,000 into a smaller and smaller space.[105] One monitoring group calculated 5,805 civilian deaths from Iraqi government and US-led coalition activities between 19 February and 19 June.[106] Even towards the end, ISIS had the organizational capacity to implement an efficient demolition of the great mosque and its landmark leaning minaret. Prime Minister Abadi came to declare victory on 9 July, but Iraq's new front-line forces had taken a major battering, which raised questions about the balance with the Shi'a PMF for the fighting that remained in Tal Afar, Hawija, and western al-Anbar. Quiet in the wings during this battle, Iran kept its clout.

93

Unlike Aleppo, where the large segment of the population hostile to Assad had mostly fled to Turkey, Sunni Arabs who left Mosul were still in Iraq and would be returning. They would be a seething mass of resentment inhabiting an urban wreck that the Iraqi state was ill-equipped to manage. Loyalties were volatile; the city would remain vulnerable to Sunni militant infiltration and influence.

Multi-dimensional chess in 2017

In early 2017, the trend since 2014 towards more decisive external interventions in Syria and Iraq reached a point at which foreign countries engaged in fighting were preponderantly calling the shots. Up to June 2014, the conflict focused on domestic disintegration in Syria. On the one hand, external entanglements with the regime and the rebels from early 2012, together with interconnection of Syria and Iraq regarding jihadist activity and Iranian interests, made the label 'Syrian civil war' dubious. However, apart from Israeli interdiction of Hezbollah weapons transfers from Syria to Lebanon, and Iranian infusion of 'advisers' and foreign militias, no foreign country was directly involved in hostilities. Syrian actors—regime, rebels, and Kurds—and incoming jihadists exercised their own momentum.

Irruption of the ISIS 'caliphate' across eastern Syria and western Iraq in mid-2014 triggered a chain reaction of adjustments to this picture. The US intervened with air power against ISIS in Iraq and Syria in late 2014. US association with Syrian Kurds against ISIS and prioritization of removing ISIS rather than the Syrian regime disturbed Turkey. Turkey and Saudi Arabia took unprecedented steps in early 2015 in terms of weapons supplies to rebels to change the balance in western Syria, to return the spotlight to what they asserted was the source of the crisis: Bashar al-Assad. Russia reacted with a sustained aerial bombing assault on Syrian rebels in late 2015, while Iranian ground-force support of Assad became more overt. Turkey finally sought to preserve some influence on the game through its own direct application of hard power in northern Syria in late 2016 (see chapter 4). Into 2017, the US added Special Force capability to aerial bombardment in the US–Iraqi and US–Syrian Kurdish campaigns in northern Iraq (Mosul) and northern Syria (al-Raqqa) respectively. Meantime, Russia, Iran, and Turkey simultaneously cooperated and jostled in western Syria after Russia's coup in Aleppo.

The post-2011 zoo of local regimes and sub-state actors in the war zone across the Fertile Crescent still exhibited autonomous tendencies. There was a notable recovery for the Iraqi regime under Prime Minister Abadi, continued strong Kurdish momentum, and recalcitrance of the Syrian regime and rebels towards their patrons. Nonetheless, as the ISIS pseudo-state shrank and Russia made its bid to lead in western Syria, the overshadowing roles of foreign states had never been so palpable.

How did the external actors interact among themselves and with local parties in the summer of 2017, and did such interaction bring real hope of better times for Syrians and Iraqis? In the Iraqi part of the eastern ISIS-focused war theatre (map 3), hope of an exit, at least to a new story, flickered. Breaking ISIS in Mosul involved the anticipated levels of destruction and population displacement, and turned into an eight-month grind, but the army's assumption of the main burden, minus the PMF, was a victory for the prime minister, the federal regime, and the US-led coalition as backer. The PMF and the Iranians found themselves, if only temporarily, on the back foot. The KRG also came out of three years of struggle against ISIS as a winner, although with qualifications. The Peshmerga had forced back ISIS when the federal authorities were barely to be seen, so it registered a reputational advance, especially with the coalition. The KRG also had expanded territory, including Kirkuk, to barter with Baghdad. Yet the war intensified the local economic contraction associated with the global oil-price decline. The KRG had to negotiate with Baghdad for any new status; each needed the other, and both had cards.

At the same time, Baghdad had a crucial test to come in reconciling itself with the smashed and destitute Sunni Arab population of central and northern Iraq. And, as the regime up to 2003 had been Sunni dominated, would Sunni Arab Iraqis ever really accept the leading political role of the Shi'a Arab majority? Could a new Shi'a–Sunni combine emerge to counter Iranian manipulation in Baghdad and southern Iraq? Or had the Islamic Republic profited from the ISIS episode to entrench its already solid stake in a part of Iraq that had once been the site and inner lands of the Sassanid Persian capital, Ctesiphon? The succession, or lack thereof, to Sistani as most respected Shi'a authority (*marja'*) in Najaf, whenever that might come, would say something. Could Turkey be a balancing external influence, especially in integrating Sunni Arabs? Or did balance require the weight of the USA, if it was not disqualified by the disaster it had inflicted on Iraq during its occupation, including partial responsibility for ISIS? Perhaps Iraq could only continue through loosening federation into confederation.

In the Syrian portion of the eastern theatre (map 3)—half of Syria—the alignment of the USA with PYD Syrian Kurds was the basis for rolling back ISIS from the north to al-Raqqa and the Euphrates banks between 2015 and 2017. In 2017, as in Iraq, the USA contributed artillery and hundreds of 'advisers' as well as air power,[107] crucial in mainly open terrain. In May 2017, the USA decided to transfer arms, including medium-calibre weapons, directly to the Kurdish People's Protection Units (YPG) militia majority in the Syrian Democratic Forces (SDF), rather than to affiliated militias that gave the SDF its Arab veneer.

Turkey, having obtained Russian permission for its push through ISIS-held territory to al-Bab, thus forestalling a continuous PYD Kurdish strip on its border at the price of leaving Aleppo to its fate, faced a new challenge. Turkey's NATO ally was choosing the PYD and its YPG military wing, offspring of Turkey's PKK enemy, as the ground force for the final battles against ISIS in al-Raqqa and towards Iraq. For Turkey, the USA was thereby supporting an entity on its border steered by PKK commanders.[108] Turks across parties feared an irredentist PKK-run show in northern Syria as even more dangerous than the PKK hideouts in the mountains of northern Iraq. Further, the USA backed the PYD in the Manbij pocket west of the Euphrates long enough to prejudice Turkey's access deeper into Syria. In early 2017, Russia patronized the Syrian regime to advance from Aleppo to the Euphrates south of al-Bab and Manbij, displacing ISIS. Turkey lost its potential land corridor to al-Raqqa.

PYD–YPG Kurds seemed to have US and Russian favour, although the connection was strictly instrumental for the great powers. The USA needed cooperative ground auxiliaries against ISIS, and Russia appreciated a constraint on Turkey, whether or not Turkey cooperated with it in western Syria. The danger was that some Syrian Kurds had developed overblown concepts of their reach both in eastern Syria and towards the Mediterranean. These ideas were beyond their capacity to sustain, and risked future conflict. As Turkey suspected, they also inclined the PYD towards openings to Bashar al-Assad.

For its part, the new US Trump administration envisaged exerting its own influence in filling the post-ISIS vacuum in eastern Syria. It indicated that it could collaborate with Russia, but knew that the Russians themselves would not supply the necessary ground forces. In the Russian option, these would have to come from the Syrian regime and Iran. The regime's track record against ISIS was dismal and its own relentless criminality put it beyond the pale, as the USA seemingly recognized by bombing it in April 2017 for its release of poison gas against civilians in Khan Shaykhun. Iran and Shi'a proxy militias were unacceptable both in a Sunni Arab environment and to top officials in the new US administration. That left the PYD Kurds with their Sunni Arab fig leaf or Turkey; in an ideal world, the Americans would have liked to put them together. The Turks canned that notion by bombing the YPG headquarters near al-Malikiyah, east of al-Qamishli, in late April 2017, to deter any transfer of weapons to the PKK. The USA indicated displeasure at the incident to Ankara.

As regards western Syria (map 3), the major development going into 2017 was Russia's enrolment of Turkey in a Russian–Turkish–Iranian framework for a prolonged truce between the regime and the rebels, now that Russia felt it had the advantage. Considering their domestic turbulence—including stress in the Turkish military after the failed coup of July 2016—and the Aleppo outcome, the Turks had no choice. They perceived that Russia wanted a political exit from the Syrian affair.[109] If so, the Russians needed to bring the top sponsor of the rebels into their process. Turkish officials also calculated that Iran and Assad remained wedded to 'the military solution'[110] and that Russia was tired of this intransigence. They hoped that such circumstances might give them capacity to persuade Putin to soften on retaining Assad.

Turkey extended cooperation in getting a representative Syrian rebel military delegation to truce negotiations in Astana in Kazakhstan, on the basis of understandings reached on 31 December 2016. Turkey and Russia would be 'guarantors' of the rebels and the regime. The Russians acknowledged seven rebel military groups with a combined strength of 51,500 fighters (Ahrar al-Sham: 16,000; Jaysh al-Islam: 12,000; Jaysh al-Mujahidin: 8,000; Jaysh Idlib al-Hurr: 6,000; Faylaq al-Sham: 4,000; al-Jabhat al-Shamiya: 3,000; and Thuwar al-Sham: 2,500).[111] Given that this excluded the Nusra front and other Salafists, the rebels seemed to be keeping up their manpower, reinforcing Turkey's bargaining hand. In May 2017, Turkey joined Russia and Iran in arranging four 'de-escalation zones' around the main rebel territories.

Turkish attention focused on the chief rebel bastion, which encompassed Idlib province and much of rural western Aleppo, with a large segment of the Syria–Turkey border. It had a swollen population after the eastern Aleppo evacuation and other inflows from areas accepting regime-imposed terms for lifting sieges. It also hosted a multiplying array of armed factions, some mutually hostile, which raised questions about its stability. For example, Jaysh al-Islam and Hay'at Tahrir al-Sham (previously al-Nusra) imported their feud from Damascus.[112] Turkey feared that involvement of Russian personnel in rebel evacuations to Idlib meant Russian collusion in 'demographic engineering',[113] and worried that the Syrian regime and Russia might intend an implosion in Idlib. An implosion would facilitate a regime military advance, and would send hundreds of thousands of new refugees into Turkey. It would also destroy Turkey's main card in facing Russia, Iran, the regime, and the PYD Kurds: the potential deployment of a viable rebel quasi-state. Turkey was already promoting refugee resettlement in the Jarabulus-al-Bab enclave, but its credibility really depended on events in Idlib. In short, Turkey's interaction with its Russian 'partner' was wary.

South of Damascus, towards Dera'a on the Jordanian border, where Syria's breakdown began in March 2011, a different balance persisted. Here Iranian strategic ambition came up against Israel; the Russians intermittently bombed rebels to indicate that they were active throughout western Syria; and the Jordanians, Saudis, Americans, and even the British worked to wipe out ISIS pockets and did not want the regime back. In mid-2017, the rebels retained positions along the Israeli-occupied Golan Heights and in much of rural Dera'a, and old FSA groups remained stronger than elsewhere. They were, however, as fractious as in Idlib, and an ISIS affiliate persevered in the sensitive corner where the Golan meets Jordan. Israel preferred the rebels, who were not a strategic challenge, to the alternative—Bashar al-Assad, Hezbollah, and Iran—who were. Iran and Hezbollah made no secret of their interest in using any regime recovery to have a base on Israel's front line. Israel therefore struck the regime and Hezbollah in this vicinity on any provocation, and encouraged the rebels.

Russia tolerated Israeli intrusion here and against Hezbollah nearer Damascus because it wanted Hezbollah's wings clipped, and to signal discomfort with its Iranian ally's sectarian predilections. Russia inclined towards refurbished Syrian regular forces in which an opposition presence would be more logical than that of Iranian-backed militias. The Russians were also cautious about the regime's Iranian-sponsored NDF: Syrians from the large Alawite and Christian minorities and loyalist Sunnis. The NDF was numerically significant but ill disciplined. Russia's problem was that it had to accept what was available.

Russia made itself the lead player in Syria from 2015 and into 2017, but the going might not stay good. Despite Turkish weakness, Iran's disability in the air and among Sunni Arabs, and distractions affecting the new US administration, Russia's lead was precarious. Putin needed Iran for ground forces as much as they needed him in the air, he needed Turkey and Saudi Arabia for any real Syrian deals, he needed Assad for his claims of 'legitimacy', he needed the USA against the jihadists, and he needed the West to supply the international sanction without which any arrangements for Syria would be dead on arrival. These needs contradicted one another. In addition, association with Assad in war crimes hurt Russia's quest for respectability as a top global player. The US cruise missile punishment of Assad over the poison-gas incident in April 2017 highlighted Russia's limitations, even in western Syria.

Shape-shifting war

A new configuration in the Quicksilver War began to crystallize through the spring and summer of 2017. Russia assisted Bashar back into Palmyra in early March, which put the Syrian regime and Iranian-steered militias into a position to bid for eastern Syria, with western Syria having become more or less quiescent. ISIS seemed at last to be cracking apart as the Mosul battle proceeded and the USA and its Kurdish and Arab auxiliaries closed in on al-Raqqa from the north and west. The USA also protected and trained rebel militiamen in the Syrian desert along the border with Jordan and Iraq east of al-Suwayda, from where they might displace ISIS at the crossroads between Syria and Iraq. Two war theatres appeared about to become three (map 3): western Syria, subject to the interplay of Russia, Iran, and Turkey; Iraq, where ISIS was being slowly ripped out of the ground in the Sunni Arab provinces; and the lands of eastern Syria that connect these two wings and are up for grabs.

For the Syrian regime, the prize is the major city of Deir al-Zor, where for five years it has maintained an outpost base. Deir al-Zor is the centre of the centre of the war zone. From here the regime can command the Euphrates Valley to the Iraqi border, recover a large part of Syria's oilfields, and undermine the Americans and the Kurds to the north, and the Americans and rebels to the south. For Iran, the prizes are the Syria–Iraq border crossings, the hinges of the war zone. They offer land access across Iraq and Syria for Iranian supplies to Iranian clients in western Syria and Hezbollah in Lebanon, a quantum improvement on Damascus and Beirut airports. Iraq and Syria would become satellite states, the Kurds would be targets, Turkey would be contained, and Israel would have its strategic environment transformed for the worse.

What's in it for Putin? Russia's strategic interests only require ascendancy in western Syria. Such ascendancy, however, propels Russia into eastern Syria to keep a hand on the regime, Iran, and the associated militias, who need Russian air power to have their prizes. It also makes what happens in Iraq significant to Russia. Iranian advances to the east are not good for Russia in the west. They complicate Russia's chances of patronizing a settlement in Syria, in order to augment Russian global impact and secure stable influence in the eastern Mediterranean. Russia needs to be in eastern Syria to register its military role in the final overthrow of the ISIS 'caliphate', but would benefit from this being in cooperation with the US-led coalition. The USA, the Kurds, and even presently blocked Turkey and dysfunctional federal Iraq can all limit Iran, which can also ease life for Putin in Syria.

A Turkish analyst shared with me the thought that sudden simultaneous late March 2017 rebel attacks in Damascus and north of Hama after regime recovery of Palmyra may have carried a Saudi–American warning to the regime not to push further east.[114] It makes a colourful little story, and would breathe new meaning into the term 'proxy'. In the event, the regime and the ubiquitous Shi'a militias probed forward from

Palmyra and south of al-Raqqa from May onwards. They challenged the US–rebel position at al-Tanaf on the southern desert border,[115] where the USA bombed them and downed an Iranian drone. In June, they bothered the SDF allies of the Americans near al-Raqqa, and the USA destroyed a Syrian regime warplane. This was getting close to inter-state warfare, and the USA and Russia patched up limited coordination of bombing of ISIS. Regime-led ground forces reached part of the Syria–Iraq border in the Homs desert and approached ISIS in Deir al-Zor, while the US-supported SDF moved carefully into ISIS-held al-Raqqa.

In May–June 2017, in Iraq west of Mosul, Shi'a PMF contingents advised by Iran's Qasem Soleimani likewise headed for the Syria–Iraq border. If Badr Brigades leader Hadi al-Amiri's comments about taking ISIS-held al-Qa'im on the border far to the south are any guide,[116] the PMF aspired to liaise with the Syrian regime for command of an area connecting Tal Afar to al-Hasakeh and extending to the Euphrates. Iran's power play across the Fertile Crescent loomed larger.

3

THE KURDS AT WAR, 2014–2017

After mid-2012, a Kurdish wing of, what was at that time, a war contained within Syria began to develop with the withdrawal of Syrian regime forces from north-eastern Syria to hold lines in the regime heartland. Local Kurds began implementing autonomy in three 'cantons' along the Syrian–Turkish border under the direction of the semi-socialist PYD, a twenty-first-century derivative of the PKK in Turkey. In the north-east, the PYD and its militia cohabited with a residual regime presence, sparred with Islamist and jihadist offshoots of the Sunni Arab rebellion, and aroused Turkish displeasure. From mid-2013 they increasingly battled Jabhat al-Nusra and ISIS jihadists, who had supply chains through Turkey and coveted the borderlands. More than 200,000 Syrian Kurds, displaced by Islamists or opposed to the PYD, fled across the Iraqi border into Kurdistan Regional Government territory.[1] Meantime, KRG president Masoud Barzani tried to patronize a rapprochement of older, more conservative Syrian Kurdish parties with the PYD, mainly arousing the suspicion of the latter.

The period from mid-2012 to the mid-2014 ISIS rampage through central and northern Iraq represented a transition in which the Syrian Kurds were both enmeshed in the Syrian war and comprised a distinctive dimension of it. In contrast, the KRG Kurds of northern Iraq stood beyond the war, challenged to a limited extent by its spillover but primarily absorbed in their tensions with Baghdad and their unstable oil-based economic boom. In June 2014, a radically different configuration took hold almost overnight, when ISIS forcibly incorporated Iraq into what became through the subsequent three years a Syria–Iraq war arena.

My discussion of the Kurdish situation in the combined war zone has three components:

a) an introductory overview of Kurdish political prospects across the whole northern and eastern margins of the Fertile Crescent, considered against the backdrop of events in Syria and Iraq since 2011;
b) a comparative exploration of the implications of the ISIS phase of the crisis for the KRG in northern Iraq and Rojava (the Kurdish zone in northern Syria); and
c) an assessment of paths out of the crisis for the KRG and Rojava in the context of international interests and interventions.

Kurdish realities

Prospects for an independent Kurdish entity anywhere in the zone of Kurdish-majority populations have been unpromising, even with the fracturing of Syria and Iraq since 2011. Kurdish majorities extend across portions of four contiguous modern countries, but two can be excluded from any scenario. In Turkey, home to more than half of the approximately 28 million people who would define their ethnicity as Kurdish, the most that Kurds might receive encompasses some further cultural and linguistic liberalization, adjustment of constitutional vocabulary about identity, and administrative devolution in the super-centralized Turkish state. Turkey has the power and legitimacy to see off the PKK challenge indefinitely, although a serious internal 'peace process' would be beneficial. In Iran, the country's 6 million or so Kurds, concentrated in provinces bordering today's Iraqi Kurdistan, are under careful surveillance. There is linguistic pluralism, especially given that the Kurdish language, whether Sorani or Kurmanji variants, is related to Farsi. As in Turkey, however, political devolution is off the table. Iran has an efficient repressive machine; it is vigilant in the light of the ill-fated Kurdish attempt to break away in the 'Mahabad republic' at a time of Iranian weakness in the late 1940s.

That leaves the Kurds of Iraq and Syria. Superficially, the multi-sided, multi-front war that developed across the Fertile Crescent out of the 2011 popular uprising in Syria gave the Kurdish-majority areas of northern Syria and northern Iraq an opportunity for decisive political assertion. A closer look, however, reveals problematic structural features, acute in the Syrian case but also operative in the most elaborate Kurdish political experiment to date: the KRG in Iraq.

First, Kurdish autonomy in Iraq and Syria—let alone separation from these states—has no proximate allies or sponsors. On the contrary, excepting Turkey's realpolitik positive relations with the KRG, the Kurds of Iraq and Syria confront uniform walls of suspicion and hostility. This differs from the situations of Abkhazia and South Ossetia in nearby Georgia, which have Russian endorsement, or Nogorno Karabakh in Azerbaijan, where local Armenians have Armenia behind them. It resembles similarly isolated Catalonia or the Basque country in Spain, but in modern times Iraq and Syria have presented the Kurds with a far nastier environment. In some ways, the post-2011 decomposition of Syria and Iraq, while it presented limited and probably temporary openings, only highlighted the absence of a real regional backer for the Kurds.

Second, geography conspires against the Kurds of Iraq and Syria. In both cases, Kurds are landlocked and depend on either their host states or Turkey for physical access to the outside world. In Syria, apart from the large minority of their number in Damascus and Aleppo, Kurds are strung out along the Syrian–Turkish border either in separated pockets or mixed with other groups, with no territorial depth and indefensible rolling plains to the south. The presence of a significant part of Syria's oil infrastructure and substantial agricultural resources only inflames Syrian Arab sensitivity about the future of the borderlands. Undoubtedly the KRG in Iraq enjoys superior circumstances. It has a more compact territory, a mountain redoubt as a refuge, and a Kurdish population of 5 million, at least three times the number of Kurds in northern Syria and an overwhelming majority of 85 per cent within the KRG. Since 2005, its autonomy and administration have had internal, Iraqi, and international legitimacy, and it commands a much larger oil resource over which its management has been partially conceded. Nonetheless, even here the leading urban centre, Irbil (Hawler), the prized town of Kirkuk, and much of the oil are strategically vulnerable on a plain wide open to the

south. Of themselves, the mountains to the rear might be a temporary refuge, but they cannot support autonomy or a state.

Third, demographic engineering, Ba'athist manipulation, and decades
of incorporation into Iraq and Syria compromised the Kurdish areas,
compounding geographical disabilities. In Iraq, Saddam's programme to
'Arabize' Kurdistan, involving population transfers in and out, weakened the Kurdish presence on the plains, leaving the legacy of 'disputed
territories'. Saddam carried out wider depopulation of Kurdish areas in
the genocidal 1988 Anfal campaign, including the gassing to death of
5,000 people in Halabja. In Syria, the governments of the 1960s and
1970s diluted the Kurdish population along the Turkish border and pursued Arabization with deprivation of citizenship, in-migration of Arabs,
and attempts to erode Kurdishness, such as banning Kurdish language
usage. A 1962 special census in al-Hasakeh province, requiring proof of
Syrian residence back to 1945, created a stateless Kurdish population
that reached 300,000 by the early 2000s[2]—a large fraction of Syria's
roughly 2.5 million Kurds. When Kurds rioted in al-Qamishli in March
2004, after a morale boost from the overthrow of Saddam in Iraq, they
met fierce repression from Bashar al-Assad's regime. Assad's 2011 offer
of citizenship for stateless Kurds would never have come without his
need for splitting tactics in a deepening crisis.

Fourth, despite painful lessons of the consequences of fratricide for
a people already facing severe constraints, the Kurds of Iraq and Syria
remain exposed to political fracturing. The KRG is bi-polar, between
parties respectively based in Irbil (Kurdistan Democratic Party—KDP)
and Sulaymaniyah (PUK and Gorran). Between 1994 and 2005, the
two cities were the foci of competing KDP and PUK entities that even
waged war with each other in 1994–7. After more than a decade of the
unified KRG, the bitterness of party disputation and the divisive party
influences within the Peshmerga armed forces remain disturbing. As for
northern Syria, the single party authority of the PYD predominated
after mid-2012. Founded in 2003 as an offshoot of the militant hard-
left Turkish Kurdish PKK, the PYD had PKK personnel and experience
to draw on to establish a military wing, the People's Protection Units
(Yekîneyên Parastina Gel—YPG), which intimidated and sidelined the
older Syrian Kurdish parties.[3]

Although the PYD has benefited from its role in defending Kurds
and carving out a territorial base for autonomy, it has also acquired

enemies within and without. Only a conclusive Turkish–PKK settlement would assuage Turkish fears of a refuge for rebel PKK 'terrorists' on the Syrian side of the border. In the future, Turkey, any Syrian regime, and even the Kurds of the KRG have incentives to play with Syrian Kurdish factionalism, especially after the destruction of the ISIS jihadist redoubts in Syria and Iraq.

Overall, despite its notable deficiencies, the KRG can conceivably aspire eventually to become an independent Kurdistan, whereas Rojava ('the west', Kurdish name for the substantially Kurdish areas in northern Syria) will be hard put to sustain its present de facto self-administration. The KRG has a much more favourable physical and human geography, constitutional autonomy arrangements within federal Iraq since 2005, decent relations with Turkey as an outlet, and a relatively robust and inclusive political infrastructure. For his part, PYD leader Salih Muslim sensibly precludes trying to cut away from Syria.[4] Even a Syrian federalism equivalent to Iraq's regular provinces, far short of the special status the KRG has already attained, with its oil rights and security authority, would have to surmount the suspicion to be expected from both any future Syrian regime and Turkey.

The PYD's Rojava is fundamentally precarious, its existence and alignments a product of fickle wartime conditions. After 2014, the USA came to see them as an effective but insufficient ground force against ISIS. After Russia elevated its investment in Syria with its bombing campaign from October 2015 onwards, the PYD became for Moscow one of the potential checks on the Syrian regime, Turkey, and Iran. The PYD is, however, vulnerable to being traded or simply trashed in dealings between Vladimir Putin and the Trump administration. Paradoxically, PYD vulnerability increases after elimination of its deadly enemy the ISIS 'caliphate'—the Americans will lose interest and the Assad regime will look to recover northern and eastern Syria.

The Kurds confront ISIS, 2014–2017

Whatever the contrasting circumstances of the KRG and Rojava, the shock of ISIS reinforced distinctive Kurdish dynamics in both Iraq and Syria. For the KRG, the August 2014 ISIS advance toward Irbil and engagement of the Peshmerga in the KRG's first war in its decade as a unified political entity only intensified estrangement from Arab Iraq. The fact that the war precipitated a large refugee inflow and coincided with a sharp economic crisis because of the steep oil-price decline through 2014–15 also concentrated attention on the KRG's domestic weaknesses. Popular alienation from pervasive public-sector corruption, failure to reduce dependence on oil rent, and fierce disputation within a still substantially tribal and patrimonial political pluralism headed these weaknesses. Amid the ISIS challenge, these were arguments for going slow on independence. However, an enforced focus on KRG vulnerabilities also intensified engagement and debate within a distinctive Kurdish political framework. The ISIS phase accelerated political effervescence within the KRG that had to come anyway on the road to further loosening of ties to Baghdad.

For Rojava, the bitter and ultimately successful defence of the town and district of Kobani (Ayn al-Arab) against ISIS between September 2014 and June 2015 also had a galvanizing effect, but rather different from that in the KRG. First, it inaugurated a military coordination with America that diverged in basic character from the long-standing military cooperation between the USA and the KRG. In Rojava, the USA, by necessity, connected with a de facto ruling party—the PYD—and its YPG militia, not with a constitutionally recognized multi-party polity and security apparatus like the KRG. Second, despite the claim of bottom-up inclusive politics in the Rojava 'cantons', military success and linkage with the USA cemented PYD and YPG supremacy over the older Kurdish parties, and over Kurds and non-Kurds alike. Whereas the KRG indulged internal political turbulence alongside its fight against ISIS after the brief existential threat passed, Rojava's more perilous geopolitical situation called forth tough management.

Stronger Kurdish dynamics stimulated by the mid-2014 ISIS blitz in Iraq and Syria particularly bothered Turkey. Turkey's AKP government of course had some responsibility for this development; in 2013 and early 2014 it was lax towards jihadists heading for Syria. While confronting ISIS after mid-2014, the KRG continued to do all possible to placate Turkey. Fortunately for Irbil, President Recep Tayyip Erdoğan and the AKP disliked Iraqi Shi'a and Iranian hegemony in Baghdad sufficiently to even contemplate KRG independence. A Kurdistan carved out of Iraq would be conservative and Sunni; it might help defuse autonomist sentiment in Syria and Turkey; and greater freedom for it to run its oil affairs would be valuable for Turkey. Rojava in northern Syria was an entirely different matter. The AKP regarded the Kobani outcome as a disaster; the PYD extended itself along the border from the Euphrates to the KRG, it became hitched to Turkey's senior NATO ally, and shock waves disturbed security across south-east Turkey. In AKP Turkey's view the PYD remained radical, secular, and socialist. It would give the PKK geographical depth, and any recognition of its autonomy would supply a precedent for devolution demands in Turkey.

From this point in the book, discussion deals with the KRG and Rojava individually. Map 4 displays the 600 kilometre Kurdish–ISIS front from south of Kobani in Syria to south of Kirkuk in Iraq, with the situations for November 2014, March 2016, and July 2017.

Kurdistan Regional Government

The ISIS surge of mid-2014 transformed a situation in which Iraq was its own arena and the KRG was in outright confrontation with Iraqi prime minister Nouri al-Maliki over finances and disputed territories. The Kurds had gained Turkish cooperation in exporting oil on their own account to and through Turkey. In response, Maliki suspended the arrangement for federal transfer of 17 per cent of Iraqi oil revenues to the KRG, which consequently could not pay its public servants' salaries. This paralleled continuing stalemate over the implementation of article 140 in the 2005 Iraqi constitution for a referendum of native residents of Kirkuk and other lands in dispute with Baghdad on joining the KRG.

Suddenly both the KRG and the Iraqi government faced a new adversary in conditions potentially advantaging the KRG vis-à-vis Baghdad, providing the former could hold its lines against ISIS. The jihadists shattered the largely Shi'a new Iraqi army in Mosul and throughout the Sunni Arab north, while the KRG promptly took control of Kirkuk and its oilfields on the perfectly reasonable argument that someone needed to secure them. The situation was particularly dire given that ISIS appropriated an extraordinary haul of new American weaponry from Iraqi army stocks around Mosul—dozens of Abrams tanks, scores of heavy artillery pieces, a veritable mountain of light and medium weapons, and 2,300 Humvees.[5]

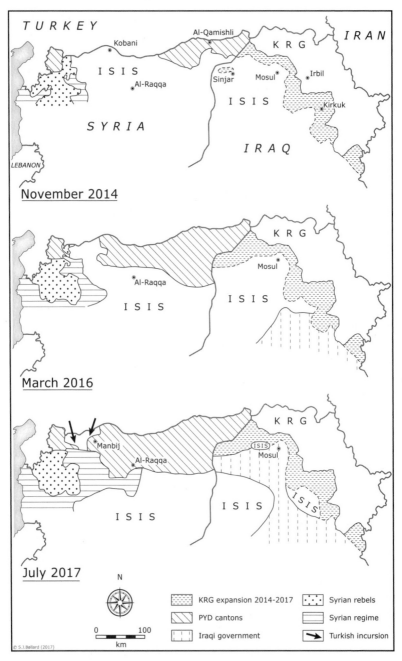

Map 4: The Kurds in Syria and Iraq, 2014–2017

A brief crisis of survival ensued for the KRG in early August 2014, when ISIS attacked the Yazidi town of Sinjar, seized the Mosul dam, and pushed towards Irbil. The Peshmerga, untested in battle for a decade and sporting obsolete equipment from the 1980s and earlier, fell back precipitously. With ISIS threatening Irbil with American arms and massacring defenceless Yazidis, the USA had no choice but to intervene with its air power, something it had avoided as long as the crisis was restricted to Syria. US aerial bombing enabled the Peshmerga to stabilize the Irbil front beyond the KRG border and to recover the Mosul dam, while US and Iraqi helicopters and Peshmerga, PKK, and YPG ground forces facilitated evacuation of about 50,000 Yazidis from the Sinjar hills.[6]

Thereafter, covered by a US-led coalition in the air, the KRG Peshmerga could consolidate its long front across northern Iraq and make offensive moves in the Kirkuk, Irbil, and Sinjar sectors. In late 2014, the Peshmerga numbered at least 100,000 soldiers.[7] At this stage they emerged as more capable than the Iraqi army and more congenial partners to the international coalition against ISIS than the Iranian-manipulated Shi'a Arab PMF, which were almost all Baghdad could immediately field. With the Iraqi government depending on the Shi'a militias simply to hold ISIS short of Baghdad into 2015 and losing al-Anbar provincial capital Ramadi to ISIS in May 2015, the Peshmerga stood out for the time being as lead ground force against ISIS in Iraq.

Equipment, training, and organizational deficiencies, however, continued to handicap the KRG forces. Western countries and the Turks helped to a limited degree with equipment and training, although the former seemed to feel that calling in air strikes compensated for ground-force vulnerabilities such as limited firepower and night-vision problems. As for organization, chains of command were complicated and cross-cutting. The main body of Peshmerga answered to both the KRG Ministry of Peshmerga and to one or other of the two main political parties: the KDP and the PUK. The parties retained their influence with the units that had been their respective paramilitaries through the half-century of Kurdish armed struggles in Iraq since the 1960s. Otherwise, the elite gendarmerie force known as the Zerevani Peshmerga came under the KRG Interior Ministry. Party connections undermined military cohesion and still carried the potential for disruption.

Regardless of such problems, the ISIS incorporation of central Iraq into its 'caliphate' temporarily humbled a demoralized Iraqi government in its relations with the KRG. Prime Minister Maliki, whose Shi'a favouritism alienated Iraqi Sunni Arabs and gave ISIS a popular base up to the western outskirts of the capital, resigned in September 2014. The new prime minister, Haydar al-Abadi, found himself boxed in by Iranian-aligned warlords, corrupt bureaucratic fiefdoms, and the populist movement of Muqtada al-Sadr. Meantime, after Kurdish expulsion of ISIS from Sinjar in November 2015, the KRG front against ISIS encompassed a large part of northern Iraq beyond KRG boundaries. These lands included the most valuable territories claimed by the KRG as Kurdish, other areas near Mosul, and assets such as the Mosul dam. The KRG could claim it was safeguarding property on behalf of Iraq and also look to deploy its gains in future bargaining.

By unfortunate coincidence, for Baghdad and Irbil alike the ISIS shock came at a time of sliding economic capacity because of the entirely unrelated steep fall in world oil prices from over $100 per barrel in mid-2014 to under $45 by the end of the year. With the enemy literally knocking at the door, the Iraqi government and the KRG scrabbled for the means to mount any sort of war effort. In these circumstances, even the incendiary issue of KRG territorial acquisitions became frozen into a hazy future. Iraq had to start again on building a new army, the KRG soon found itself challenged to keep up with civil servant and Peshmerga salaries, and the KRG in particular had to cope with a large new refugee inflow. Foreign workers and professionals fled, and projects of all descriptions were thrown into uncertainty. One might ask what had happened to some of the considerable revenues from the immediately preceding good years, for there to be rapidly developing penury among the population by 2015. Plainly the KRG needed to show more concern about its own sink-hole of corruption if the home front was to be kept supportive of the administration.

Both under severe pressure, the KRG and the Iraqi government smoothed over their oil-revenue dispute in December 2014. The KRG would supply Iraq's state organization for oil marketing (SOMO) with 550,000 barrels a day, including 300,000 from Kirkuk, and Baghdad would resume paying Kurdistan's 17 per cent share of Iraq's oil proceeds.[8] For the KRG it was an irritating reiteration of economic integration with Iraq, but for its part Baghdad had to acknowledge that the KRG commanded Kirkuk. In any case the arrangement frayed in early 2015. Baghdad failed to deliver full payments, claiming it was not receiving contracted amounts of oil. The KRG ridiculed the claim, indicated that it would hold buyers liable for payments, and again turned to independent oil sales. The venom in KRG–Baghdad economic interactions even when they were allies in warfare illustrated the deep instability of federal Iraq.

Full KRG sovereignty over oil resources, contracts, and sales was an appealing aspiration in such conditions. In late 2014, before prices slipped below $60 per barrel, the three-year outlook for oil production within its boundaries, already up to over 300,000 barrels per day from almost nothing in 2009,[9] indicated that the KRG might be able to meet its budget obligations without anything from Kirkuk. This seemed a plausible basis for political independence. The prospect vanished through 2015 as prices dropped below $40 per barrel. Even with the addition of Kirkuk output, the KRG earned $630 million per month in sales through its pipelines into Turkey—short of the $850 million needed to pay civil and military salaries and the oil companies.[10] In early 2016 a shutdown in the pipeline across Turkey demonstrated KRG vulnerability to Turkish security problems and political priorities. Oil companies also became less optimistic about KRG reserves and geological favourability.[11] In March 2016, the Iraqi state company operating the Kirkuk field chose to inject its 150,000 barrels per day of production into the ground rather than add it to the 450,000 barrels of KRG exports through Turkey.[12] This expressed Baghdad's determination to compel the Kurds to accept its oil policies and cease unilateral exports.

Here the KRG–Baghdad oil dispute intersected decisively with the joint military campaign against ISIS and the vital interests of the United States in that campaign. With reconstructed Iraqi army units performing creditably in central Iraq against ISIS in Ramadi and Falluja, capturing the former in February and the latter in June 2016, the USA wanted to advance planning for the battle to rid Mosul of ISIS. Success would smash the terrorist nerve centre in Iraq. The Peshmerga controlled land west, north, and east of Mosul that Iraqi forces needed to use for the offensive. They also needed Kurdish logistical and operational collaboration in the Mosul countryside. The KRG made clear that it would be easier to be helpful if Baghdad was not so obstinate about oil.

Seasoned US envoy Brett McGurk conducted shuttle mediation from April until late August. An agreement emerged to share the Kirkuk output equally between the KRG and Baghdad, with the Kurds committing to full, enthusiastic collaboration in the Mosul battle. The Kurds also promised not to enter Mosul, a primarily Sunni Arab city, where they had no desire to get mired anyway. In late September, KRG president Barzani visited Baghdad for the first time in three years, even having a friendly discussion of independence with Prime Minister Abadi. Iraqi troops and US advisers moved into place south of Mosul, with the senior Iraqi general effusive in praise for 'unprecedented' Peshmerga cooperation.[13] The way was open for driving towards Mosul within a few weeks.

While the KRG's oil-rent economy sputtered and contracted—precisely when it seemed to have most promise, and in the days of most need—the Kurdistan region also faced waves of displaced people fleeing ISIS. Up to June 2014, the KRG received about a quarter of a million refugees, mainly Kurds, from the disintegration of Syria. The mid-2014 ISIS surge precipitated a much greater tide of fugitives from areas of Iraq taken by the jihadists. These included more than 50,000 Yazidi Kurds, more than 100,000 Christians from Qara Qosh and other environs of Mosul, and at least 1 million Sunni Arabs, probably around 1.5 million in total.[14] Proportionate to its own population, by late 2014 the KRG hosted numbers greater than the Syrian refugee load carried by Jordan and approaching that carried by Lebanon. Irbil received considerable support from international agencies, but there was heavy pressure on resources, employment, and social cohesion amid economic and military crisis. The Sunni Arab majority of the incomers presented demographic and security worries for Kurds. Was there ISIS infiltration that might interact with local religious radicalism?[15] Nonetheless, shouldering the burden registered the KRG as a responsive government apparatus in the eyes of the international coalition confronting ISIS.

Even before the ISIS crisis and the parallel economic recession, political horizons shortened among the KRG population. In January 2005, an informal referendum of 2 million voters participating in KRG assembly and Iraqi parliamentary elections in the Kurdistan region showed 98 per cent Kurdish endorsement of independence.[16] In September 2012, when a sample of 2,500 in Duhok, Irbil, and Sulaymaniyah answered the same question, support was 56 per cent.[17] On an emotional level, probably nothing had changed; on a practical level, 'no' responders wanted a better-developed economy first and feared external repudiation of the KRG, including a hostile US reaction. There was also a party undercurrent of Duhok and Irbil—KDP- and Barzani-dominated provinces—expressing more favour for early independence than the PUK and opposition stronghold of Sulaymaniyah, on the Iranian border. With PUK founder Jalal Talabani holding the ceremonial presidency of the new Iraq, plus suspicion of KDP motives, a reserved outlook in Sulaymaniyah was predictable.

Differences on implementing Kurdish independence—few disagreed on the principle—accompanied rancour among the KRG political parties on President Masoud Barzani's command of executive authority since 2005, meaning KDP pre-eminence. Ironically, the emergence of the reformist and anti-corruption Gorran movement, splitting from the PUK in 2009 and displacing it as second party after the KDP in the KRG assembly in 2013—a healthy blow to KDP/PUK duopoly—accentuated political volatility in the ISIS crisis. The KDP and PUK kept their long-standing decisive influence within the Peshmerga and wielded financial and patronage resources that Gorran lacked.

To compensate, Gorran joined the KRG coalition government in 2013, most prominently taking the Ministry for Peshmerga. This deal with the KDP, which conceived Gorran as a block on PUK resurgence, intensified Gorran's need to keep its momentum by flaunting anti-establishment credentials. Its leader, Nawishirwan Mustafa, promoted a shift from a presidential to a parliamentary regime.[18] Meantime, the Gorran–PUK split and other infighting debilitating the PUK made both parties more vulnerable to Iranian pressure. Ultimately, Iran sought to influence them to contain the KDP and the Barzani clan.

Gorran went along with an extension to Masoud Barzani's presidency when it joined the administration in 2013, but in August 2015 combined with Islamist parties and some PUK members to oppose another extension, proposing that a new president should either be elected by the people, with ceremonial functions, or by parliament,

115

with executive power. A KDP deputy ridiculed these ideas: 'How can you have a president elected by parliament with more power than a popularly elected president?'[19] The KDP turned to the Kurdistan Consultative Council, set up in 2008 to adjudicate administrative disputes, to authorize Barzani's extension to August 2017 with all powers intact. Gorran could not give way, especially after its flirtations with Barzani's party had cost it votes in the 2014 Iraqi general elections, and it loudly protested at the new extension.

Together with KRG bankruptcy and failure to pay salaries, the dispute inflamed popular discontent. In early October 2015, demonstrations by unpaid civil servants in Sulaymaniyah degenerated into street riots. A crowd set a KDP office ablaze and six people were killed. In response, the KDP had the parliamentary speaker, who was a Gorran deputy, and four Gorran government ministers banned from entering Irbil.[20] Gorran ceased to participate in the regional administration; general Kurdish concern not to undermine morale on the front against ISIS ensured that the street upheaval was not repeated, but the political impasse became protracted. A senior PUK personality, attending a PYD congress in northern Syria, let loose his fury against the KDP: 'If Masoud Barzani decides to separate Kurdistan from Iraq, then we will separate Sulaymaniyah from Kurdistan and attach it to Iraq.'[21]

On 17 May 2016, Gorran signed a political alliance with the PUK against the KDP. Its alternative of street protests was obviously not practical while the Kurdistan region was at war with ISIS. Gorran thereby returned to the embrace of the segment of the ruling class that it had supposedly repudiated. In September, the Iranian consul in Sulaymaniyah strove to patch up relations between estranged wings of the PUK headed by Jalal Talabani's deputy, Barham Salih, and Talabani's wife, Hero Ibrahim Ahmad.[22] The latter faction railed against the former: 'Your only goal is to keep piling up your wealth, after you usurped thousands of dunums of land and took over huge businesses.' Gorran embarrassingly declared its 'neutrality', which made its accusations of 'monopolization' against the Barzanis ring hollow. President Barzani did not appear to be in imminent danger from this dissonance, but the overall political decomposition made a regression to 'the rule of two administrations' seem as plausible as the KDP's independence project. Meanwhile, the exertions of the Peshmerga and coalition air power in slowly corroding ISIS around Kirkuk and Mosul continued as if in an alternative reality.

Rojava

Whatever its difficulties, the KRG conducted its military campaign after June 2014 against a single enemy—the ISIS jihadists—from a legitimized contiguous territorial base and with decent international relations. If frictions with Iraqi Arabs and the Iraqi regime were to return to the bad old days, it would be after ISIS. Syrian Kurds lived in more mercurial circumstances, certainly after the emergence of Syrian Kurdish cantons along the Turkish border and the displacement of less steely Syrian Kurdish parties by the PYD in mid- and late 2012. At the outset in 2012, the Jazira, Kobani, and Afrin cantons (map 1) were widely separated from one another, had potentially hostile Sunni Arab opposition factions as immediate neighbours, and had virtually no licit access across the Turkish border. Jazira and Kobani lacked defensible topography and were wide open to infiltration. The PYD had to share the largest canton, Jazira, with intelligence services that the regime kept in place.

Through 2013, Syrian Kurdish relations with the mainstream Syrian opposition were mostly cool. Kurdish National Council (KNC) opponents of the PYD managed to get the National Coalition to take the word 'Arab' out of the 'Syrian Arab Republic', but otherwise the opposition viewed PYD Kurds as both separatist and serving Assad. Many Kurds in turn saw the Arabs as chauvinist. From mid-2013, fighting developed between the YPG paramilitary force of the PYD and a varying assortment of jihadist and Syrian opposition militias. The YPG expelled al-Nusra jihadists from Ra's al-Ayn at the western extremity of Jazira canton, also taking the border crossing, and in October made a crucial advance southward to improve the viability of Jazira. They took the Rmeilan oilfield, seized the border post and military installation at Ya'rubiya, widening their access to the KRG and Iraq, and consolidated a territorial linkage with the city of al-Hasakeh, which they cohabited with regime forces. The logical interest of the regime was that Kurds, jihadists, and opposition militias kill one another, but that the Kurds be left standing, suitably weakened, safeguarding the real estate until the regime was able to return and take it all back.

Into 2014, the PYD had no friends among external powers dabbling in Syria's war. Along its border Turkey preferred the regime, the opposition, and the Islamists to the PYD Kurds. Indeed, the regime presence in al-Qamishli meant that the city's border crossing intermittently operated for civilian supplies, which also gave some relief to the PYD administration. At this stage, the only Russian and Iranian interest was that the PYD remain split from the Arab opposition and maintain an ambiguous position on the future of Bashar al-Assad. The PYD obliged by taking part in the National Coordination Committee (NCC), a soft 'opposition' front tolerated by the regime. The Iranians, of course, wanted Kurdish autonomy terminated with an overall final victory for the Syrian regime and themselves. Having to accept the KRG in Iraq was bad enough. The Russians and Americans were barely engaged with the Kurdish dimension of the Syrian breakdown between 2011 and 2014, but the Russians had a historical association with the semi-Marxist PKK.

ISIS took firmer shape as the leading existential threat to Rojava in March 2014 when it probed YPG forward positions near Tell Abyad and on the Kobani margins. Of course, ISIS detested the Kurdish emphasis on ethnic rather than religious identity, and regarded PYD secularism, socialism, and gender equality as the most flagrant godlessness, but the main PYD offence for the ex-Ba'athist Iraqi officers and Chechens prominent in ISIS military affairs was that it impeded communications into Turkey. By early 2014, Tell Abyad represented the only border crossing not covered by the expanding Jazira and Kobani cantons.

After ISIS combined eastern Syria and western Iraq to make its 'caliphate' in June 2014, a showdown with the PYD was inevitable as soon as ISIS chased rival jihadists out of Syrian oilfields and subdued Syrian Arab tribes. Certainly, it looked to eliminate the Yazidis and forward Peshmerga positions in northern Iraq, and even to make a move on Irbil, but otherwise the KRG did not represent an immediate target, because it wasn't on the way to or from anywhere. In contrast, when ISIS asserted command of the Syrian side of the Turkish border north-east of Aleppo, Kobani beckoned as a glaring geographical interruption north of the 'caliphal' headquarters in al-Raqqa.

In July 2014, ISIS launched an assault that the YPG managed to fend off. For ISIS, the whole border east of Aleppo was the target, and

Kobani only the beginning. It had to have the freest possible access for thousands of foreign jihadist recruits transiting Turkey, as well as to its terrorist cells in Turkish cities and Europe. Also, the broader its presence along the border, the broader its possibilities for penetrating and intimidating Turkey; Erdoğan and the AKP were so focused on the PYD's border holdings that they did not seem to recognize the implications of the looming alternative.

In mid-September, ISIS launched its major offensive against the Kobani canton, deploying several thousand jihadists, and weapons captured from the Syrian regime, along with American equipment from Mosul. By early October the YPG, with a thousand or so fighters, including hundreds from the PKK and its own women's contingent, was reduced to a pocket in Kobani town, on the Turkish border, and virtually all the cantonal population fled into Turkey. With Turkey set against helping the PYD, and ISIS on the verge of a new coup, the US-led coalition tentatively stepped in with air power, increasing the backup as the YPG demonstrated resilience. Turkish Kurds slipped across the border to reinforce the YPG, and Turkey reluctantly allowed a contingent of Peshmerga to come with artillery from Iraq and to enter Kobani, as well as Free Syrian Army troops who hated the jihadists. By late January 2015, the YPG finally gained the upper hand in the town after a grinding attrition in which ISIS lost around a thousand personnel compared with about 300 from the YPG and allies.[23] By mid-March it recovered all the lost countryside.

The Kobani battle was the biggest reverse for ISIS in the first year of its 'caliphate', and the achievement transformed the standing of the PYD and Syrian Kurds. In October 2014, US secretary of state John Kerry remarked that preventing the fall of Kobani did not reach the level of a 'strategic objective';[24] in February 2015 he termed the victory 'a big deal', especially as ISIS had defined Kobani as a 'symbolic and strategic objective'.[25] From barely being on the US radar, the YPG now became the favoured American ground-force partner against ISIS in Syria. The discrediting of the US programme to persuade Syrian Arab rebels to shift priorities from Assad to ISIS by September 2015, when trainees gave their US equipment to Jabhat al-Nusra jihadists,[26] consecrated the YPG's status. The following month the YPG consented to a US-promoted rebranding of itself at the head of a new front of Arab and other non-Kurdish factions.[27] The YPG drew on FSA allies in the Kobani fight, and adopted the banner of Syrian Democratic Forces (SDF); 25,000 YPG Kurds initially comprised the large majority of SDF troops, but by May 2016 Arabs numbered about 6,000 and were increasing.[28]

Unfortunately, just as the Kobani struggle opened the door to Washington for the PYD, it confirmed Turkey and Rojava in their hostile view of each other. PYD leader Salih Muslim accused Turkey's AKP government of betting on the fall of Kobani and fingered cross-border movement of arms and reinforcements to ISIS, 'although I don't know to what degree the Turkish state may be involved in that'. He 'believed that they [the AKP] want demographic change in the whole Kurdish area [of northern Syria]. … Perhaps they prefer the creation of a Sunni [Arab] state [there].'[29] The deep freeze with Turkey in turn made the PYD's longer-term partnership with the USA uncertain, because of the fundamental importance for America of relations with Turkey.

For the moment, PYD advances on the ground through 2015 buttressed the immediate viability of Rojava. In June 2015, the YPG seized Tell Abyad, thereby achieving a continuous geography of the Jazira and Kobani cantons and depriving ISIS of its last border outlet east of the Euphrates. Turkey angrily accused the YPG of conducting ethnic cleansing of non-Kurds around Tell Abyad, but the evidence was debatable. In November and December, the new SDF cleared ISIS from about a thousand square kilometres south-east of al-Hasakeh, impressing the Americans and firming up collaboration. Jazira–Kobani now had a decent agriculture and oil base, while the regime continued partially to pay public-servant and teacher wages. On the other hand, this was achieved through expansion beyond the Kurdish zone into Arab tribal lands, and the regime kept a bureaucratic stake in Rojava only to ease its own ultimate reassertion.

To the west, the isolated Afrin canton stood as a testament to continued economic interactions across front lines.[30] Afrin produced olive-oil-based soap and jeans for much of Syria, and did its business at a cost in transport charges and backhanders regardless of a Turkish blockade and the fluctuating tempo of hostilities here and there. Into 2016, Afrin and Jazira cantons hosted Arabs, Kurds, and others fleeing western Syria turmoil and ISIS rule to the east; Kurds were in any case a shaky majority across Rojava.

As for rudimentary governance in place of the Syrian regime, between 2013 and 2016 the PYD formulated local administrations in the three cantons.[31] In contrast to the KRG, with its established apparatus and multi-party politics, the PYD was a single party starting from zero in an emergency—features that encouraged arbitrary behaviour. It coopted its own cadres, others ready to work under its umbrella, and cooperative Arabs, Turkmen, and Assyrian Christians. These staffed interim multi-ethnic municipalities, legislatures, and executives, with Kurdish preponderance. In theory, in a bottom-up democratic socialism, local populations would elect the municipalities, which would then elect the cantonal legislatures. In practice, PYD appointment operated until the first municipal elections in March 2015. At the upper level, the PYD announced autonomous cantons in November 2013, and the interim authorities declared a federation of northern Syria in March 2016. The PYD configured itself as the leading component of a multi-ethnic rather than Kurdish structure; this would be a model for a federalized Syria. The decentralized democratic hierarchy concept followed recommendations of PKK leader Abdullah Öcalan, in turn derived from the ideas of the American Murray Bookchin.[32] Otherwise, the PYD-steered administration declared Kurdish, Arabic, and Syriac as official languages and implemented gender balance, for example with co-chaired executives.

The PYD-driven project for Rojava had two adversaries who would be around longer than the ISIS pseudo-state: Turkey and the Ba'athist Arabist Syrian regime of Bashar al-Assad—the latter with Iran lurking behind it. Turkey was an open book; it publicly identified the PYD as a subordinate of the PKK, and all else followed. The Assad regime moved behind curtains of deceit: the PYD could be handy as a temporary ally of convenience to bother rebels in north-west Syria; the regime's Russian guardian wanted the PYD in play; and liquidation of Rojava was a long-term goal. The KRG also had enemies, but what the Syrian Kurds faced was proportionately more formidable. The only relief, apart from a United States that could vary unpredictably from president to president, was the hatred of Erdoğan for Assad, and the contempt of Assad for Erdoğan. Two developments in 2016 illustrated what Rojava was up against.

First, given the collaboration of the YPG-led Syrian Democratic Forces with the USA and the rift between Turkey and Russia after the direct Russian aerial intervention on behalf of Assad, the PYD was tempted to act to reduce the remaining gap in its border holdings (map 4). That ISIS occupied a large part of the gap was actually helpful to the PYD, because a move against ISIS as the partially Arab SDF could have US bombing support as well as a US veto against Turkish interference.

In December 2015, the SDF probed across the Euphrates into the ISIS-held Manbij district in defiance of Turkey, which was furious but impotent. In February 2016, the PYD took advantage of a Syrian regime operation with Russian bombing support against rebels north of Aleppo, sending the SDF east from Afrin to seize a strip of rebel territory up to the ISIS zone. In response, Turkey used artillery to shell the SDF, and facilitated the transfer of hundreds of Syrian Islamist fighters into the rebel border pocket. This provoked Russian and American warnings to Turkey, but the Turks did manage to deter the SDF from attacking the border town of A'zaz. In May–August 2016, the SDF mounted a major move in coordination with American Special Force advisers and bombing to take the Manbij district and town from ISIS.

Turkey was now frantic, and resolved to take any chance to cross the border and block what was left of the Syrian Kurdish border gap. In late August, ISIS provided the chance with a suicide bombing in Gaziantep, and the Turkish army and allied Syrian Arab rebels cleared ISIS from the border between Jarabulus and A'zaz. They then moved south towards al-Bab to block the Kurds. US vice president Joe Biden, visiting Ankara on the day of the Turkish border thrust and put on the defensive by Turkish speculation about US sympathy for the failed mid-July 2016 military coup attempt against the AKP government, ordered the Kurds to leave Manbij and withdraw back across the Euphrates or lose US backing.[33] The SDF, having made considerable sacrifices against ISIS through the summer, moved some personnel but largely stayed put. There was no further comment from the Obama administration, but the Turkish air force now bombed the SDF from time to time, also without American comment. The Syrian Kurds had received a warning of what being a new American friend might mean if this ever conflicted with a US–Turkey rapprochement.

The second development was between Rojava and the Syrian regime in eastern Syria, in al-Qamishli and al-Hasakeh. Regardless of PYD participation in the tame Assad- and Russian-approved NCC 'opposition' and preference to put off trouble with the regime, cohabitation of the two towns with regime personnel, facilities, and checkpoints as well as small loyalist militias meant continuous friction and intermittent incidents. In April 2016, tensions between the PYD's Assayish security organization and regime militias (Ba'athists and loyalist local Arabs and Christians) boiled over into two days of clashes in al-Qamishli with dozens of deaths. On 17 August, an altercation between PYD Assayish personnel and the regime's NDF militia in al-Hasakeh escalated into clashes across the town between the YPG and regime regular troops. The next day the regime mounted its first air raids on Kurdish forces since creation of the cantons in 2012. A 'government source' termed the strikes a message to cease demands that 'trespass on national sovereignty'.[34] The Americans warned the regime to desist and made deterrent air patrols; the Russians oversaw mediation from the regime-controlled airport in al-Qamishli.

Regime spokesmen bared their fangs. The governor of al-Hasakeh in the same breath asked for YPG 'mercy' and threatened to turn the town into a 'heap of rubble' (*kawmat hajar*).[35] Assad's national security chief Ali Mamlouk flew in and promised that 'he would smash both al-Qamishli and al-Hasakeh over the heads of their inhabitants' if YPG advances did not end immediately.[36] The fighting died down by 24 August with the YPG increasing its share of al-Hasakeh from about half to 90 per cent. The Syrian Kurds, however, had had a clear signal about what to expect in the north-east if Russia and Iran helped Assad towards his repeatedly expressed goal of recovering all of Syria. They received another such signal when the December 2016 collapse of Syrian rebels in eastern Aleppo neutered PYD autonomy in the Kurdish suburb of Shaykh Maqsud and terminated YPG use of it as a lever between the regime and rebels.

Kurdish paths

In mid-2017, after three years of the ISIS phase in the Syria–Iraq war zone, the strategic circumstances of Kurdistan in Iraq and Rojava in Syria differed substantially. To put it succinctly, the KRG at least vaguely matched potential resources to ambitions, whereas Rojava plotted a track to increasing overstretch. The YPG–SDF expanded to over 50,000 troops,[37] but both the recruitment reservoir and the mobilized strength were probably only about half of that of the KRG Peshmerga. Though relatively effective and battle hardened, the YPG had to fall back on conscription within the cantons while its alignment with non-Kurdish allies in the SDF was tailored more to American than to Kurdish requirements.

As for belligerent opponents, the KRG faced one enemy—ISIS—and other parties with whom it had delicate relations—the Iraqi government, Shi'a Arabs, the PKK, and Iran. Especially with the close American commitment in Iraq, the KRG could be reasonably confident that more serious friction with the 'frenemies' could be postponed until after disposal of ISIS. In contrast, adversaries of the PYD's domination of much of northern Syria—Turkey, the Syrian regime, Iran, and imported Shi'a militias—were ready to squeeze Rojava even while work against ISIS remained unfinished. A tentative US umbrella kept them at bay, but at a cost—service as a US ground force against ISIS in al-Raqqa involved YPG–SDF losses, and there was no clear American plan for future phases. Still, Syrian Kurds had no choice but to cling to the USA because Turkey wanted to strip them of this association.

Ironically, while they sought to displace each other with the USA, the Syrian Kurds and Turkey's AKP government had a common interest in the USA keeping the Syrian regime, Iranian-backed militias, and Russia away from al-Raqqa. Also, when Turkey pushed into northern Syria in August 2016 against both ISIS and the YPG–SDF, Syrian Kurds acquired an interest in ISIS and Turkey abrading each other—as did Russia and the Syrian regime. To call this a tangled web is wholly inadequate.

The question for the KRG in 2017 is not survival but the feasibility and desirability of bidding for independence in the prevailing conditions. On the one hand, the internal economic crisis and political factionalism argue for the prioritization of lessening dependence on oil rent and of bureaucratic reform. As for externalities, the USA plainly prefers resuscitating 'federal' Iraq, into which it has invested so much. Given that in 2016 the USA committed about $900 million to Peshmerga salaries and armaments in the context of the campaign against ISIS in Mosul,[38] relieving the KRG's overall financial position, President Barzani is not well placed to disturb Washington. At the same time, the political and security volatility in Turkey since 2015 has raised questions about its reliability as a land corridor to the world. Certainly, both the US and Turkish dimensions point, more than before ISIS, to a vigorous negotiating effort with Baghdad for a confederation. This would help pacify the USA and ensure redundancy in land corridors.

There are of course risks in standing still. Arab Iraqis have generally favoured a strong central regime, and before 2014 a majority of Shi'a and Sunni Arabs alike preferred a unitary to a federal state.[39] Iran tends in the same direction, particularly if it has chief steering influence in Baghdad. If there can be real reconciliation between Shi'a and Sunni Arabs after ISIS, which is unlikely but not impossible, the KRG could come under pressure for erosion of its authority. The USA itself was not enthusiastic about ethnic federalism when it patronized the new Iraqi constitution in 2005. It inclined towards each provincial unit being multi-ethnic with federalism as a device to embed pluralist politics rather than to express different national identities.[40] For some in the KRG, particularly the KDP, the USA providing Baghdad with an enhanced air force, including F16 fighter-bombers, is a warning of trouble ahead—promoted by the power that is also its own ally.[41] Before ISIS, Kurdistan was on the verge of front-line hostilities with Nouri al-Maliki's government, and in 2017 still lacks air defence capability.

Beyond the bonhomie of Kurds and Iraqis in the wake of the Mosul battle there remains the unfinished business interrupted by ISIS in June 2014: Kirkuk, other disputed territories, oil, and sovereign powers. For the KRG the sacrifices and burdens of the ISIS phase, including 1,614 Peshmerga deaths between June 2014 and November 2016[42] and the strain of hosting refugee numbers equivalent to almost one-third of the KRG's own population, call forth rigidity in facing Baghdad. In June 2016, a senior PUK official, Saadi Pira, insisted that there was no daylight between the PUK and KDP on basics. He supported an early independence referendum, slating the 'sectarian, chauvinist, and racist' mentality of 'the governments in the region', including Iraq and Iran.[43] The ISIS phase entrenched aspirations for territorial expansion, a rounded-out resource base, and effective sovereignty. The strain of the crisis, however, also imposed realism; most in the KRG accept that the best route is through an understanding with Baghdad on a continuing common framework.

In mid-2017, the KRG controlled lands beyond its official boundary equivalent to more than a half of its own territory (map 4). The KRG held some of these lands before June 2014, but it acquired most in the process of pushing out its defence line against ISIS. For the KRG, the whole area is 'disputed territory' subject to Kurdish claims on the basis of historical occupation prior to 'Arabization'—importation of Arabs and expulsion of Kurds—implemented by Saddam Hussein's Ba'athist regime. KRG officials, notably from the KDP, insisted that the KRG would not surrender lands it regards as originally Kurdish, meaning the bulk of the territory between the official KRG boundary and the Peshmerga front lines of mid-2017.[44]

Heading Kurdish claims is the city, province, and oilfields of Kirkuk, Iraq's original lead oil reservoir before the opening up of oilfields in the Shi'a Arab south. Before the 'Arabization' of the 1970s onwards, Kirkuk town had a rough balance of large Kurdish, Turkmen, and Arab communities, with Kurds having the demographic advantage in the province as a whole. For Kurds in Iraq, Kirkuk is the most significant Kurdish historical centre, from its function as the Baban emirate seat in the seventeenth and eighteenth centuries. Iraq reluctantly conceded article 140 in the 2005 federal constitution that provides for a referendum of the native population of Kirkuk and other disputed areas, as established by a census. The constitution specified that the referendum would happen by late 2007, but the federal government stalled. With a Kurdish demographic edge gradually consolidated since 2003 with the return of displaced Kurds, the KRG wanted Kirkuk's geopolitical situation resolved in its favour. Turkmen and some others would like a special separate status for Kirkuk, but that is not the prevailing Kurdish sentiment. Otherwise, in Ninewa province, the KRG looked to extend itself towards the outskirts of Mosul and along the Iraq–Syria border to Sinjar (Shingal in Kurdish); the KRG sees the Yazidis as Kurds.

Apart from the overall quarrel with Baghdad, problems emerged in the disputed territories among Kurds, and between Kurds and others, even close to the front line with ISIS. The Kurdish parties and the KDP and PUK sections of the Peshmerga eyed the division of influence in Kirkuk and its oilfields. There were clashes between the Peshmerga and Shi'a Turkmen fighters in Tuz Khurmatu, and between the Peshmerga and the Shi'a PMF militias at the far southern end of Kurdistan, in

Diyala province. Human Rights Watch reported Kurdish demolition of deserted Arab homes and villages in disputed rural areas in Kirkuk and Ninewa provinces between September 2014 and May 2016.[45] In response, the KRG blamed ISIS improvised explosive devices and coalition bombing.[46] The danger for the Kurds was that any such demolitions could stimulate the antipathy of the large Sunni Arab tribes of northern Iraq. The KRG could do without extra complications in its situation in northern Iraq as it moved into a critical new phase in its relations with the Shi'a Arab-dominated Iraqi regime.

The disputed territories are intimately bound up with oil because the KRG would like to improve its own resource base with nearby oil and gas, particularly given Kurdish land claims. Oil, in turn, is at the focus of Kurdish interest in the KRG having more sovereign rights on its territory, including new territory. The 2005 constitutional arrangement underpins a messy division between federal government command of established oil and gas fields and production, which covers Kirkuk, and KRG claims to rights over new discoveries within its post 2005 boundaries. Baghdad questions the KRG claims, which raises doubt over KRG capacity to guarantee deals and contracts. Legal ambiguity can scare off foreign companies. The KRG would also like one day to get beyond the complicated haggling over transferring its earnings from oil sales to Baghdad in exchange for a fixed 17 per cent share of overall Iraqi oil revenues, based on population. The share was decent enough—and even advantageous—up to 2017, but the picture will change when the potential proceeds from the KRG's own production surpass 17 per cent of Iraq's total earnings. At that point, it would be logical for the KRG to aspire to full recognized independent sovereignty over its resource base.

Sovereignty also involves security powers. Under regional autonomy the Peshmerga have been recognized as a security force, but they are supposed to receive new equipment via Baghdad and they are technically subsidiary to the Iraqi armed forces. Under security sovereignty they would be a separate army empowered to demand and receive supplies directly from source. Since 2014, the KRG has repeatedly complained about delays in delivery of American weapons routed through Baghdad. A 2016 US Department of Defense report delicately refers to 'uncertain shipment and delivery times throughout the supply chain'.[47]

Where, then, do prevailing circumstances leave the KRG for after ISIS? A KDP-promoted drive for independence in the aftermath of the elimination of ISIS and a resurgence of Iraqi state authority faces public trepidation, problematic economic viability, domestic political crisis, and external disapproval. Yet the 2005 framework has significant economic and security deficiencies and is vulnerable to erosion by Baghdad and foreign powers.

One option would involve two stages. First, the KRG would resurrect constitutional article 140 and concentrate on implementation of the census and referendum for Kirkuk and other disputed territory. This would not be linked to anything beyond the existing constitution. Thereafter, the KRG would open the possibility of a confederal structure with Baghdad, with a clear plan for economic coordination as well as cooperative foreign and security policies in the context of two sovereign units in free association.[48] It is worth recalling that Austria-Hungary operated a system of dual sovereignty for decades after the *Ausgleich* (compromise) of 1867 and only broke apart under the immense strain of the First World War.

During the first stage, which would take one or two years, the KRG would pursue reforms in the spheres of administrative transparency and corruption reduction, using these measures and the disputed territory efforts to heal its fractured domestic politics. It would also embark on a major diversification programme to help shrink the bloated public sector, with vigorous promotion activity abroad for aid and investment. There are decent prospects that continuing oil sector development in tandem with the diversification can assist with viability.

On moving to the second stage, the KRG would publicize the confederal project in the international arena. It would emphasize the strategic and commercial benefits of anticipated geopolitical stabilization for Iraq, Iran, and Turkey. In the eventuality of Baghdad refusing to play, believing that victory over ISIS, Iranian endorsement, and recovering military capability mean it can ignore the KRG, the KRG would suggest a referendum of its population on the confederal plan and appeal to the international community. The KRG has potent infrastructural and diplomatic assets in its location at the strategic intersection of Iraq, Turkey, Iran, and Syria. It can, for example, be a handy partner for Turkey and Russia in helping them to deal with the Kurdish factor across northern Syria.

Certainly, Rojava draws psychological and, to a degree, material comfort from having the KRG as a Kurdish backstop. The political relationship since the PYD set up the three Syrian Kurdish cantons in 2012–13 has been erratic. In a conference in Irbil in July 2012, Masoud Barzani tried, with ephemeral results, to paper over the cracks between the PYD and the conservative KNC, the latter being a collection of older Syrian Kurdish parties.[49] Barzani's KDP gets on better with more traditional Syrian Kurdish groups and has little sympathy with the socialist and PKK orientations of the PYD. Flirtation with the PYD and PKK on the part of some PUK officials confirms KDP reservations. In May 2013, Barzani closed the Iraq–Syria border between the KRG and Rojava when the PYD arrested Syrian KDP protestors,[50] and closed it again in early 2016 when the PYD excluded the KNC from revenue sharing.[51] In the latter incident, the PYD suspected Turkish involvement, while in a March 2016 interview Barzani openly identified the PYD with the PKK.[52] In parallel, the KRG supported a Rojava Peshmerga of several thousand fighters, drawing on Syrian Kurds sympathetic with KNC parties. In early 2017, Rojava Peshmerga clashed with PKK and Yazidi fighters in Sinjar region, close to the border.

Despite such perturbations among Kurds, the Iraq–Syria (that is, the KRG–PYD) border has mostly been open for Kurdish commercial exchanges and weapons transfers, with the KRG as a refuge for civilians if needed. In his series of interviews with *al-Hayat* in July 2015, PYD leader Salih Muslim heaped praise on Barzani as 'one of the precious symbols' of the Kurds and stressed that the KRG was the main original weapons source for Rojava.[53] When asked about the first US weapons drop in Kobani in October 2014, he specified that these came from Peshmerga stocks. In September 2015, Muslim met Barzani and US envoy Brett McGurk in Irbil to discuss the joint effort against ISIS.[54] Many in the KRG political class may not like PYD hegemony over Rojava, but they will be disturbed by any open threat to overthrow Rojava autonomy.

Turkey's antipathy towards the PYD and continuing conviction that the organization dabbles with Bashar al-Assad and channels weapons to the PKK highlight the dangers of Syrian Kurdish dependence on

Presidents Trump and Putin and on Rojava's increasingly cocksure ruling party. Syrian Kurds would be unwise to read too much into Russian
toying with 'federalism' for Syria. The Syrian regime will resist anything beyond cosmetic administrative decentralization in a continuing
'Syrian Arab Republic', and Russia will in the end give priority to its
main anchor in Syria. Assad and Iran will aspire to overturn the PYD,
by violence and/or by splitting tactics among discontented Kurds and
between Kurds and others. They will start with undermining and
enveloping whatever local council the USA and the SDF set up in al-
Raqqa, especially after they get full command of the more important
eastern Syrian city of Deir al-Zor.

Turkey's immediate interest, in contrast, is simply to have the Syrian
Kurdish cantons contained, preferably under revamped management,
and to have them detached from the PKK. Turkey presumably does not
want to extend its battered armed forces into new parts of northern
Syria, but its temper is short. The KRG can be a useful interlocutor,
using this position to save what can be upheld for Syrian Kurds. In sum,
the KRG has prospects amid difficulties; Syrian Kurds face a grimmer
outlook after ISIS, with powerful opponents weighing their chances and
the survival of the cantons in question.

A throw of the dice

For the KRG, the war period from 2014 to 2017 saw domestic weaknesses accentuated, and entailed a high price in blood for the
Peshmerga troops. Negligence and sectarian bias in Baghdad plainly had
a role in the initial explosive spread of ISIS, including towards Irbil, and
did not encourage Iraqi Kurds to savour perpetuation of the political
tie to Iraq. On the positive side of the ledger, the war enabled the KRG
to expand into the lands it claimed, especially Kirkuk, and thereby also
to push back the terrorists on behalf of everyone. After all the sacrifices
there should be serious enhancement of the KRG's status.

Even as the campaign to destroy ISIS in Mosul proceeded in late
2016 and into 2017, KRG president Masoud Barzani could look ahead
to narrowing horizons for the KRG. The horizon for his own legacy
was also shortening, and the KRG was only a half-way house to his
Kurdistan. Giving a speech in Ba'shiqa town after the Peshmerga liber-

ated it from ISIS in November 2016, Barzani talked tough.[55] He casti-
gated Nouri al-Maliki as an unnamed 'scourge' who had wanted
American F16s so he could bomb the Kurds. The Peshmerga would not
withdraw from areas liberated before the Mosul offensive. Referring to
his September 2016 visit to Baghdad, when Prime Minister Abadi had
been chiefly anxious to have everyone on board for Mosul, Barzani said
he found the Iraqi government open to negotiating independence. The
KRG, however, would turn to a referendum if this didn't work out.

Barzani's nephew Nechirvan Barzani, head of the KRG government,
stressed in December 2016 that independence would be for 'the Kurds
of Iraq only', while the president's chief of staff Fuad Hussein noted
that 'the road to independence begins from Baghdad and then passes
Tehran and Ankara'.[56] Hussein suggested a widely representative committee to bargain with Baghdad, including Turkmen and Assyrian
Christians. *Al-Hayat* claimed that the Barzanis were running ahead of a
continuing political crisis in the KRG,[57] with PUK and Gorran officials,
themselves divided, barking at their heels. Another spur was a new plan
by Baghdad to reorient Kirkuk oil exports to go via Iran rather than via
Turkey under KRG supervision.[58] It was perhaps not coincidental that
Barzani went to Ankara to see President Erdoğan twice in a week in
February 2017, although Mosul and the Syrian Kurds were also pressing topics.

In late March 2017, the independence issue moved beyond conventional on–off dimensions when the governor of Kirkuk, a Kurd from
the PUK rather than Barzani's KDP, entered the fray, raising the KRG
flag alongside its Iraqi counterpart on public buildings. Governor
Najmaldin Karim had a reputation for hard-nosed promotion of provincial authority, for example squeezing out Shi'a Turkmen security
officials appointed from the Shi'a-controlled Interior Ministry in
Baghdad.[59] The Iraqi parliament demanded that the Kurdish flag come
down, and the Kirkuk provincial council responded on 4 April by
'deciding' to hold a referendum on integration of the province into the
KRG.[60] Local Arabs adopted a conciliatory tone, with sharper reactions
from Turkmen. There was a surreal quality to these events while the
Iraqi army was engaged in a fierce battle with ISIS in the old city of
Mosul and ISIS remained in Hawija, just down the road from Kirkuk.
The logic, however, related to the wider future settling of accounts in

post-ISIS Iraq. Iran warned of 'separatism'; Erdoğan, in contrast, voiced Turkey's requirement that the flags come down in relatively mild language, observing that Kirkuk 'is not just for the Kurds'.[61]

De facto Peshmerga command of Kirkuk province apart from Hawija in 2017, an outcome of the war that began in Syria in 2011, obviously shifted the equation regarding KRG independence. It meant that, unlike before June 2014, independence would have to go together with resolving the situation of the disputed, now KRG-occupied territories. Governor Karim provided Barzani with the basis to reverse priorities in dealing with Baghdad. The KRG referendum would now come first, and talks with the federal government thereafter. The Kirkuk referendum would be folded into the wider referendum. In early April 2017, Barzani took up the coalescence with alacrity, because he conceived the referendum result would be leverage in both the talks and the international community.[62]

Western members of the US-led coalition did not like this complication while work against ISIS remained, but for the KRG the tail-end of the campaign against the terror group dragged interminably. Perhaps miscalculating prime minister Abadi's own circumstances and ambitions in Baghdad, Barzani saw reasons to seize the moment, before the KRG's geostrategic significance for outsiders declined, before Baghdad consolidated restored command of Arab Iraq, and before Iraq acquired F16s from the USA and 'several hundred' T90 tanks transferred from Syria by the Russians.[63] On 7 June, the KRG, without the Gorran movement, announced 25 September 2017 as the referendum date. It would be a simple yes/no vote on independence and it would include Kirkuk and KRG-held Makhmur, Sinjar, and Khanaqin. It would be a non-binding opening to talks with Baghdad. Both Iran and Turkey stood against it. Iran's national security chief Ali Shamkhani warned a PUK delegation that the referendum would service 'arrogant and imported plots'.[64] Turkey's position assumed key significance. Would Erdoğan, regardless of grandstanding, live with a result used simply to guide bargaining? Here Iraqi government resurgence, with eventual 'reconstruction' and other commercial prospects, affected the picture for Turkey, perhaps not favourably for the KRG.

4

TURKEY AND THE WAR ZONE

Since the late twentieth century, the emphasis in Turkey's policies towards Syria and Iraq has shifted from hard power to soft power and back again. In the 1990s and up to the election victory of the modestly Sunni Islamist-inclined Justice and Development Party (AKP), relations with the Arab Middle East were awkward. The priority along the Syrian and Iraqi borders was suppression of the rebellious Kurdish PKK. Turkey browbeat the Syrian regime because of its patronage of the PKK, and mounted raids into Iraq to attack PKK refuges in the mountains of Iraqi Kurdistan.

Between 2002 and 2011, the AKP implemented a new policy of openness and close commercial ties with Turkey's surrounds, termed 'zero problems with neighbours'. In the cases of Syria and Iraq, this dovetailed with a sharp decline in the PKK security challenge and a conciliatory AKP approach towards Kurds within Turkey. By 2010, Turkey's relations with Syria, with a free-trade agreement, visa relaxation, and security and political collaboration, showcased Turkish foreign minister Ahmet Davutoğlu's 'strategic depth' in links particularly with Middle Eastern, largely Sunni Muslim, former Ottoman lands.[1] Relations with Iraq were more ambiguous because of Turkey's rejection of the US-led invasion of Iraq in 2003 and the replacement of Saddam Hussein with a new Shi'a-dominated regime oriented towards the USA and, increasingly, Turkey's old Middle Eastern imperial rival Iran. Even here, however, Turkey presented itself as a partner for the Kurdish north and a friend of Baghdad.

Turkey's 'zero problems' soft-power approach fell apart with the 2011 street uprising in Syria against President Bashar al-Assad and the parallel turn in Iraq towards Shi'a Arab sectarian assertiveness at the expense of Sunnis under Prime Minister Nouri al-Maliki. Assad rebuffed brotherly Turkish advice to make serious political reforms, and a personally affronted Turkish prime minister Recep Tayyip Erdoğan moved abruptly to promoting regime change in Damascus. Subsequent Turkish backing of Syrian Sunni Arab armed factions as the Syrian uprising became a civil war by early 2012 also cut across relations with Baghdad. The dominant Shi'a forces in the Iraqi regime favoured Assad, and by 2013 Iraqi Shi'a militiamen were established in Syria to assist the regime. Erdoğan and Maliki traded insults from early 2012 on. After 2011, all that remained of Turkey's 'zero problems' policy was its robust commercial and political cooperation with the KRG in northern Iraq, cooperation that of course only further annoyed Baghdad.

Developments in Turkish policy towards Syria and Iraq through the three phases illustrate the significance of both personal agency and synergies between foreign policy and Turkey's domestic affairs. The fervent pursuit of the convergence of AKP Turkey with Bashar al-Assad's repressive and ramshackle Syrian state depended heavily on the personal commitments of Erdoğan and Davutoğlu. Similarly, the bitter divorce in 2011 owed much to the personal prickliness of both Erdoğan and Assad. As for the role of the shifting Turkish domestic environment, the 'zero problems' foreign policy came with the dramatic electoral swing in 2002 that made the AKP Turkey's first single-party government since the 1950s. The return to a security-oriented outlook along Turkey's south-east Anatolian margins after 2011 marched in step with rising authoritarian assertion from both the AKP and its leader as both felt more assured of indefinite domestic political primacy. It intertwined with the faltering of AKP openings to Turkey's Kurdish population and renewed security deterioration between the Turkish state and the PKK.

Turkey's post-2002 outlook on Syria and Iraq also echoes the historical preoccupations of the two great empires whose Anatolian core of power modern Turkey has inherited: the Ottoman sultanate and medieval Byzantium. In the mid- and late twentieth century, Atatürk's Turkish republic sought to downplay the preceding Ottoman imperial past and its eastern, Islamic, and even Balkan connections in favour of the integration of Turkey with the 'advanced world' of Western Europe and North America. In the early twenty-first century, the pious, conservative AKP looked to resuscitate the Ottoman and Islamic commonalities of Turkey with its immediate neighbourhoods in a rebalanced world-view. Given that Istanbul and Turkey had been the Ottoman centre, 'neo-Ottomanism' involved a patronizing attitude that made the new fraternity rather brittle. AKP Turkey was deeply sincere, but in its *tour d'horizon* the new countries that came out of former Ottoman provinces were by definition not equivalent to the Turkish centre. For its part, the Syrian regime had no problem with Turkey's initiative in 2008 for indirect mediation between Syria and Israel, and welcomed the new business partnership between Aleppo and nearby Turkish cities. Bashar al-Assad, however, was not interested in Ottoman revivalism; in August 2011, he reminded Davutoğlu that the Syrian president was not an Ottoman provincial governor.[2]

AKP Ottoman nostalgia persisted beyond the death of 'zero problems' soft-power foreign policy, but with an altered connotation. The idea of a commonwealth of former Ottoman lands, at least in the Middle East, shrank into a protective impulse regarding Sunni Muslims. In this frame, Turkey sought from late 2011 onwards to rise to the challenge of the Syrian regime's onslaught on the Sunni Arab armed rebellion in peripheral and suburban Syria. AKP Turkey would resume the Ottoman mantle of dominant Sunni Muslim polity.

The East Roman state at its medieval peak following invasion of northern Syria by the emperor Nicephorus Phocas in the 960s contributed a template for managing geopolitical flux along Turkey's southern Anatolian margins. Byzantine emperors and their deputies, the dukes of Antioch (Antakya) and Edessa (Şanlıurfa), engaged with fragmented Syrian politics and oversaw an imperial frontier running through the same terrain as the modern Turkish–Syrian border. The Ottomans of course faced rebellions, autonomist movements, and infighting among Arabs and Kurds across their Syrian and Iraqi provinces, but these were internal affairs like Turkey's issues with Kurds in south-east Anatolia— not foreign relations across an outer imperial border. AKP 'neo-Ottomanism' gives ideological assurance to Turkey's power projection into post-2011 Syria and Iraq, publicly justified as security interests; Byzantine experience echoes into the detailed issues Turkey faces in projecting influence. My purpose is to dissect Turkey's policy and performance in confronting geopolitical disintegration in Syria and Iraq. My starting point, as with the initial breakdown in Syria, is structure and agency. Ethnosectarian fragmentation and involvement of multiple external powers represented the structural situation in the developing war zone after 2011, constraining agents. Yet the whole context that came out of the 2011 breakdown in Syria itself derived to a large extent from the character and behaviour of a single agent: President Bashar al-Assad of Syria. Hence structures and agency arise out of each other. As Anthony King comments, we need to get beyond 'the pernicious individual–society dualism' that obscures 'the genuine basis of human society, interaction'.[3] Turkey's Recep Tayyip Erdoğan and other external agents have reacted to a crisis that they did not bring into being, but they have affected its elaboration. There is also the interaction between Turkey's leadership and that other structural context—the domestic environment.

Erdoğan has very much had his own style of navigating both the crisis and the accompanying domestic circumstances. Erdoğan's 'evangelism',[4] risk-taking, self-assurance, erratic impulses, and religiously inclined neo-Ottoman world-view have accorded the interactions among himself as chief Turkish agent, the Syria–Iraq war zone, and domestic affairs a special flavour. His AKP colleague Abdullah Gül would have mapped a different trajectory, and the opposition Republican People's Party would have done its best to insulate Turkey altogether. However, the sheer scale of Assad's Syrian train-wreck would have severely tested any Turkish foreign policy, on both the moral and material levels. Without Erdoğan and Davutoğlu there would have been less of the neo-Ottomanism, but playing neo-Byzantine geopolitical chess along the frontier would still have been unavoidable.

As for the actual Turkish trajectory that has eventuated, I suggest four broad observations:

a) Individual agency within the Turkish leadership and among its allies and opponents has been critical.

b) Between 2011 and 2014, Turkey miscalculated its capacities in the Syrian and international environment, with frustration leading to permissiveness towards Islamist radicals.

c) Domestic diversions and constraints have consistently hobbled Turkish engagement with Syria and Iraq.

d) Turkey only began to display intermittent traces of coherent strategy in 2015–16, with mainly poor results to date.

After reviewing and comparing Turkey's affairs in Syria and Iraq between 2011 and 2014, the Syrian wing of which has received perceptive attention in the literature,[5] I consider Turkish interplay with local parties, Russia, Iran, and the United States in northern Syria and Iraq from early 2015. The best that can be said for Turkey's situation in 2017 is that it is still in the game, and the game is still far from over.

Turkey's contracting horizons, 2011–14

In 1030, the Byzantine emperor Romanus III Argyrus demanded the submission of Aleppo, which was already a cooperative protectorate paying tribute to Constantinople. Romanus, who was incompetent in military affairs, crossed the border to A'zaz in high summer with a poorly organized force lacking proper water supplies. The Aleppans compelled him to retreat in humiliation and disarray, but then came to terms with the highly competent duke of Antioch, recognizing the basic disparity in power and that Byzantium could not let humiliation stand.[6]

In late 2011, AKP Turkey put itself in a similar position to Romanus when Prime Minister Erdoğan embraced regime change in Syria, in reaction to Bashar al-Assad's rejection of Turkish appeals for political reform. Turkey hosted rebels and dissident Syrian officers as well as the Syrian National Council (SNC) of squabbling political exiles, and Erdoğan evidently expected that declaring Bashar fallen would make it so.[7] There was the seductive model of swift autocrat removal in Tunisia and Egypt, together with misreading of the Alawite sectarian entrenchment of the Syrian security machine, the commitments of Iran and Russia to Assad, and the determination of the Syrian leader to ride out the storm. Unlike the Aleppans in 1030, Assad had no thought of pragmatic bending, and Turkish–Syrian relations became a bitter personal vendetta.

Within Turkey, the political situation in 2011 and subsequent years encouraged hubris at the top. After eight years of electoral supremacy, the AKP achieved its best ever voting share in June 2011, just under 50 per cent; the army's former political clout had been wiped away, with the officer corps cowed by coup-plot allegations and show trials; and 2010 constitutional amendments opened the way to the AKP replacing the old secular elite in dominating the judiciary. Given that Erdoğan and Davutoğlu dictated Middle Eastern policy, Erdoğan's distraction into cementing himself at the summit of AKP majoritarian democracy meant that dealing with developments in Syria and Iraq drifted into autopilot punctuated by fitful interventions.

Domestic political and economic affairs imposed tight constraints. First, public sentiment ran against military incursions into northern Syria. Most of the non-AKP half of Turkey—the secularists, hard nationalists, and the Alevi minority—had no problem with the Syrian regime. Even Erdoğan's pious Sunni core constituency was unenthusiastic about risks and casualties. Second, the political battering of the armed forces raised questions about the morale of officers and men, especially in a 'war of choice'. Third, Turkey had highly significant economic relations with Russia and Iran, the backers of the Syrian regime. Russia, for example, supplied more than half of energy-poor Turkey's natural gas plus lucrative contracts for Turkish construction companies. Potent commercial lobbies had influence within the AKP constituency and within the government itself. None of this was conclusive, but it made military deployment across the border a gamble when Erdoğan was also playing a high-stakes domestic game.

The main point was that tipping Syria towards regime change required hard power, whether directly or via massive bolstering of a coordinated armed opposition. Erdoğan blustered against Assad, but was reluctant to invest the full means; Turkish policy therefore lacked legs. When the rebels launched major attacks in Aleppo and Damascus from July 2012, in Aleppo coming into poorer suburbs from the countryside near the Turkish border, Turkey simply facilitated transfers of personnel, weaponry, and finances through its territory. In the process, Turkey, Saudi Arabia, Qatar, and private Arab oil-state financiers tripped over one another in sponsoring different Sunni Islamist groups. They thereby hurt the opposition by contributing to fragmentation, boosting religious hardliners, and weakening politically flexible factions that the international community might conceive as part of an alternative regime. In AKP neo-Ottoman imaginings, the Muslim Brotherhood represented a congenial network for Turkish influence among Sunni Arabs across the Middle East. In Syria, Erdoğan and the AKP turned to Brotherhood militia offshoots such as Liwa al-Tawhid in Aleppo whereas the Saudis, who distrusted the Brotherhood, sponsored alternatives such as Jaysh al-Islam in the Damascus countryside.

Turkish and Arabian Peninsula input was enough to cause serious difficulty for the regime in late 2012, but not enough to break it. This situation precipitated two further developments that complicated the arena for Turkey. Iran and Russia escalated their reinforcement of the regime, including the import of Shi'a militias from Iraq and Lebanon, Iranian organization of new mainly Alawite paramilitaries, and Russian provision of hardware. Meantime, the regime withdrew forces from north-east Syria to hold the lines in Aleppo and Damascus. This allowed the Syrian Kurdish PYD, as noted an affiliate of the PKK, to assert control of 'cantons' in Kurdish-populated areas along the Syrian side of the Turkish border. The PYD's interaction with the PKK enabled swift establishment of its armed YPG when turmoil enveloped Syria in 2011–12. Wielding the YPG, the PYD could marginalize the older Syrian Kurdish parties of the KNC. The KNC was prepared to collaborate with the Turkey-based Syrian opposition SNC if the latter acknowledged Kurdish identity and grievances. Turkey reacted to the PYD-controlled cantons with coolness and suspicion, while Syrian Sunni Arab opposition politicians cut the ground from under the KNC by maintaining a Syrian Arabism not significantly different from that of the Ba'athist regime.

For Turkey, the PYD represented a surrogate for the Syrian regime and the PKK. The PYD shared the major border city of al-Qamishli with the regime, which kept the airport, the army base, intelligence capability, and residual territory that virtually bisected the largest PYD canton. The PYD also joined the internal Syrian political 'opposition', the NCC, regarded by the armed opposition and the exiles as a regime tool. PYD leader Salih Muslim vigorously claimed hostility to the regime and denied any interest in Syrian Kurdish independence.[8] Turkey, alarmed by the PYD project for a federal Syria, was not convinced. Nonetheless, in July 2013 Foreign Minister Davutoğlu invited Muslim to Ankara to explain his perspectives.[9] Muslim met Foreign Ministry undersecretary Feridun Sinirlioğlu and the national intelligence agency (Milli İstihbarat Teşkilatı—MİT) chief Hakan Fidan. Davutoğlu had already laid down demands: no PYD support for Assad; no pre-empting of wider Syrian agreement on a new Syria; and no involvement in 'aggression against Turkey'.[10]

At the time, it suited Erdoğan and Davutoğlu to be a little tolerant. Turkey had closed border crossings to PYD areas except for occasional humanitarian deliveries, but could not clamp down hard on illicit cross-border traffic while it turned a blind eye to cross-border flows benefiting the Syrian opposition and Islamist militias. In this context, just before the invitation to Muslim, the PYD expelled the jihadist Jabhat al-Nusra from the border town of Ra's al-Ayn and took the Syrian side of the local crossing, demonstrating military effectiveness and disrupting Syrian Islamist links into and out of Turkey. More broadly, through 2013 the AKP still sought a domestic Turkish understanding with the PKK, with exchanges of ideas between the MİT and imprisoned PKK leader Abdullah Öcalan; détente with the PYD complemented this initiative.

As for the main regime–opposition contest in Syria from 2012 into 2014, Turkey promoted humanitarian corridors into northern Syria, together with a no-fly zone to deter the regime from aerial bombing of civilians.[11] Rising numbers of Syrian refugees in Turkish border cities from Antakya to Şanlıurfa, reaching half a million by mid-2013, gave added impetus to hard-power schemes. In theory, with NATO endorsement and some technical assistance, Turkey had the air and ground forces to do the job itself. In practice, Turkish domestic constraints and the risks to relations with Russia and Iran deterred Erdoğan. He looked to delegate the heavy lifting to Western partners on the basis of a Libya-style 'responsibility to protect'. This especially meant US president Barack Obama, who exhibited desultory readiness to bolster the dwindling array of non-Islamist rebels but who was mainly concerned to get out of Middle East conflicts. Anyway, Russian rejection of regime change ruled out UN Security Council endorsement.

Erdoğan was thus bound to be disappointed. The ultimate letdown came in the wake of the 21 August 2013 sarin gas attack on opposition suburbs of Damascus. The US administration had previously declared that any substantial release of poison gas was a red line likely to trigger direct military punishment; according to the Americans, the Syrian regime transgressed the line on 21 August. President Obama came to the brink, but the Russians offered him an exit with Syrian chemical disarmament. Erdoğan had pinned his hopes on a vigorous US response changing the whole Syrian equation, and was furious with what he viewed as Obama's backsliding.[12]

Thereafter Turkish policy toward Syria became entirely incoherent. Casting about for anything that might damage Bashar al-Assad, Turkey blinked at jihadists as well as Islamists exploiting its territory and facilities for funnelling recruits and supplies to Syria. The potent new terrorist group ISIS that was setting up in eastern Syria in 2013 and early 2014 knew how to take advantage. It wasn't even interested in Turkey's priority of the Syrian regime; it simply wanted land in Sunni eastern Syria and western Iraq at the expense of anyone. Indeed, as far as can be discerned, ISIS had a cosy tacit understanding with Assad's apparatus by which they both focused on mutual opponents in the Syrian opposition. ISIS also constructed a network of cells in Turkey that it could later use against its host.[13] For their part, in late 2013 Davutoğlu and Foreign Ministry officials explored Iranian peace ideas for Syria but, according to the Iranians, talks collapsed over Turkish insistence that Assad be barred from any Syrian elections.[14] In 2013–14, this all coincided with Erdoğan's distraction into facing down the May–August 2013 Gezi Park protests, coping with December 2013 corruption allegations, campaigning against the 'parallel state' of former Gülenist allies, and converting himself from prime minister into elected president in August 2014.

In early 2014, MİT arms trucking into Syria intercepted by the unwitting gendarmerie, promotion and abandonment of a Syrian rebel operation south of Antakya, and a weird scheme for an army raid across the border indicated policy on autopilot. The newspaper *Cumhuriyet* reported both the MİT incident and clandestine artillery support for the rebel toehold on the coast.[15] In the latter case, Turkey seems to have retracted cover for the rebels coincident with a June 2014 visit by Iranian president Hassan Rouhani to Ankara, illustrating the contradiction between aiding Syrian rebels and pursuing commercial deals with

Iran. The army raid idea involved protecting a small Turkish enclave on the Euphrates, with a sensitive discussion among national security officials leaked onto YouTube. The government's furious reaction to the media exposure contributed to constriction of the press and internet.

What of Iraq while Turkey lost its way in Syria? In Iraq as in Syria, Turkey's horizons contracted northward from 2011.[16] Aspirations for leading influence in an Ottoman-derived commonwealth of nations, realized through kindred spirits in Damascus and Baghdad, shrank into Byzantine-style strategic and borderland preoccupations in the cold reality of the Syria–Iraq conflict zone. This was not how it seemed when Erdoğan visited Baghdad, Najaf, and Irbil in March 2011, emphasizing sectarian and ethnic outreach by going to see both Shi'a grand ayatollah Ali al-Sistani and KRG president Masoud Barzani.[17] This certainly expressed an expansive Ottoman-style outlook, and AKP Turkey seemed fully competitive with Iran in Baghdad. Alas, the projection collapsed in less than a year. By late 2011, Turkey and the Iraqi government were on opposite sides in the Syrian crisis. In December 2011, as soon as the USA had pulled its last troops out of Iraq, Prime Minister Maliki supported murder charges against Sunni vice-president Tariq al-Hashimi. The latter fled to the KRG and Ankara. In January 2012, Erdoğan termed Maliki 'oppressive' and advised the Shi'a Iraqi leader not to be like the Sunni Umayyad caliph Yazid. Maliki warned Erdoğan against 'meddling' in Iraq and making Turkey a 'hostile state'.[18]

Turkey now turned to consolidate its already strong political and commercial ties with the Kurds of Iraq, just as its affairs with the Syrian Kurdish PYD deteriorated. Being reduced to northern Iraq, where it had a strong local partner, was of course much more comfortable for Turkey than its situation vis-à-vis the desolated and politically splintered landscape of northern Syria. By 2013, the KRG was Turkey's third-largest export market, worth $8 billion per annum, and Turkey had a massive investment in local infrastructure.[19] In 2014, Turkey took the KRG's side in its dispute with Baghdad over oil revenues, and piped KRG unilateral oil exports to the Mediterranean.[20] Baghdad regarded this as complicity in an illegal enterprise. For Turkey, the KRG was an important potential energy source, possibly including gas, and Barzani offered himself as a facilitator in the AKP's 'Kurdish opening' inside Turkey. Between 2011 and 2014, Turkey moved from commitment to a unified Iraq to readiness to contemplate greater KRG devolution. Here Turkey expected the KRG to respect its parallel connections with the Sunni Arabs and Turkmen of Mosul and Kirkuk. The main complication—apart, of course, from Baghdad—was Iranian rivalry: Iran had friends and capability in Sulaymaniyah, the KRG's second city, to play against Irbil, the Barzanis, and Turkey.

Iraq and Syria coalesced in a train-wreck of Turkish policy in June–July 2014, when ISIS deployed assets assembled in the two countries to break the Iraqi regime in western Iraq, consolidate its base in eastern Syria, and declare an avowedly terrorist 'caliphate' integrating these territories. Despite MİT interchange with various Syrian factions, there is no evidence that Turkey had any appreciation of the ISIS trajectory, a serious intelligence lapse shared with Western and Arab states. The flow of jihadist recruits across Turkey from Europe, the Caucasus, and North Africa together with growth of ISIS infrastructure in Turkey facilitated development of the dangerous new pseudo-state. Through 2013–14, Turkey focused too narrowly on Bashar al-Assad and the Kurdish PYD and missed important parts of the picture, including the Syrian regime's common interests with ISIS.

In Iraq, the fall of Mosul to ISIS in June 2014 included the seizure of the Turkish consulate with forty-nine Turkish staff. This crippled Turkey for a critical three months, during which its KRG ally faced a severe challenge from ISIS, and relied on US air power to stabilize the situation in July–August. The USA had an obligation to the Kurds of Iraq because ISIS had captured American equipment that boosted its firepower and mobility. Regardless, however, of US carelessness in providing the Iraqi army with material that ended up in 'the wrong hands', influence on the KRG swung in favour of the USA and other Western powers, the Iranians registered a helping hand, and Turkey was hardly visible. Into late 2014, Kurdish Peshmerga fighters secured Kirkuk, gave Irbil decent forward defence, and expelled ISIS from the Mosul dam. The USA and the PKK salvaged Yazidi Kurds near Sinjar. The KRG complained about its deficient weaponry, but more than ever looked to the West—not Turkey—for rectification.[21] In October, Turkey restored room for manoeuvre with a humiliating prisoner swap with ISIS, including recourse to the Liwa al-Tawhid militia in Aleppo to release ISIS detainees.[22] Nonetheless, with Mosul's Sunni Arabs in ISIS hands or scattered, and with the KRG emphasizing other ties, Turkey's standing in northern Iraq was at a low ebb.

In Syria, a chain reaction of events following ISIS's proclamation of its 'caliphate' commanded from al-Raqqa led to Turkey's discomfiture on its own border. In September–October 2014, ISIS lunged into the Kurdish PYD Kobani canton, to widen its control of the Syrian side of the Turkish border north of al-Raqqa (map 2). Kobani was isolated from the main PYD area to the east and particularly vulnerable. The ISIS attack was accompanied by beheadings of American and British hostages, and the USA reacted by extending its aerial bombing of ISIS into Syria, including Kobani. For its part, Turkey moved troops and tanks to its side of the border with Kobani town, and in October the Turkish parliament voted to allow incursions across the border. The AKP government, however, indicated that it would not help the PYD, that it regarded the PYD as 'terrorists' on the same level as ISIS, and that it had strong reservations about the USA giving priority to destroying ISIS over the removal of Bashar al-Assad, whom Erdoğan and other AKP leaders viewed as the source of the mess.

Turkey allowed several hundred thousand Kurdish refugees to enter its territory and camp there, but Turkish forces sat motionless on the border while only US airdrops and air strikes sustained the PYD's YPG militia. Turkish Kurds protested furiously against AKP indifference through October and November; around thirty died in violent demonstrations, and the credibility of Turkey's domestic Kurdish opening was compromised.[23] Turkish permission for contingents of KRG Peshmerga to reinforce Kobani made no difference to the new rift between the government and Turkish Kurds.

In February 2015, the PYD succeeded in pushing ISIS out of Kobani town. By late June they linked the Kobani countryside with the main PYD Jazira canton, expelling ISIS from the intervening border town of Tell Abyad. As in northern Iraq, events in northern Syria left Turkey's standing in tatters. The PYD was riding high; the Syrian regime proclaimed that Turkey helped terrorists; the USA was suspicious of its NATO ally; and ISIS and PKK challenges within Turkey paralleled Turkish impotence in Syria and Iraq.

TURKEY AND THE WAR ZONE

Turkey the bold, 2015–2016

Like the Byzantine Emperor Basil II in the early eleventh century, in early 2015 the Turkish president Recep Tayyip Erdoğan had to find his way amid fragmented rump state, semi-state, pseudo-state, and sub-state actors along a similar south-east Anatolian frontier. Unlike Erdoğan, reduced between 2011 and 2015 from regional leader to a two-bit player, Basil had serious respect from Muslim entities ranging from hill and desert clanships to competing factions in Aleppo to the Kurdish Marwanid principality to the Fatimid caliphate further south.

Apart from a desultory role in playing among Syrian opposition groups, in early 2015 AKP Turkey commanded little respect from either local entities or their foreign backers. Bashar al-Assad felt he had the upper hand as Turkey floundered among the Islamists, and Assad's Russian and Iranian patrons believed Turkey emasculated by its commercial interests. The Iraqi regime detested the AKP and looked to the USA and Iran. For the Syrian Kurdish PYD cantons, Turkey had moved from being unfriendly to being an enemy, while their new American patrons had almost given up on Turkey being useful against ISIS. The KRG had watched ISIS devalue the Turks. The ISIS 'caliphate' derided the AKP: in October 2014, even as the AKP spurned the PYD in Kobani, ISIS threatened to 'conquer' Turkey and overthrow Erdoğan.[24]

For Turkey, the Kobani affair and US involvement in it diverted attention from the primary confrontation between the Syrian regime and opposition in western Syria. Sheer frustration motivated Turkey to light a fire under Bashar al-Assad. The only practical means of doing so was to force military coordination among the competing Syrian opposition groups and transfer new weaponry to the factions in north-west Syria. For such an initiative, Erdoğan and the MİT needed a Sunni Arab partner, and in January 2015 Saudi Arabia, hitherto out of phase with Turkey and playing with different rebels, presented itself. Saudi Arabia acquired a new monarch with the death of King Abdullah on 23 January. King Salman's youngish and activist inner circle determined to counter what they perceived as Iranian outflanking of the kingdom via Syria and Yemen. Erdoğan travelled to Saudi Arabia on 2 March, and the two leaders agreed 'on the need to increase support for the opposition in Syria'.[25]

In north-west Syria support meant a generous flow of Saudi-acquired TOW anti-tank missiles and other equipment across the Turkish border, excepting surface-to-air missiles, which the Americans banned. The Turks and Saudis worked to persuade the big Islamist groups to come together in Jaysh al-Fath (the Army of Conquest), also cooperating with other Islamists such as Faylaq al-Sham and factions derived from the original FSA. The regime was stretched thin in holding towns and communications, and the opposition offensive beginning in March 2015 soon achieved results. By June the combined force drove the regime out of the towns of Idlib, Jisr al-Shughur, and Ariha and advanced in the hills of the coastal Latakia province. The exiled opposition coalition chief Khalid Khoja noted: 'The Saudi–Turkish coming together has strengthened the accelerated progress of the revolution.'[26] The regime also fell back in Dera'a province on the Jordanian border. On 26 July, Assad made unprecedented admissions: 'Sometimes, in certain conditions, we have been compelled to let go of some areas. ... It has been necessary to specify critical areas for our armed forces to hang on to. ... [Everything] is available, but there is a deficiency in human energy.'[27]

At the same time, Turkish foreign minister Mevlüt Çavuşoğlu repackaged the earlier Turkish calls for security zones and humanitarian corridors as a more specific scheme for a 'safe zone' for Syrian refugees and the opposition inside northern Syria.[28] Turkey would lead in throwing ISIS out of an area north-east of Aleppo as far as Jarabulus on the Euphrates, and extending at least 25 kilometres south of the Turkish border. This idea surfaced directly after Turkey agreed to US use of the Incirlik air base for bombing ISIS, which helped the USA to endorse the safe zone. Through early 2015 Turkey also acknowledged its problems with ISIS use of its territory, and worked to choke off ISIS cross-border traffic. The AKP was firming up a more credible Syria strategy. First, the safe zone would place Turkish-backed rebels on the fringe of Aleppo with Turkish military cover, which would complicate regime military activities. Here Erdoğan proceeded by stealth; the USA did not want to send 'the wrong message' to the Syrian regime, and even preferred that the safe zone be termed the 'ISIS-free zone' to stress that ISIS was the target.[29] Second, the plan would prevent the PYD Kurds from establishing continuity along the border, pushing west across the Euphrates to link with the outlier Afrin canton.

In the event, new twists in Turkey's domestic scene and counter-moves by other international players foreclosed early implementation of this first direct Turkish hard power gambit. Already on 7 June 2015 the shock loss of the AKP's overall majority in parliamentary elections discouraged an adventure across the border. President Erdoğan could not stomach coalition construction and wanted a pretext for new elections; without recovery of the majority there was no chance for his dream of an executive presidency.

On 20 July 2015, ISIS provided Erdoğan with his route to new elections with a bomb attack on Kurdish PYD supporters in the Turkish town of Suruç, near Kobani. A radical PKK splinter group, blaming the AKP for fostering ISIS in Turkey and Syria, then attacked Turkish police posts. Erdoğan took these events as an occasion for a token strike against ISIS in Syria, but mainly to hit the PKK in Turkey and northern Iraq. Defending Turkish security promised to be a vote winner by undercutting the hardline Nationalist Action Party in parliament. However, the security crisis had to be in Turkey, not northern Syria—the latter would cost votes. Some in the PKK welcomed a breakdown, because it might derail Kurdish political rivals, who had surpassed the 10 per cent threshold in the 7 June elections. From late July, the government and the PKK entered hostilities, ISIS fed the security angst with another mass-casualty bombing in Ankara in October, and the AKP regained its parliamentary majority in the 1 November elections. The breakdown with the PKK in turn sharpened conflict between Turkey and Syrian Kurds; Turkish bombing of PKK camps in KRG territory complicated relations with Iraqi Kurds; and Russia and Iran found Erdoğan's domestic absorption handy for their own riposte to Turkey in Syria. The malignant synergy of Turkish internal developments and Turkey's affairs in the Syria–Iraq war zone could not have been starker.

Purposeful Turkish–Saudi coordination in early 2015 probably startled Russia and Iran. It seems that Iran and Lebanese Hezbollah had no confidence in Syrian regime staying power against the rebel offensive, and Iran sounded the alarm in Moscow as early as March.[30] It suited President Vladimir Putin to have the Iranians come to him as supplicants; the Iranian commander in Syria and Iraq, General Qasem Soleimani, showed up in Moscow in July for detailed planning.[31]

Thereafter the Russians took their final decision for direct military intervention. According to one credible source, the safe zone idea, inevitably meaning a no-fly zone as well, was the last straw.[32] Erdoğan's electoral and PKK preoccupations handed Russia time to assemble aircraft and logistics in Syria. At the end of September, Putin unleashed Russian airpower against 'terrorists'. Russia claimed it was combating ISIS, but this was a smokescreen for smashing the real opponents of the Syrian regime and checkmating Turkey and Saudi Arabia.

Through the following nine months, until the regime surrounded eastern Aleppo in July 2016, the Sunni Syrian armed opposition, confronting a great power and a regional power as well as the regime and foreign Shi'a militias, held up well. The regime advanced in the Latakia hills and near Damascus, but the opposition improved its lines north of Hama. This would have been impossible without continuation of inputs from Turkey. Russian aircraft therefore struck up to the Turkish border, and on 24 November 2015 the Turkish air force downed a Russian bomber after it briefly violated Turkish air space while hitting Syrian Turkmen rebels. It was the first time since the Korean War that a NATO country destroyed a Russian air-force plane.

Vladimir Putin, shocked and enraged, imposed painful sanctions on Turkish businesses and trade. The Russians also made it clear that Turkish planes entering Syrian air space would face similar treatment, which rendered any safe zone unviable. An immediate implication, not lost on the Russians, was tipping of the psychological balance along the Turkish border in favour of the Kurdish PYD. In October 2015, the PYD presented its YPG as the core force of the new SDF coalition with small Arab and other rebel groups, thereby making itself more attractive to the USA as a ground ally against ISIS. In February 2016, Turkey could only watch while the new SDF piggybacked on a regime–Russian operation cutting Aleppo from the A'zaz–Kilis border crossing to extend the Afrin canton at the expense of the opposition factions. In May 2016, the USA approved and backed a YPG–SDF offensive across the Euphrates against ISIS, culminating in the capture of the significant town of Manbij by early August (map 4). For Turkey, the PYD was bridging the gap between Kobani and Afrin, while Russia twisted the knife by hinting that Syria might have a federal future.[33] The USA remained impatient with what it regarded as deficient Turkish commitment against ISIS. Meantime Russia and the USA experimented with Syrian 'cessations of hostilities' and discussed who was and wasn't a 'terrorist' as if Turkey hardly existed.

Given his irritation with Western criticism, his Saudi partner's pre-occupation with bombing Yemen, and his preference to isolate Syria from his desire to get on with Russia, Erdoğan soon sought repairs with Putin. He also sought a way round blockage of the proposed safe zone, into 2016 increasingly spurred by the PYD designs on Manbij, within the only space left for the safe zone. In a revealing December 2015 interview with the Saudi satellite channel al-Arabiya, Erdoğan represented the safe zone as of 'the utmost importance'; he described his lobbying for it at the November 2015 Group of Twenty (G-20) Summit.[34] It would extend 45 kilometres into Syria (twice the depth of the July version); Turkey would build a city for Syrian refugees; the 'moderate opposition' would provide security; there would have to be a no-fly zone; and the safe zone would resolve the issue of Syrians fleeing to Europe. This was a bid for a Turkish role in Syria's future on an impressive scale, and it certainly had more than a whiff of the old Ottoman world of Turkish–Sunni Arab togetherness. But how could it be got past Putin's Middle East, not to mention an Iran extending itself across the Fertile Crescent?

Erdoğan began reaching out to Putin in April 2016 using military, business, and political connections.[35] Hulusi Akar, chief of the Turkish General Staff, linked with a textile merchant who knew the Dagestani leader who knew Putin's chief adviser. Drafts of a letter of remorse from Erdoğan regarding the two dead pilots went back and forth before Putin accepted a formulation midway between 'sorry' and 'apologize'. The Russians had a long-term interest in decent relations with Turkey, and the Kazakh president mediated. The letter went public on 27 June, Erdoğan praised Putin, and Russia lifted some sanctions. Turkey ceased to condemn Russian bombing in north-west Syria, and Turkish officials even indicated that Assad might stay in power into a Syrian 'transition', although this was also contradicted.[36] Putin hastened to congratulate Erdoğan on his survival of the 15 July 2016 coup attempt.

Nonetheless, the rebel offensive that briefly broke the regime–Russian siege of eastern Aleppo in early August received supplies from Turkey.[37] Was Turkey playing a double game? By this point, Turkey was fully engaged against ISIS after a terrible 28 June ISIS suicide attack on Atatürk Airport in Istanbul. On the US precedent, Russia could hope that Turkey had swapped its insistence on Assad's early removal for prioritizing combating 'terror'.

A testing time for Turkey's rapprochement with Russia came after a 21 August ISIS bombing of a wedding in Gaziantep, leaving fifty-four dead. Turkey immediately declared that it would eliminate ISIS from the Syrian side of the border. The Turks, however, had to obtain suspension of the Russian veto on their aircraft flying into Syria. The Russians knew full well that Turkey's real objective was to forestall the PYD Kurds from taking al-Bab and establishing their territorial continuity along the Syrian side of the border. There was not much left of the gap between the new YPG–PYD positions in Manbij and the PYD finger jutting east from Afrin, and the Turkish government was nervous. The situation obviously suited the Russians, who were probably not averse to the Kurds getting a little closer to al-Bab. As for ISIS, it was in Turkey's way and clearing it was the self-defence justification for the incursion.

Putin's price for acquiescence was that Turkey back away from supporting the rebels in Aleppo, easing the conditions for the final regime–Russian–Iranian push. The Turks had no choice but to satisfy the Russian president. Having done that, Erdoğan had the reward of at last being able to implement his safe zone, which he had first promoted under other vocabulary in early 2012. Turkey swiftly assembled commandos, armour, and artillery to buttress several thousand Syrian opposition fighters, and on 24 August plunged into Syria, first expelling ISIS from the border town of Jarabulus. The Turkish army, debilitated by purges before and after the July 2016 coup plot, proceeded carefully amid warnings about erosion of its capability at both command and field levels.[38] Erdoğan defined al-Bab and a 5,000 square kilometre expanse as the initial aim of Operation Euphrates Shield (map 3).[39]

For Turkish officials, removing 'terrorism' covered the Kurdish YPG militia as well as ISIS, and they demanded that the YPG–PYD surrender Manbij and withdraw east of the Euphrates. The PYD, confident of American backing, held firm in Manbij, but the Kurds did not have the heavy weaponry to root out hundreds of ISIS fighters entrenched in al-Bab. Turkey therefore had a little time, at least until Assad and the

Russians were finished with Aleppo and turned their exertions east-wards. Turkey, however, had a serious nut to crack in al-Bab.

Putin evidently had a touch of seller's remorse about giving Turkey its direct entry into Syria. Certainly, the Russians were on guard,[40] and by late September they added to the price of allowing Turks as close to Aleppo as al-Bab: Turkey should not just forsake the eastern Aleppo pocket, but should press to have rebel fighters removed from it, most immediately Jabhat al-Nusra.[41] Erdoğan assented during a phone call with Putin, but then stalled: for AKP Turkey footholds in northern Syria are vital to the security of Anatolia, given Syrian regime enmity and PYD advances. The same had been the case for medieval Byzantium. Basil II reacted sharply to any challenge to his allies in Aleppo from the Fatimid authorities in Damascus—this was his *casus belli* in the east.[42] In 995, receiving an appeal from Aleppo after the Fatimids defeated his agent the duke of Antioch, the emperor moved the main field army from the Balkans across Anatolia in only two weeks, to appear unexpectedly outside Aleppo. The Fatimids hastily withdrew. Northern Syria has no less significance for modern Turkey. For President Erdoğan, Assad's Russian-supplied December 2016 victory in Aleppo was a deep wound; Assad had crowed that Aleppo would be Erdoğan's 'graveyard'.[43]

Between August and November 2016 Operation Euphrates Shield eliminated ISIS in a border strip inside Syria from Jarabulus westward to al-Ra'i, meeting the rebel-controlled A'zaz pocket. Turkey stiffened a collection of former FSA and Islamist units, including a large number of Syrian Turkmen fighters, with hundreds of Turkish Special Force troops and heavy equipment. They deepened the strip to about 15 miles (more than 20 kilometres) through October, and approached al-Bab from the north by early November 2016. At al-Bab, ISIS put up a stubborn defence that took more than three months, many casualties, and significant Turkish aerial bombing to overcome. Meantime, with Aleppo back under regime command, regime troops with Russian air cover pushed across the southern outskirts of al-Bab to link with the PYD Manbij enclave and reach the Euphrates River. Turkey found its offensive constricted on three sides by the Syrian regime, the PYD, and Russia. For example, on 24 November 2016, the first anniversary of the Turkish downing of the Russian plane, a regime airstrike outside al-Bab killed four Turkish soldiers. Erdoğan phoned Putin twice and sent Foreign Minister Çavuşoğlu and MİT chief Fidan to Tehran. He sought assurances that it wasn't a Russian airstrike, and solicited Russian and Iranian toleration of his operations.[44]

In the final phase in January–February 2017, the chastened Turks received occasional Russian air support, raising an obvious question about the health of the Turkish air force after the July 2016 coup, and FSA units fought regime troops at Tadaf beyond al-Bab. Amid such confusion, Turkish-led contingents cleared al-Bab of ISIS and declared its capture on 23 February 2017. Erdoğan had intended to extend the safe zone further south as access for Turkish and allied forces to join the USA in taking al-Raqqa from ISIS, displacing the US-aligned PYD-dominated SDF in a high-profile liberation of the ISIS 'capital'. In October 2016, he told President Obama: 'We have this power ... what are they [the PYD]? They're a simple terror organization.'[45] In contrast, US commanders had become comfortable with the SDF, and apparently were dismissive of the Turkish alternative.[46] Anyway, Erdoğan was both excluded from Aleppo and blocked from eastern Syria by his new Russian friends.

The Turkish prime minister Binali Yıldırım nonetheless put on a brave face and on 29 March declared Euphrates Shield an unqualified success. The Turkish newspaper *Milliyet* reported the high price of the 'success': 67 Turkish soldiers killed and 245 wounded in the seven months, together with 600 dead among the allied FSA fighters.[47] The Turkish army claimed that the overall operation killed 2,288 ISIS jihadists and 322 'PKK–PYD' personnel.[48] These were fearsome numbers for a relatively short-lived, peripheral front. If accurate, the ISIS toll indicated the formidable scale of Baghdadi's 'caliphate' and once more raised the question about how it had become so extensively entrenched so rapidly. The Kurdish toll warned that the PYD was ready for casualties and would not be a pushover if it stayed coherent. Turkey's own losses already put it second to Iran in deaths suffered by an external power in Quicksilver War hostilities.

What were the benefits for Turkey of a half-achieved safe zone (map 3)? Although it may be true that the lands from the border to al-Bab have no 'inherent strategic importance',[49] they could be made to have significance into the longer term as a base area for rebels and returning

Syrian refugees, the latter eventually being a source for more rebels. If substantial non-jihadist rebel groups persevere to constrain the Hay'at (al-Nusra) jihadists in Idlib, the combination with the safe zone could be a serious card for Turkey and the Syrian opposition. On the other hand, if the Syrian regime and Iran gain the upper hand on the ground in post-ISIS eastern Syria, the safe zone would be exposed to diplomatic and even military pressure. In this situation—yet another irony—Turkey could come to share an interest with the PYD Kurds.

Whereas in western Syria in 2015–16 Erdoğan managed to inflate Turkey's role into real, if fragile, significance, in Iraq Turkey remained crimped during the ISIS phase. In this theatre, there were again echoes of Byzantium. Emperor Basil II had a friendly Kurdish buttress east of the Euphrates in the person of the Marwanid amir Muhammad al-Dawla in Diyarbakır, rather like the KRG and the Barzanis. The Marwanids even supplied a contingent for Byzantine use in Aleppo.[50] Like Erdoğan, Basil had a strained relationship with Baghdad, in Basil's case meaning its Shi'a Buyid rulers from the Iranian plateau. The Buyids gave refuge to the Byzantine rebel Bardas Skleros, who had played a part resembling the PKK, the coup plotters, and the Gülenists of 2015–16, all rolled into one. Overall, however, for both Basil and Erdoğan the eastern wing of the Fertile Crescent was of less strategic concern than Syria.

Through 2015, Turkey continued a commercial partnership with a KRG beset by falling oil prices and dissent over extension of Masoud Barzani's presidential term. The Turks kept an open mind on independence, but there was sourness over friction between Kurds and Turkmen in Kirkuk and the AKP–Kurdish breakdown in Turkey. The Turks inflicted local casualties while bombing the PKK in the KRG's mountains while the KRG's Peshmerga forces passed a thousand deaths in confronting ISIS. Turkey also joined Iran, the USA, and Britain in containing KRG infighting.[51] One leader from Barzani's Kurdistan Democratic Party accused Iranian General Qasem Soleimani of instigating the trouble, and the Iranian consul-general flaunted his influence.[52] Turkey had concerns, but was one voice in a foreign crowd. Ironically, while the USA and the EU opposed an independence referendum and strove to reconcile the KRG and Baghdad, Turkey seemed disengaged.

In March 2015, Turkey turned to the Sunni Arabs of Ninewa province and established a small military base on KRG-controlled 'disputed territory' near Ba'shiqa to train Peshmerga and a Sunni militia for deployment in the coming battle for Mosul. Athil al-Nujayfi, former Sunni Arab governor of Ninewa, endorsed the move; Baghdad ignored it, but protested when Turkish reinforcements arrived in December 2015.

Turkey's presence dropped out of sight while the Iraqi regime concentrated on recovering Ramadi and Falluja. Inflammation only ensued when Baghdad finally focused on Mosul in late 2016. In late September, the Turkish parliament voted a routine extension for the 2,000 troops stationed in northern Iraq to safeguard Turkey against 'terrorists'.[53] The Iraqi parliament promptly demanded their removal. On 11 October, Erdoğan retorted in a manner reminiscent of Ottoman scolding of an errant province. It was up to Turkey to 'expend an effort if Iraq and Syria are in trouble … we do not need to take permission'. As for Iraqi prime minister Haydar al-Abadi: 'You are not my quality … who is this? Iraq's prime minister? Know your place.'[54] Abadi's office denied any legitimacy for Turkey's presence; Erdoğan claimed to have a duty to prevent 'demographic change', meaning an intrusion of Shi'a militias from the south; and the irritated Americans, trying to corral mutually suspicious forces to liberate Mosul, declined to consider the Turks part of the US-led coalition.[55] The USA relented with the beginning of the Iraqi army offensive in late October. Turkey became a peripheral participant, steering Sunni Arab and Turkmen fighters and backing KRG operations.

Erdoğan's intrusions, however, had more relevance to the balance across northern Iraq after the Iraqi recovery of Mosul. First, hostility to the Iraqi Shi'a PMF pressing forward in non-Shi'a Iraq implied general Turkish patronage of Iraqi Sunnis, including Kurds.[56] Second, bellicosity towards the PKK or PYD extending from Syria into the Sinjar hills reflected Turkish–Kurdish antagonism along the Syrian–Turkish border. Third, Turkish interaction with the KRG could affect the viability of post-ISIS Iraq.

Turkey in a new strategic landscape, 2017

In late 2016 and early 2017, Turkey found itself in a delicate situation with Russia and Iran in western Syria at the same time as it did not see eye to eye with the USA regarding the end-game against ISIS in eastern Syria. Turkey's assets across the war zone encompassed its influence with Syrian rebels, its new military presence north-east of Aleppo, and its capacity to be helpful to the USA, the Iraqi government, and the KRG in northern Iraq. These were not negligible, but they were devalued by the deterioration in Turkey's relations with its Western allies through the Syrian crisis since 2011. Problems between Turkey and the West, especially the USA, in turn made Russia more confident that it had the upper hand over a Turkey estranged from its NATO partners.

On the US side, a hangover continued from earlier American suspicion of Turkish interaction with hardline Islamists in Syria. The Obama administration took a distant and cerebral view of Turkey's domestic pressures while warfare metastasized to Turkey's south. Washington perceived Erdoğan as intemperate and increasingly authoritarian and Turkey as losing value as a NATO partner. For its part, Turkey continued to resent Western softness towards Assad and what it perceived as US disregard of Turkey's fears of Syrian Kurdish linkage to the PKK within Turkey. Even after receiving bumped-up EU aid in 2016, Turkey felt that its shouldering of the burden of 3 million Syrian refugees remained insufficiently appreciated in the West. After the failed coup attempt of 15 July 2016, Erdoğan and other Turks observed that the USA and other Western countries did not rush to condemn the coup plotters. A conviction formed that some in the West would not have been unhappy to see Erdoğan fall. Certainly, there seemed to be a lack of Western sensitivity to the comprehensive Turkish allergy to military coups. In contrast, Putin was on the phone virtually immediately. The Russians could see the potential for playing on Erdoğan's resentments and thereby gradually corralling Turkey.

All this fed into Turkey's contradictory gyrations towards Russia. Even after bowing over Aleppo, the Turks floated a plan in November 2016 that was obviously a non-starter in Moscow: the city would become a 'safe zone' with removal of 'foreign forces', meaning the Shi'a militias as well as Jabhat al-Nusra.[57] On 29 November 2016, Erdoğan declared in a speech in Istanbul that 'we went into Syria to put an end to the tyrannical Assad's regime and not for anything else'.[58] He defined the Syrian regime as a 'terrorist state'. The next day the Kremlin demanded an explanation;[59] after a phone exchange with Putin the same evening, the Turkish president climbed down and Foreign Minister Çavuşoğlu clarified that the 'terrorist' targets of Euphrates Shield were ISIS and al-Nusra, not Assad.[60] Meantime, also in November, Turkey set up the Ankara talks between Russia and Syrian rebels, after transferring Turkmen and other armed rebels out of Aleppo to Jarabulus from late August on, to fight ISIS rather than Assad.[61]

Through mid-December 2016, Turkey entered its first cooperative venture with Russia inside Syria in jointly sponsoring evacuation of remaining fighters and civilians from eastern Aleppo. This helped Russia to finish with Aleppo smoothly, without last-minute human rights embarrassments. On 19 December, when a Turkish police officer assassinated the Russian ambassador in Ankara, shouting 'Don't forget Aleppo', Erdoğan phoned Putin to assure the Russian leader of his horror and complete cooperation against terrorists. On 20 December, the Turkish, Russian, and Iranian foreign ministers met in Moscow to issue a 'Moscow declaration' that formally inaugurated a tripartite framework for overseeing Syria. Turkey went along with a Russian and Iranian drive that took advantage of the presidential hiatus in the USA between Obama and Trump in a way that could only leave a sour taste in Washington. The declaration was bland, but without any direct mention of transitions or a new constitution, thereby signalling Turkish acceptance that Assad's future was not on the table. Instead, the 'Syrian government' would simply negotiate with the opposition on reinstatement of the 'Syrian Arab Republic'. The newspaper Cumhuriyet had no doubt of the implications, headlining the 'collapse' of the six-year Turkish policy of regime change.[62] Turkey's interest in having Hezbollah equated with the Sunni jihadists also met absolute Iranian rejection.

A week later Russia and Turkey agreed to a ceasefire between the Syrian regime and rebels beginning on 1 January 2017. They then organized the first-ever direct talks between the Syrian regime and armed opposition groups in Astana, the Kazakh capital, to discuss pacification of the various fronts in western Syria. The talks took place on 23–24 January and, as expected, simply produced a restatement of positions. At this stage Iran was content to have the regime speak for them both, and Turkey's role in pressing mainstream rebel factions into the process gave the Turks more prominence. Turkey and Russia were both sensitive about exclusion of the West and the UN, and carefully reserved serious political movement for the established Geneva track, which they insisted must include their Iranian partner. In parallel, Turkey indulged further contortions regarding the future of Assad. The Turkish deputy prime minister Mehmet Simsek told a session at the World Economic Forum in Davos on 20 January that Bashar was to blame for 'the suffering of the Syrian people', but that Turkey 'could no longer insist on a settlement' without him.[63] Simsek's office denied the remarks, and—more important—President Erdoğan still could not stomach such a position.

Turkey had two worries about Russia in early 2017. First, in late January the Russians leaked their own proposal for a Syrian constitution.[64] On the one hand, it was evidence of Russian commitment to a political rather than military resolution. In addition, provision for a strong executive presidency hinted that Russia was not wedded to Assad, who they knew was unacceptable to most of the international community. However, the draft referred to the 'Syrian Republic' rather than the 'Syrian Arab Republic', and provided for 'autonomy of Kurdish regions'. Russia had already expressed openness to the PYD Kurdish proposal for a federal Syria, even regardless of the refusal of the Syrian regime.[65] For Moscow, it was something to hold over the head of Bashar, and perhaps also a warning to the Turks.

Second, Turkey was unhappy with ambiguity over the geographical extent of the ceasefire and continued hostilities near Damascus.[66] According to a Syrian rebel official, 'the Russian enemy' wanted the East Ghouta exempted,[67] presumably so that the regime could further consolidate its military advances in the environs of the capital. Through January 2017, regime forces and Hezbollah took villages in the Barada Valley west of Damascus, an important water source for the city. From February to April 2017, the regime shelled and attacked the East Ghouta, making gains in the Qaboun area closest to central Damascus. For Turkey, Russian aerial involvement could only feed lingering doubts about Russia's ultimate purpose.

On 4 May 2017, in the fourth Astana session on military de-escalation between regime and rebels, Turkey, Russia, and Iran agreed to be joint sponsors of four de-escalation zones in western Syria (map 3). East Ghouta became one of these, but it was a neutered East Ghouta. The regime moved into the Qaboun and Barzeh districts in an early

May evacuation deal, which coincided with ISIS and Hay'at (al-Nusra) pulling out of south Damascus suburbs by arrangement with the regime. In a repeat of May 2016, internecine fighting inside East Ghouta eased regime truncation of rebel territory. Bashar al-Assad now had a grip on the Syrian capital unprecedented since 2012—after Aleppo, another poke in the eye for Erdoğan.

The other de-escalation zones were the Idlib–west Aleppo–north Hama rebel heartland in north-west Syria; the rebel holdout north of Homs; and the Dera'a–Quneitra rebel spread on the southern border. Hostilities would be suspended for six months, except against ISIS and Hay'at (al-Nusra) jihadists, with extension in the hands of the guarantors. Iran assumed a more active role as a guarantor, restricting Turkish–Russian bilateralism. Turkey had an interest in an observer presence around Idlib, and debated with the Russians whether there would be on-the-ground supervision.[68] The southern zone was complicated because of US, Jordanian, Saudi, and Israeli roles. Overall, Turkey was now locked into its collaboration with Russia and Iran, especially considering Erdoğan's unusual personal submission to Putin, and locked out of the US-directed campaign against ISIS in eastern Syria. Russia's seniority and supremacy could probably only be jolted by a falling-out with Iran or an unlikely US assertion in western Syria.

In making al-Bab a cul-de-sac, Russia and the Syrian regime physically blocked Turkey from joining the US operation to liberate al-Raqqa from ISIS. There was also a widening gulf in comprehension between the NATO allies. Turkey felt that the USA was preferring the PYD associates of PKK terrorists who threatened Turkey's territorial integrity. For its part, the USA perceived Erdoğan's own political manoeuvres as substantially responsible for destabilization within Turkey since the Gezi Park protests of summer 2013. It also perceived the Syrian Kurds as a reliable instrument against ISIS, with a solid track record. It was not concerned with the PYD's monopolistic political practices in its cantons and its interactions with Russia, the PKK, and the Syrian regime.

US officials could readily compare Turkey's threat to attack the PYD–YPG in Manbij if the US did not compel Kurdish withdrawal with Turkey's deference when the Russians covered Syrian regime infiltration into Manbij to buttress the same Kurds.[69] The USA ignored Turkish warnings that Kurds capturing Arab al-Raqqa would soon bring ethnic troubles because the Americans felt that they already had the answer. Between March and May 2017, the USA oversaw a successful preliminary SDF attack on the Tabqa dam area, mainly involving Arab SDF militiamen backed by US Special Forces. From the US perspective, the Arab component of the SDF was expanding satisfactorily and was a known quantity compared with Turkey's Arab auxiliaries. Besides, after the Syrian regime cut Turkish land access from al-Bab, Turkey would have to drive through PYD lands to get to al-Raqqa. That would involve complexities that the USA did not need.

Given the circus in Washington in the early months of the Trump presidency, the fight against ISIS became delegated to the defense secretary, James Mattis, and the US military. They knew that the PYD Kurds, with whatever Arabs, were a narrow base for moving deeper into eastern Syria in competition with the regime, Russia, and Iran for a final reckoning with ISIS in Deir al-Zor. They would have liked to have a NATO ally that was also a regional power on board. Yet Erdoğan has been a difficult number for them. He applauded the Trump administration executing the first-ever US strike against Assad on 7 April 2017 in punishment for use of chemical weapons that were supposed to have been eliminated under Obama's shoddy 2013 disarmament deal. Here Turkey's president cut across his Russian friends and their theatrical condemnation of the USA. But he demanded more, meaning the USA taking risks with Russia, at the same time as he carried on working with Russia and Iran. Then came the 25 April Turkish air strike against the YPG in north-east Syria, followed by border clashes compelling the USA to run border patrols to keep Turkey and the Syrian Kurds apart. Erdoğan both gave the USA cause to sideline him and the Russians cause to bottle him up.

Frustrated in Syria, Turkey did not find Iraq any easier. Into mid-2017, the various parties calculated their futures as Iraqi forces steadily ground down ISIS in the north-eastern quadrant of the war zone. Turkey conceived itself as having a protective function for a shattered Iraq against Iranian ambition, and as being the best-placed outside power to help reintegration of the wrecked Sunni Arab provinces. The Iraqi federal government and the USA were both wary after the little storm over Turkey's Ba'shiqa military base; Prime Minister Yıldırım made a damage-control visit to Baghdad in early January.[70] Turkey was concerned in early 2017 that post-ISIS Mosul should recover as a principally Sunni city and that Turkish-trained Sunni Arab and Turkmen fighters should have a role in guarding local security. Turkey also joined Saudi Arabia to encourage Sunni Arab personalities to work with Baghdad to reconstruct Iraqi politics.[71]

Consternation about Turkey's intentions resurfaced in Iraq when President Erdoğan gave April interviews predicting an al-Bab-style Turkish military intervention for northern Iraq,[72] and condemning the Iraqi Shi'a PMF (which included 3,500 Turkmen from Tal Afar)[73] as a 'terrorist' extension of 'Persian expansion policy'.[74] Turkey's potential missions included protecting Iraqi Turkmen in Tal Afar and Mosul from the PMF and hitting the PKK in the Sinjar hills. The idea of a ground operation was disturbing. Otherwise, Erdoğan expressed Turkish suspicion of Iran that raised questions about how long the two could be on the same team in Syria. The Turkish president asked: 'Who are the PMF? Who is backing them?' The Iraqi prime minister's office responded that the PMF 'is a recognized force by law'; Turkey should stay out of 'internal affairs'.

In northern Iraq, the PMF was only one dimension of 'internal affairs' and Turkish–Iranian friction as the ISIS story approached an ending in the ruins of Mosul. Most important was the trajectory of the Kurds of the KRG after ISIS, and the fate of what might be termed Kurdish spoils of war: de facto KRG control of Kirkuk and extensive other 'disputed territories'. Despite encouraging KRG defiance of Baghdad from time to time, Turkey preferred to see Iraq maintained and the KRG shrunk back to its pre-June 2014 dimensions. This did not match with Kurdish flag-raising in Kirkuk in April 2017 and KRG president Barzani's renewed push for an independence referendum.

In the end, Turkey flinched from 'Balkanization' of Iraq.[75] On the one hand, it encouraged the KRG and Rojava Peshmerga presence in Sinjar against the PKK and PYD in these strategic hills verging the PYD in north-east Syria. Sinjar was way beyond recognized KRG boundaries. Turkey also depended on the KRG as a strategic balance against both the PKK and the Iranian-backed Shi'a PMF. It didn't mind the Peshmerga stationed outside the KRG if it was countering the PMF. It also welcomed Barzani in Ankara in February with a show of the KRG flag; Barzani might still be helpful in calming tensions within Turkey.

TURKEY AND THE WAR ZONE

On the other hand, Turkey was sensitive about the large Turkmen community in Kirkuk city and province, and preferred a special status for Kirkuk separate from the KRG. It also had lingering fears that a KRG cut away from Iraq might have ripple effects in Turkey. How would Turkey view a negotiated Iraq–KRG confederation?

Frustration?

Turkey's affairs in Syria and Iraq after the Arab Spring arrived in Syria in 2011 were largely Recep Tayyip Erdoğan's affairs. The shift from excoriating US-led regime change in Iraq in 2003 to promoting regime change in Syria in 2011 and expecting the USA to do the work was the whimsy of a strong-willed individual. The AKP's neo-Ottoman fancies as expressed in Davutoğlu's 'strategic depth' and Erdoğan's rhetorical flourishes could not turn Turkey from a regional into a great power. Erdoğan has been Turkey's leader since 2002, but these are not the days of Yavuz Sultan Selim who overthrew the Mamluks at Marj Dabiq in 1516 and marched to Damascus and Cairo. Erdoğan took Dabiq from ISIS in October 2016, but Vladimir Putin ensured that Aleppo stayed out of reach.

AKP Turkey has had limited room for manoeuvre in the crowded Syria–Iraq arena. Erdoğan faced a fragmented strategic landscape in the Fertile Crescent similar to that vexing his East Roman predecessors. Nicephorus Phocas and Basil II were more favourably endowed in that they had armed forces in better shape and were not cramped by greater powers like the USA and Russia. They could throw around hard power in Syria, but were also careful about overreach. Romanus III illustrated the short distance from hubris to humiliation.

In terms of agency, Erdoğan determined Turkey's quicksilver role in Syria and Iraq between 2011 and 2017; by 2011, he had overawed AKP colleagues and the state apparatus. Blunders multiplied: picking dubious Syrian clients, losing focus on the Syrian regime with the Syrian Kurdish distraction, and myopia regarding the jihadists and ISIS between 2012 and 2014. Erdoğan's diversion into domestic conflicts and ambitions got in the way of coherent policy regarding Syria and Iraq. Even the 2015 coordination with Saudi Arabia and the 2016 safe zone did not involve realistic presidential calculation of the Russian factor.

QUICKSILVER WAR

As Russia and Iran promoted a major swing in the military balance towards the Assad he detested, Erdoğan faced basic questions. Could he sustain Syrian rebels and safe zones while placating Putin and the Shi'a Iranian theocracy? Should he bring the USA and the West back into his equation? Might he make a new 'opening' to Kurds? How far could a Turkish military hobbled by Turkey's domestic turbulence carry hard power proclivities in Syria and Iraq? The structures that hemmed him in were, in part, his own products.

EPILOGUE

Sassanid Persian rulers reached across the Fertile Crescent in the 250s and 611 to seize Antioch (Antakya), deep within Roman territory. In the 1620s, the Iranian Safavid shah Abbas the Great occupied much of Ottoman Iraq and expressed an interest in Aleppo. Into the modern era, much has changed. The Turkish republic is the heir of East Rome and the Ottomans, and there are real world powers that have concerns in the space between the Mediterranean and the Persian Gulf. It seems, however, that the appetite of the power on the Iranian plateau has not changed. More than merely conserving an established strategic position with the Syrian regime and Lebanese Hezbollah, holding a defensive 'resistance' line against the USA and Israel, does today's Islamic Republic pursue a long-term offensive project from Iraq to the Levant? Are there signs in the energetic travels of the omnipresent General Soleimani? Could Iran rather than Russia emerge as eventual leading winner among external states involved in the Quicksilver War?

Into 2017, commentators surveyed Iran's participation in the unfolding struggle for the ISIS succession in eastern Syria and Sunni Arab Iraq.[1] One widely held view is that Iran wants a land bridge under its hegemony across Iraq and Syria to Lebanon's Shi'a community and the Mediterranean, as part of a bid to become the primary regional power. To further such a scheme the Iranians command or influence around fifty local and foreign militias in Syria mustering more than 60,000 fighters, according to the Arabic daily *al-Sharq al-Awsat* in August 2017.[2] These militias are crucial to the viability of the Assad regime. In Iraq, Iranian penetration of the Shi'a PMF assures it of a similar number. Tehran thereby has powerful leverage in Baghdad.

In the summer of 2017, Iranian-patronized Alawite elite units, together with Iranian-coordinated Lebanese Hezbollah and Iraqi Shi'a, have been essential to the Syrian regime's drive to Deir al-Zor and into the south-eastern desert. When they meet the Iraqi army accompanied by the PMF rolling ISIS up to the border from the other side, Iran can calculate putting together Iraqi and Syrian client states for strategic domination of the Fertile Crescent. But what about the complications of Russian and US interests, Israel and Turkey, Iraqi and Syrian Kurds, significant Iraqi Shi'a disquiet with Iranian domination, and Sunni Arab detestation of Iran across what are mainly Sunni Arab territories? Together these complications would seem to be insurmountable. Further, as regards conventional military equipment, Iran has a hard-power deficit in relation to other regional powers such as Israel and Turkey, aside from its missiles, and has to fall back on its elite special units, covert activity, and its admittedly impressive array of clients.

In facing world power players, Iran has both assets and limitations. In eastern Syria, its ground-force presence confers an advantage over its Russian ally. In both Syria and Iraq, Iran has its potent, relatively low-cost mobilization of militias, with stiffening from Islamic Revolutionary Guards. Iran can also hope that the USA is impeded by division of air space with Russia in eastern Syria, and by strategic incompetence under the Trump presidency. In this respect, US-supported movement of YPG and Syrian Sunni Arab fighters towards Deir al-Zor city and east towards the border with Iraq must be disconcerting for Iran and Assad, especially if the Russians are diffident.

Russia's own ambitions for a leading role in the eastern Mediterranean restrict the room for Iran on the Mediterranean shore. Russia is jealous of its hard-won leading role in western Syria, which has made it an arbiter among the other states involved in the war zone. In July 2017, Jordan and the USA, tired of Syria, readily agreed to Russian-enforced pacification of regime–rebel fronts in south-west Syria. Russia achieved Jordanian distancing from the rebels, and could exploit Israeli alarm about Iranians and Hezbollah possibly moving up to the Jordanian–Syrian border and the Golan Heights under Russian cover. Russia could also choose to tolerate Israeli strikes against Syrian regime, Iranian, and Hezbollah targets. On 7 September, Israel used Lebanese air space to hit Syrian facilities west of Hama where Iran was beginning missile production and the Syrian regime conducted chemical weapons research.[3] It was not clear whether Israel took a risk with the Russians, in answer to their sidelining of Israeli concerns in south-west Syria. In any event, the attack showcased that in the air Iran was both exposed to Israel and dependent on Russia, and neither was about to let Iran forget such realities.

Otherwise, Russia has established a formidable distribution of personnel from the margins of Idlib south to the Jordanian border in order to monitor various front lines, has its own penetration of Syrian regime regular forces and what remains of the NDF, including in eastern Syria, and has good reason to keep a close eye on Bashar al-Assad. For its part, the USA has a ground presence, allies, and air power in eastern Syria and Iraq that easily match Iran's assets. The main question is whether or not the American enterprise across the Fertile Crescent has any coherent direction under Donald Trump.

For Iran, Turkey and the Kurds represent an integrated issue. Turkish fury over the US alignment with Syrian Kurds, and apprehension about the KRG's most serious push for independence since its creation opened opportunities with Ankara. Iran knows that however testy Iranian–Turkish relations become, the PKK, Syrian Kurds, and a KRG independence referendum can act as reset buttons. Hence the chief of staff of the Iranian armed forces travelled to Turkey in August 2017, in the first such visit since the 1979 revolution in Iran. President Erdoğan, who had condemned 'Persian expansion policy' in April, welcomed his guest amid talk of possible joint Turkish–Iranian actions against the PKK across northern Syria and Iraq.[4] Nonetheless, in a longer view, Turkey cannot accept Iranian hegemony directly to its south. Turkey's relations with Iran are destined to more zig-zags as long as Iran backs a Shi'a militia role in northern Iraq and seeks land access to the Mediterranean. As in dealing with Iran and Israel, Russia can play above and between Iran and Turkey.

In Baghdad, the Iraqi Shi'a Arab political map shifted in the summer of 2017, making Iranian string-pulling a more intricate undertaking. Prime Minister Abadi showed interest in setting up his own electoral bloc, although without leaving the Da'awa Party, and the popular independent Muqtada al-Sadr planned to reorganize his support base with more incorporation of civil society elements.[5] Ammar al-Hakim abandoned his family's declining Supreme Islamic Council, founded in exile in Iran. His move accentuated polarization between proponents of the Shi'a leadership of Grand Ayatollah Sistani in Najaf and those loyal to Iranian supreme leader Ali Khamenei.[6] A front resistant to Tehran—Abadi, Sadr, al-Hakim, and others, with Sistani in the rear—continues slowly to evolve. It aspires to neutrality between Iran and the Arab states of the Persian Gulf, and has informed Tehran that Iranian efforts to reconcile Shi'a parties must involve Iran reducing its pressures on the Iraqi government.[7] On 30 July, Sadr visited Saudi Arabia for talks with Crown Prince Mohammad bin Salman. The Iranian-aligned Badr organization felt obliged to applaud,[8] but Tehran could only be irritated. A week later Sadr called for complete assimilation of the PMF into the main body of the Iraqi army.[9] Into the future, Iran's sway over nearly 20 million Iraqi Shi'a is uncertain.

Both Iran and the Sunni Arab oil principalities have inflamed Sunni–Shi'a and Sunni–Alawite animosity through their operations in Syria. With respect to Iran, the more charitable but less credible reading is that the Iranian theocrats are simply too arrogant to appreciate consequences. The other is that the Iranian regime has done its cost–benefit analysis and calculated the consequences as manageable. First, thanks to three years of ISIS, the Sunni Arab presence in eastern Syria and western Iraq will be so debilitated that it will be incapable of bothering Iran's land bridge. Second, after the military campaigns are done the Syrian regime and Iraqi Shi'a will handle security, without visible Iranians. Third, Iran and Lebanese Hezbollah will shift from their Syrian warfare to beating the war drums against Israel. The calculation here is that the Israeli–Palestinian affair will be sitting stagnant, untreated, and ripe for exploitation. At this point the human rights abuses of the Syrian regime, in which Iran has been a fellow-traveller, together with the indignities of Iranian supremacism, will presumably be forgotten and Sunni Arabs will come running to Iranian leadership.

On the other hand, Iran's sectarian adventures across Syria may ultimately backfire. It is not easy to imagine the anger that millions of battered, humiliated, displaced Syrians who sympathized with the insurrection feel towards the Iranian regime, which joins Assad in wanting them scrubbed out of history. Three million of them sit across the border in Turkey and can be the basis for an indefinite insurgency if President Erdoğan feels that Iran and Russia devalue Turkey. There is a good chance that an international settlement for Syria, tailored to the convenience of Iran and Russia, will degenerate, after an interlude of reimposed dictatorship, into more years of violence. Erdoğan has leverage, especially as Iran cannot use the Kurdish card, and the Iranian regime would have to prop up Assad through recrudescence of the war with enhanced risks of collision with Turkey. Russia can use the Kurdish card, but once more that puts Tehran in hock to Moscow.

Overall, when we consider the array of competing interests, the Iranian example illustrates that the war zone is not amenable to easy supremacy for any single external power, and particularly not a regional state compelled to align with a world power.

What then of projected futures for local players? The outlook in late 2017 is clearly in favour of near-term consolidation of the Syrian regime and the Iraqi federal government, in other words superficial restoration of the pre-war status quo. ISIS has knocked revisionism off the Western agenda, another ISIS service to Bashar al-Assad and the Iranians.

In comparing Iraq and Syria, Iraq entered 2011 with both a pluralist regime and rampant sectarian sentiment among Iraqi Arabs. Saddam Hussein's Sunni-based apparatus had smashed a Shi'a uprising in the early 1990s, and the USA promoted the Shi'a majority into power after 2003, with Sunnis deeply aggrieved. Syria, in contrast, proceeded into its 2011 street protests with a monolithic despotic regime and activists earnestly proclaiming ethno-sectarian harmony. In Iraq, identity politics were already out in the open, in a pluralist system framed by these politics. In Syria, identity politics soon burst into the open, as the regime saw its interest in encouraging sectarian and ethnic splitting, both of its opponents and the population in general. In this respect, Iraq's more fully developed sectarian acrimony was a bonanza for the Syrian regime, with Iraq's Sunni jihadism and Shi'a fear and pride as resources to be imported into the Syrian war arena, the first to break up the rebels and the second to stiffen the regime. In 2017, in both Iraq and Syria, outside powers seek to put the lid back on identity politics.

In the Syrian case, Jordan and Saudi Arabia have told the mainstream exile political camp of the National Coalition and its 'high negotiating commission' that they have to accept perpetuation of Assad in accordance with Russian preferences. The situation of the Syrian rebels in western Syria in late 2017 is abysmal. In late July, the Hay'at Tahrir al-Sham (al-Nusra) jihadists hijacked military domination in the heart of the main rebel Idlib enclave at the expense of non-jihadist but mainly Islamist militias. It appears that Syria's armed opposition cannot rise above petty factionalism and sectarian promotion of hardline Sunni Islamism. These proclivities have been accentuated by the long, bitter resistance to the regime, and they primarily benefit the regime. Obdurate Islamism guarantees that the outside world will turn away from the rebels.

Under the exclusion of jihadists from 'de-escalation', the Syrian regime, Russia, and Iran have perfect justification to attack Idlib. The regime is delighted but the Russians, with their investment in 'de-escalation' and diplomacy, are probably less so—the regime cannot move without the Russians. Turkey has the task of somehow shrinking al-Nusra, before time runs out.[10] European states may suspend civilian aid infusions,[11] given al-Nusra's terrorist status. The Russians have made pointed comments about the dangers of 9,000 Hay'at jihadists in Idlib, the major part of what their specialists estimated as 15,000 in western Syria in August 2017—considerably more than the 9,000 the Russians claimed was the surviving complement of ISIS in Syria.[12] In late September, Russian and regime aircraft struck across Idlib, breaking a half year lull and killing scores of civilians as well as jihadists and fighters from 'Astana factions', after a Hay'at attack on Russian military police in north Hama.[13] There was no international reaction and Turkey was forced to watch. In October 2017, the Turks implemented a limited military deployment into the Idlib enclave; Russia could hardly oppose such 'stabilization'.

Jihadist supremacy among rebels and a looming battle for Idlib weakens Syrian opposition negotiators, although the mainstream exiles remain defiant towards the regime and its backers. To add to their woes, US secretary of state Rex Tillerson indicated in July 2017 that Bashar al-Assad's situation and therefore the whole negotiating process is in Russia's hands.[14] In other words, the Russians own the show, which may in the end turn out to be not so convenient for Moscow. The USA has also reiterated that it has no concerns in Syria apart from destroying ISIS, as if there was no connection between Assad's behaviour since 2011 and surging jihadism.

US insistence on a narrow focus in a multi-dimensional game raises the question of what will happen 'after ISIS' in the relations between the USA and the PYD–YPG Kurds. Are the Turks really supposed to believe US secretary of defense Mattis that the YPG will meekly hand back all their American weapons when the YPG knows that the USA will then vanish into the sunset, deserting its associates? The US message to old and new allies that they had best keep their powder dry and look to themselves as soon as American self-interest in their welfare slips is dangerous, especially with allies on the brink of hostilities with each other. One Turkish idea, for example, is for Turkey to seize the PYD Kurdish Afrin canton,[15] which would enable Turkey to link its al-Bab safe zone with Idlib and exert more sway over armed rebel factions.

Federal Iraq's resurgence may be all smoke and mirrors if it is on the basis of Iranian steerage of Baghdad and imprisonment of Kurds, Sunni Arabs, and unwilling Shi'a in such a satrapy. The credibility of Iraq's rough electoral pluralism will evaporate if there is not Iraqi Shi'a Arab autonomy from Iran. For the foreseeable future, Sunni Arabs will depend on Baghdad for the rebuilding of their lives. Their provinces are derelict and oil-poor, while their politicians, emerging from the shadow of jihadism, lack any serious coherence. There is risk of a despairing relapse into insurgency if their concerns are not handled carefully. In any case, if sectarian rancour does not deflate, Arab Iraq will sooner or later splinter again.

For their part, KRG Kurds mostly want release from the Iraqi Arab disaster that has intruded so heavily on them through the Quicksilver War. This comes on top of a longer-term sentiment that Iraq has only brought them misery. In an August 2017 interview with *al-Sharq al-Awsat*, KRG president Barzani accused Baghdad of tending towards a '[Shi'a] sectarian religious state'.[16] He lamented that Iraq's Sunni Arabs failed to formulate a unified voice through the ISIS challenge and wallowed in 'nostalgia'.

On 25 September 2017, Barzani's referendum went ahead on a 72 per cent turnout with 92 per cent voting for independence. Sulaymaniyah exhibited a lower turnout; the Gorran and PUK abstainers also wanted a new country, just not under the KDP. The conclusive Kurdish 'Yes' elicited clear answers about the KRG's situation going forward. The Iraqi government demanded that the KRG repudiate its 'unconstitutional' referendum. It embargoed international flights to Kurdistan, imposed economic sanctions, and threatened 'all means'. In Shi'a Arab politics, Abadi lacked options; Iran and its allies would cut him off at the knees if he faltered. Baghdad's reaction clarified that Iraq simply would not conceive releasing the Kurds.

Abadi looked to political dissension, financial erosion, and morale cracking within the KRG. Iranian General Qasem Soleimani worked on splitting Sulaymaniyah from Irbil, not a difficult assignment. Abadi assembled the Iraqi army outside Kirkuk, some of it fresh from operations against ISIS in nearby Hawija, and including Shi'a PMF with sectarian banners. In mid-October 2017, to Kurdish dismay, this force swiftly seized the city and its oil-rich environs from the KRG Peshmerga, who withdrew virtually without resistance. There was no mystery; Iran advised PUK Peshmerga not to fight, and KDP units had to retire with them. Courtesy of the USA, the reconstructed Iraqi army already enjoyed the preponderance of force. De facto control of Kirkuk was the major Kurdish gain from confronting ISIS. To lose it in such a way was a stunning humiliation. The KRG bowed to circumstances, including Iraqi bombardment, by pulling back from other disputed districts to its recognized core, while maintaining its claims under constitutional article 140.

PUK founder and former Iraqi president Jalal Talabani died in the midst of the drama. His widow and sons called for joint administration of disputed land with the federal government, and for dialogue under the 'ceiling' of the Iraqi constitution. Into the future, the KDP can claim massive majority Kurdish public backing for KRG sovereignty, but it doesn't mean anything if the KRG collapses. Kurds are also exposed to population manipulation in the lost disputed lands, undercutting article 140. Iranian supreme leader Khamenei's adviser Ali Akbar Velayati illustrated what the KRG was up against when he crowed that 'the defeat of the Kurds in Kirkuk has scuttled the Barzani conspiracy backed by the Zionist entity'.[17]

International responses facilitated Iraqi rejection. The USA, France, and Britain indicated that the KRG Kurds were being a nuisance, and termed voting in disputed territories 'provocative'. US secretary of state Tillerson declared the referendum 'illegitimate', with impatience similar to his attitude towards the Syrian opposition. Iran and Turkey breathed fire. Iran championed isolation of the KRG; all the same, while it wanted Barzani deflated, Iran was probably wary of an inflated Abadi taking advantage in the Shi'a arena in 2018 Iraqi elections. For its part, Turkey felt in a bind; it preferred to freeze the KRG status quo indefinitely. Complaining of lack of consultation from Barzani, President Erdoğan rounded on Turkey's KRG friends, but was reluctant to inflict mutual commercial damage.

Russia monitors the commotion. It backs Iraq's integrity but departs from Turkey and Iran in approving Kurdish national aspirations; Putin looks to have his cake and eat it. For Russia, the Kurdish belt across the Fertile Crescent is a prize, awaiting the hoped-for US ditching of Syrian Kurds. Further, in 2017 Russia has been moving into KRG oil, a much more inviting commercial prospect than eastern Syria and not to be compromised by other players. Russia's problem in northeastern Syria is that Assad wants Kurdish Rojava cancelled, discomforting Moscow. The winding-up of the ISIS phase makes KRG and Rojava developments into 2018 of close interest.

An even more serious prospective conjunction in the Quicksilver War, which would ensure more hostilities down the track, is acquiescence of a disengaged international community in a Russian–Iranian-dictated settlement refloating the Syrian regime prettied up with cosmetic embellishments. Assad and the Syrian security machine, authors of calamity, would carry on. The conjunction may or may not be preceded by another military round in western Syria taking advantage of rebel disarray that has become simply suicidal. In the aftermath, a culled and cowed Syrian population would be corralled into a sham referendum. Russia, Iran, and the regime are confident that the hundreds of thousands of dead will swiftly fade from memory as their camp polishes its tendentious narrative of righteousness against 'terrorism', and the West 'moves on'.

Given the grim Syrian opposition circumstances in 2017, did the protesters who became rebels choose a ruinous road from the outset in 2011? Did they foolishly miscalculate the entrenchment of a regime that had a formidable social and sectarian base quite different from the situations of the Tunisian and Egyptian autocrats? First, the long road of the six years has had ups and downs and could have taken different directions; for example, the rebels have good reason to complain that the West encouraged then betrayed them. Second, civil disobedience was never going to budge a pitiless regime brandishing fearsome military instruments. Third, the choice facing Assad's opponents was appalling. Either they knuckled under to an implacable police state that offered no credible relief on any horizon or they pursued a confrontation in which the regime would burn the country rather than concede anything. Did the warping of Syria through the decades of tyranny mean that by 2011 it was simply too late to go through anything except hell itself to try to get to a better world?

Along the way, we have the question of accountability for the top man-made catastrophe of the twenty-first century to date. The evidence against the Syrian regime since 2011 is mountainous. Anyone wanting an education could start with the February 2017 Amnesty International Report *Human Slaughterhouse: Mass Hangings and Extermination at Saydnaya Prison Syria*, investigating extrajudicial executions estimated at between 5,000 and 13,000 at this site alone between September 2011 and December 2015.[18] Amnesty International has also reported on war crimes in ISIS, jihadist, and rebel prisons in north and north-west Syria, but assesses that 'the vast majority of detention-related violations since 2011 have been carried out by the Syrian authorities'.[19]

What has happened in charnel houses like the Sednaya prison is only one illustration of the Syrian regime's routine perpetration of mass murder and crimes against humanity; and this is putting aside other questions such as regime responsibility for the descent into war. In addition to prisons that are death camps, we can count barrel bombs packed with shrapnel and indiscriminately dumped on civilians, regular aerial bombing of hospitals, poison gas attacks, and much more. Accountability is especially important in Syria because of the implication of state personnel and institutions, especially the criminality at the summit of the state. There have been atrocities and severe abuses in Iraq, with ISIS the worst of the perpetrators, but regime involvement is at a special and extraordinary level in Syria. In addition, Syrian developments led the way in the chain of causation that produced a common war zone in Iraq and Syria. We know that Bashar al-Assad will never face international justice. One can only ask that all democracies boycott any reconstruction being overseen by a Syrian regime that continues to feature the present ruling clique. Also, that all democracies maintain a diplomatic boycott. It is an insult to expect our tax payers to reward Bashar al-Assad for wrecking Syria, creating an international human catastrophe, and fertilizing jihadist terrorism.

Ideas for peace after the Quicksilver War—indeed, ideas without which there will not be a peace that is more than an interlude—are easy to propose. Syria should get a comprehensive fresh start with a real democratic, independent, pluralist regime. There should be accounting for war crimes. Iraq should acquire a more transparent, less sectarian pluralism with diminished foreign manipulation. Kurds should get a place that they can call their own—meaning the existing pluralist KRG entering negotiations to become a sovereign polity, in confederal partnership with Iraq. Unfortunately, opponents of such changes have the upper hand at the time of writing. No ideas for more decent political arrangements look like becoming outcomes, more than six years into warfare.

Syria's complete fresh start depends on sustained commitment from the international community, therefore on agreement between the USA and Russia to fashion UNSC resolution 2254 into a radically new dispensation. Iraq's destiny depends on understandings among Shi'a Arabs, Kurds, and Sunni Arabs on political futures. In late 2017, annihilation of the ISIS 'caliphate', with thousands of its foreign jihadists killed and others scattering, leaves a dead zone. Assad gears up to reassert Syrian regime command, while the Iraqi government has recovered Sunni Arab Iraq. PYD Kurds in Syria have tempted fate by unfurling PKK leader Abdullah Öcalan's portrait in al-Raqqa, a red flag to Arabs as well as Turks. KRG Kurds have found that Iraqi and regional balances remain against them, but they still want sovereignty. Baghdad brandishing threats, bribery and institutional attrition will not persuade the Kurdish 20 per cent of Iraq to feel Iraqi. Anyway, for a time, thanks to the USA and Iran, Baghdad again has its own functioning hard power. Damascus is more dependent on its backers, and the regime-rebel contest in western Syria has yet to play out. The interesting new factor is Turkey's use of its 'partnership' with Russia and Iran to entrench itself among the rebels of north-west Syria, potentially shrewd strategic gaming. More broadly, Assad's belligerence despite his own circumscribed capability, the deep Iranian and Russian investment in his regime, the Saudi-Iranian feud, and American policy drift indicate turbulence into 2018. Syria's post-2011 black hole remains, as does the toxic little universe within its event horizon. Only Syrian hopes of a new dawn can reverse the sectarian and Islamist inflammations.

Into 2018, Iraq is again on its own pathway while Russia promotes diplomacy for a reconstituted Syria, with Iran and Turkey as partners. Russia needs Assad's regime, but also a settlement, to anchor its interests and prestige. Iran's reach across the Fertile Crescent would collapse without Assad. Turkey's Erdoğan, even as Putin's partner, still can't stomach Assad. Turkey will guard its position in northern Syria, where its strategic concerns are existential in contrast to those of Iran and Russia. For its part, Saudi Arabia is re-tightening its endorsement of Syrian opposition demands for Assad's early removal. The Saudis are reacting to Iran toying with their brutal botch-up in Yemen and asserting superiority across their north, from Baghdad to Beirut. The Turks and Saudis may enable military blockage of the regime in north-west Syria. As for negotiations, the Syrian political opposition, barely tolerated by Syrian rebels as their de facto representative, prefers the 'legitimate' UN Geneva framework for Syria to a Russian supervised track. It intends to dissect every detail of a new constitution and UN-managed elections. For the Syrian regime, it is preposterous that the 'victor' concede anything. For the opposition, it is unendurable that murderers command the state.

What of the USA? In pursuing ISIS, the USA has bombed across Syria and Iraq, made local alliances, and brought in thousands of personnel. Failure to find respectable answers, whether between the Syrian Kurds and Turkey or for Syria's future, is dereliction. Secretary of State Tillerson says that 'the reign of the Assad family is coming to an end'. No-one contemplating the vacuity of the Trump administration would be holding their breath.

GLOSSARY

Where possible, armed Syrian rebel factions are classified in the glossary as large (10,000 plus fighters), middle-sized (4–10,000), or small (less than 4,000). These are very rough estimates, mainly following Stanford University's *Mapping Militant Organizations* and a partial listing in *al-Hayat*, 1 January 2017.

Abu al-Fadl al-Abbas Brigade: Pro-Syrian regime Shi'a armed faction formed in 2012 to defend Shi'a holy sites. Manpower mainly drawn from Iraqi Shi'a with input from the small Syrian Shi'a community.

Adalet ve Kalkınma Partisi (AKP): Turkish ruling party since 2002. Has preserved single party majority in parliament with brief interruption in 2015.

Ahrar al-Sham (Free Men of Syria): Large rebel Salafist armed faction primarily in north-west Syria. Founded in 2011 with Hassan Abboud as leader.

Alawite/Alevi: Distinct religious groups with names derived from Caliph Ali, first imam of the Shi'a. Alawites (Syria) believe Ali has divine attributes. Alevis (Turkey) do not conceive him in such terms, and have a free-ranging mystical orientation different from that of Alawites. Both differ radically from Twelver Shi'a, despite a historical link.

Albu Assaf: Sunni Arab clan that has headed the Dulaym tribal conglomerate in Iraq's al-Anbar province.

Albu Bali: Small Iraqi Sunni Arab tribe in al-Anbar province associated with opposition to ISIS.

175

GLOSSARY

Albu Risha: Small Iraqi Sunni Arab tribe in al-Anbar province associated with *sahwa* tendency and opposition to ISIS.

Asa'ib Ahl al-Haqq (Bands of the Right-Minded People): Large Iraqi Shi'a militia supported by the Iranian Quds Force. Split from Mahdi Army in 2006. Headed by Qais al-Khaz'ali. Major component of PMF.

Asifat al-Shamal (Storm of the North): Small Syrian rebel armed faction formed in 2011 in A'zaz north of Aleppo. Took over Bab al-Salameh border crossing in 2012. Links with both FSA and Islamic Front.

Ba'ath (Resurrection): Secular Arab nationalist party founded in Damascus in 1943 by Michel Aflaq (Orthodox Christian) and Salah al-Din al-Bitar (Sunni Muslim).

Badr Brigades: Iraqi Shi'a military formation. Originated in exile in Iran in the 1980s. Covering political party (Badr organization) headed since 2009 by Hadi al-Amiri. Major component of PMF.

Da'awa (Call): Senior Iraqi Shi'a Islamist party. Founded in 1957 to oppose secularism. Core of State of Law parliamentary coalition after 2009. Party of Prime Ministers Maliki and Abadi.

de-Ba'athification: Removal of former Ba'ath Party members, mainly Sunnis, from Iraqi bureaucracy and military since 2003. Has assumed sectarian connotations with the new Shi'a ascendancy.

Desert Hawks: Elite militia of Syrian army veterans that emerged in 2013 and has taken initiatives for the regime in the Homs desert and Latakia hills.

Dulaym: Largest Sunni Arab tribal conglomerate in Iraq. Spreads into eastern Syria. Constituent clans supported US-backed *sahwa* in 2007, and some opposed ISIS in 2014.

Farouq Brigades: Early FSA armed rebel faction originating in Homs and Rastan in mid-2011. Splintered in 2013; thereafter many members drawn into Salafist groups.

Fath al-Sham (Conquest of the Levant): Palestinian Sunni jihadist group used by the Syrian regime to destabilize Lebanon.

GLOSSARY

Faylaq al-Rahman (al-Rahman Legion): Former FSA group in East Ghouta since 2013. Fluctuating in membership and in long-standing conflict with Jaysh al-Islam. Small.

Faylaq al-Sham (The Syrian Legion): Alignment of nineteen mildly Islamist rebel armed factions, formed in March 2014. Based in Idlib and rural Hama. Unlike most such conglomerates, stayed together into 2017. Middle-sized.

Free Syrian Army (FSA): Loose alignment of armed Syrian rebels stiffened by regime military defections, launched in mid-2011. Overshadowed by Islamists and Salafists by late 2012, and always splintered among regions. Attracted Western favour.

Gorran (Change): Kurdish political party formed in 2009 by Nawishirwan Mustafa in split from PUK and in opposition to KDP and PUK domination of KRG in northern Iraq. Overtook PUK in 2013 KRG assembly elections.

Harakat Hazm (Resolute Movement): Group of ex-FSA factions in north-west Syria in 2014. Beneficiary of CIA arms provision. Dissolved after humiliation by al-Nusra in 2015.

Harakat al-Nujaba (Movement of the Superior Ones): Iraqi Shi'a militia that emerged out of Asa'ib Ahl al-Haqq and Kata'ib Hizballah in 2013, backed by Iran. Important role in fighting around Aleppo, 2015–16.

Hay'at Tahrir al-Sham (Council for the Liberation of the Levant): Second rebranding of Jabhat al-Nusra, January 2017. Alignment with Nur al-Din Zanki movement and three smaller Salafist groups.

Hezbollah (Party of God): Militant Lebanese Shi'a movement founded after Israeli invasion of Lebanon in 1982. In coordination with Iran, sent thousands of militiamen into Syria to back Bashar al-Assad from late 2012 onwards.

ISIS: See Islamic State in Iraq and Syria. Acronym often reduced to IS (Islamic State).

Islamic Front: Coalition of Syrian rebel Islamist and Salafist armed factions formed in November 2013 (Ahrar al-Sham, Jaysh al-Islam, Liwa al-Tawhid, Suqur al-Sham).

GLOSSARY

Islamist: Proponent of subordinating government and society to one or other interpretation of Islamic values.

Islamic State in Iraq (ISI): Violent Sunni jihadist group emerging out of al-Qaeda in Iraq in 2006.

Islamic State in Iraq and Syria (al-Dawlat al-Islamiya fil-Iraq wa al-Sham—DAESH) (ISIS): Reformulation of ISI in 2013 to include Greater Syria.

Jabhat Fath al-Sham (Conquest of the Levant Front): Rebranding of Jabhat al-Nusra in July 2016 after announcement of separation from al-Qaeda. Media claim that Qatar pressed for this separation.

Jabhat al-Nusra (The Support Front): Established in 2012 by Abu Muhammad al-Jawlani of ISI as the first jihadist rebel movement against the Syrian regime. Wants Islamic emirate in Syria. Large. See Jabhat Fath al-Sham; Hay'at Tahrir al-Sham.

al-Jabhat al-Shamiya (The Levant Front): Re-emergence in Aleppo in late 2014 of shrunken Liwa al-Tawhid, linking with other Islamist rebel factions. Participated in Operation Euphrates Shield. Small.

Jaysh al-Fath (Army of Conquest): Alliance of Salafist, jihadist, and ex-FSA factions for 2015 rebel offensive in Idlib province.

Jaysh Idlib al-Hurr (Free Idlib Army): Coalescence in September 2016 of three FSA factions: Liwa Suqur al-Jabal, Division 13, and Northern Division. Based at Ma'arrat al-Nu'man and Kafr Nabl. Fighters involved in Operation Euphrates Shield. Middle-sized.

Jaysh al-Islam: (Army of Islam): Large rebel Salafist armed group primarily in East Ghouta. Coalescence of Damascus factions under Zahran Alloush in 2013.

Jaysh al-Muhajirin wa al-Ansar (Army of Migrants and Helpers): Small Sunni jihadist group formed in Syria in 2013, mainly for foreign fighters. Chechens particularly prominent. Flirted with ISIS, then joined al-Nusra in 2015.

Jaysh al-Mujahidin (Army of Strugglers): Conglomerate of ex-FSA and mildly Islamist armed factions, formed in January 2014 on similar model to the SRF. Persisted into 2016 in Aleppo countryside.

GLOSSARY

Jihadist: Muslim who advocates violence to impose Islamic rule or authority.

Jubbour tribe: Mainly Sunni Arab tribe in northern Iraq, around Tikrit. Major segments fell out with both Saddam Hussein and ISI/ISIS.

Jund al-Aqsa (Soldiers of the Aqsa Mosque): Sunni jihadist splinter from al-Nusra in Syria, emerging in 2013. Flirted with ISIS and clashed with Ahrar al-Sham in 2016. Small.

Justice and Development Party: See Adalet ve Kalkınma Partisi.

Kata'ib Hizballah (Battalions of the Party of God): Large pro-Iranian Iraqi Shi'a militia formed by Abu Mahdi al-Muhandis in 2007. Links with Badr Brigade, Iranian Revolutionary Guards, and Hezbollah. Component of PMF.

Kurdish National Council (KNC): Assemblage of older Syrian Kurdish parties opposed to PYD domination of Rojava. Kurdish autonomist with a conservative flavour, and backed by KDP since formation in 2011.

Kurdistan Democratic Party (KDP): Leading Kurdish political party in Iraq and KRG. Kurdish nationalist; otherwise ideologically pragmatic. Led by Barzani family since founding in 1946.

Kurdistan Regional Government (KRG): Kurdish autonomous area and government in northern Iraq, formally established in 2005 as a special super-provincial component of the new federal Iraq. Has own security force (Peshmerga) and border authority.

Liwa al-Tawhid (Oneness of God Brigade): Coalescence of Aleppo rebel militias in July 2012. Muslim Brotherhood-style programme. Fell out with FSA. Middle-sized force, but declined after leader Abdul Qadir Saleh killed by regime air strike, November 2013.

local coordinating committees (LCCs): Networks of Syrian civilian activists that emerged to service the 2011 protest movement. Most viewed the shift from civil disobedience to armed insurrection as counter-productive.

Mahdi Army: Iraqi Shi'a Arab militia created by Muqtada al-Sadr in 2003. Populism and nationalism uncomfortable for USA, Maliki government, and Iran. Disbanded in 2013 as al-Sadr moved more into civilian politics.

Milli İstihbarat Teşkilatı (National Intelligence Organization—MİT): Agency responsible for Turkey's internal and external intelligence activities. Lead Turkish institution involved in Syria and Iraq, with strong 'special operations' orientation.

Muslim Brotherhood: Sunni Islamic revivalist movement founded by Hassan al-Banna in Egypt in 1928. Branches in other Arab countries. Gradualist strategy to Islamize society and the state.

Muslim Brotherhood in Syria: Branch founded 1946. Hama uprising in 1982 smashed by regime. Movement in exile sidelined by Islamists within Syria in post-2011 war period. Qatar, Turkey have favoured factions with Brotherhood associations.

Naqshbandi army: Iraqi Ba'athist fusion after 2006 with Naqshbandi Sunni Sufi religious order to form insurgent groups under Izzat Ibrahim al-Douri. Briefly helped ISIS in June 2014.

National Coalition of Syrian Revolutionary and Opposition Forces: Umbrella for exiled Syrian politicians and groups. Established in December 2012 with Western, Arab, and Turkish backing. Derided by many rebels within Syria.

National Defence Forces (NDF): Paramilitary units, mainly drawn from Alawites and other minorities, established by the Syrian regime from early 2013 to buttress depleted regular forces. Iranian and Hezbollah planning and support.

Nur al-Din Zanki movement: Syrian Islamist rebel group significant in Aleppo from 2012. Received Saudi support. Prominent in infighting in eastern Aleppo on eve of rebel Aleppo collapse. Drifted towards al-Nusra in 2016.

Operation Euphrates Shield: Turkish incursion to al-Bab in northern Syria.

Patriotic Union of Kurdistan (PUK): Kurdish political party in Iraq and the KRG. Jalal Talabani emerged as leader after 1975 split from KDP. Left inclined, and originally more urban than the KDP.

Peshmerga (those who face death): Armed wing of the Kurdish national movement in Iraq since the 1960s. Split between KDP and PUK. Since 2005, the recognized armed force of the KRG.

PKK (Kurdistan Workers' Party): Founded as a small Marxist group among Turkish Kurds in 1974. Rebelled against the Turkish state and viewed by Turkey as separatist–terrorist. Leader Abdullah Öcalan captured in 1999.

Popular Mobilization Forces (PMF): Broad alignment of Iraqi Shi'a paramilitaries put together in mid-2014 to face ISIS. Iranian-oriented core, but also major independent Shi'a input.

PYD (Democratic Union Party): Dominant Syrian Kurdish political movement since 2012. Recent (2003) offshoot of Turkish Kurdish PKK. Distrusted by both Turkey and the KDP.

al-Qaeda in Iraq: Created in Iraq in 2003 by Jordanian freebooter Abu Mus'ab al-Zarqawi, with reluctant conferring of franchise by al-Qaeda chief Usama bin Laden. Spearhead of Iraqi Sunni jihadism against the USA, the Shi'a, and the new Iraqi regime, 2003–6.

Quds Force: External wing of Iran's Islamic Revolutionary Guard Corps. Since 2003 headed by General Qasem Soleimani.

Sahwa (Awakening): US-assisted mobilization of Iraqi Sunni Arab tribes tired of jihadists against al-Qaeda in Iraq and the ISI, 2006–2008. Later starved of support by Maliki government.

Salafists: Sunni Muslims who look back to an imagined community of the first Islamic generations in the seventh century as the model for Islam. From *salaf* (ancestors).

Saraya al-Salam (Peace Companies): Partial resuscitation by Muqtada al-Sadr of the Mahdi Army as his contribution to the PMF to fight ISIS. Al-Sadr hostile to PMF transfers to Syria to prop up Bashar al-Assad.

Southern Front: Post-February 2014 alliance of dozens of ex-FSA and mildly Islamist Syrian rebel factions in Dera'a and Quneitra provinces to face the regime and its allies. Support from USA, Saudi Arabia, and Jordan. Very large (30,000).

GLOSSARY

State of Law coalition: Iraqi political alignment centred on the Da'awa Party, established by Prime Minister Maliki for the 2009 provincial and subsequent elections.

Suqur al-Sham (Hawks of Syria): FSA-connected Syrian rebel faction with military and civilian wings created in late 2011. Hardening Islamist orientation from 2013. Joined Ahrar al-Sham, March 2015. Middle-sized.

Surge: Short-term infusion of 20,000 additional US troops into Iraq in 2007 for concentrated security effort in Baghdad and al-Anbar province (paralleled by Sahwa).

Syrian Democratic Forces (SDF): Syrian Kurdish YPG initiative in October 2015 to form multi-ethnic military alignment against ISIS including secularist Sunni Arab FSA groups and Arab tribal, Assyrian Christian, Turkmen, and Circassian contingents.

Syrian Martyrs' Brigade: Secularist FSA faction formed in Jabal al-Zawiya by Jamal Ma'arouf in late 2011. Took initiative to establish wider SRF in 2014.

Syrian National Council (SNC): Initial assemblage of the exiled Syrian opposition in Turkey in August 2011. Criticized for Turkish-promoted Muslim Brotherhood influence. Largest bloc in 2012 National Coalition. Chairman Orthodox Christian George Sabra.

Syrian Observatory for Human Rights (SOHR): Network across Syria coordinated from Britain by Rami Abdulrahman. Maintains count of deaths from violence, limited to identified victims. Disparaged by regime sympathizers, but generally conservative and below UN estimates.

Syrian Revolutionaries' Front (SRF): Broad alliance of ex-FSA secular or mildly Islamist factions in north-west Syria. Formed in December 2013 to confront ISIS and as a counterpoint to the Islamic Front. Fell apart in north by early 2015.

Takfiri: Muslim who declares that another Muslim is an unbeliever. Involves an implicit or open invitation to commit violence against people labelled as apostates.

GLOSSARY

Tiger Forces: Elite Syrian regime Special Forces organized in late 2013 under highly capable Alawite officer Suheil al-Hassan. Highly mobile among fronts. Critical for regime in Aleppo fighting.

TOW (Tube-launched, Optically-tracked, Wire-guided): US made anti-tank missile

Yarmouk Martyrs Brigade: Syrian rebel group founded in 2012 in area abutting Golan and Jordan. At first linked to FSA, then affiliated itself to ISIS through late 2014. Fluctuating links with Islamic Muthanna group, hostile to al-Nusra and Southern Front.

YPG (People's Protection Units): Military wing of Syrian Kurdish PYD and chief ground-forces ally of the USA against ISIS in Syria. Core force of SDF. Includes women's units.

NOTES

INTRODUCTION

1. James Breasted, *Ancient Times: A History of the Early World* (Boston: Ginn & Co., 1916), pp. 100–2.
2. William McCants, *The ISIS Apocalypse: The History, Strategy, and Doomsday Vision of the Islamic State* (New York: St Martin's Press, 2015), pp. 74–5.
3. Denise Natali, 'The Kurdish Quasi-State: Leveraging Political Limbo', *Washington Quarterly* 38:2 (2015), pp. 145–64.
4. For critical observations, read Lionel Beehner, 'How Proxy Wars Work and What That Means for Ending the Conflict in Syria', *Foreign Affairs*, 12 November 2015, https://www.foreignaffairs.com/articles/2015-11-12/how-proxy-wars-work
5. Estimates for deaths from violence in Syria in 2011–16 go as high as 400,000, or even more. See, for example, Ian Black, 'Report on Syria Conflict Finds 11.5% of Population Killed or Injured', *The Guardian*, 11 February 2016, http://www.theguardian.com/world/2016/feb/11/report-on-syria-conflict-finds-115-of-population-killed-or-injured
6. Iraq Body Count, *Documented civilian deaths from violence*, https://www.iraqbodycount.org/
7. Halford Mackinder, *Democratic Ideals and Reality: A Study in the Politics of Reconstruction* (London: Constable & Company, 1919).

1. WAR ZONE TAKES SHAPE, 2011–2014

1. For comparison with the Thirty Years War, see Brendan Simms, Michael Axworthy, and Patrick Milton, 'Ending the New Thirty Years War', *New Statesman*, January 26 2016, http://www.newstatesman.com/politics/uk/2016/01/ending-new-thirty-years-war. For comparison with Hungary in 1848–9, see William Harris, 'Syria's Firestorm: Where From? Where

To?', *Ortadoğu Etütleri* 6:2 (2015), p. 9. For descriptions of sieges in early modern Europe that bear more than a passing resemblance to the Syrian regime's investment of Damascus suburbs, consult Lauro Martines, *Furies: War in Europe, 1450–1700* (New York: Bloomsbury Press, 2013), pp. 103–41.

2. Leo Tolstoy, *War and Peace*, translated by Anthony Briggs (London: Penguin Books, 2006), pp. 667–71 and 912–14.

3. Margaret MacMillan, *History's People: Personalities and the Past* (Melbourne: The Text Publishing Company, 2015), p. 4.

4. Lara Marlowe in the *Irish Times*, 19 February 2005, http://www.irishtimes.com/opinion/bringing-lebanon-together-1.416615

5. Bashar al-Assad presidential inauguration speech, http://www.presidentassad.net/index.php?option=com_content&view=article&id=438:president-assad-2000-inauguration-speech-july-17-20003&catid=106&Itemid=496

6. Alan George, *Syria: Neither Bread nor Freedom* (London: Zed Books, 2003) gives a valuable interview-based survey of the period.

7. Carsten Wieland, *Syria—A Decade of Lost Chances: Repression and Revolution from Damascus Spring to Arab Spring* (Seattle: Cune Press, 2012), pp. 148–50 and 52–153.

8. Wieland, *Syria—A Decade of Lost Chances*, pp. 21 and 119.

9. *Al-Sharq al-Awsat*, 29 July 2011.

10. Bassam Haddad, *Business Networks in Syria: The Political Economy of Authoritarian Resilience* (Stanford: Stanford University Press, 2011).

11. Peter Gleick, 'Water, Drought, Climate Change, and Conflict in Syria', *Weather, Climate, and Society* 6:3 (2014), pp. 331–40.

12. Francesca De Châtel, 'The Role of Drought and Climate Change in the Syrian Uprising: Untangling the Triggers of the Revolution', *Middle Eastern Studies* 50:4 (2014), p. 527.

13. De Châtel, 'The Role of Drought', p. 532.

14. Sami Nazih in *al-Ra'i al-'Am* (Kuwait), 15 October 2005.

15. UN Security Council, S/2005/203, *Report of the Fact-finding Mission to Lebanon inquiring into the causes, circumstances, and consequences of the assassination of former Prime Minister Rafik Hariri*, 24 March 2005, p. 5, http://www.undemocracy.com/S-2005–203

16. *Al-Qabas* (Kuwait), 29 October 2005, citing unpublished testimony by Rød-Larsen to the UN commission of inquiry into the Hariri assassination.

17. United Nations, *Note of the Secretary-General's Meeting with His Excellency President Bashar al-Assad of Syria Held at the Palace in Damascus on 24 April 2007*, p. 4 (a copy in author's personal collection).

18. Bashar al-Assad, quoted in *al-Hayat*, 6 May 2001: 'They try to kill all

the principles of the Semitic religions with the same mentality involved in the betrayal and torture of Christ and in the same way they tried to deceive the prophet Muhammad.'

19. *Al-Safir*, 16 August 2006.
20. *Al-Sharq al-Awsat*, 26 February 2010.
21. Michael Weiss and Hassan Hassan, *ISIS: Inside the Army of Terror* (New York: Regan Arts, 2015), pp. 104–5.
22. Weiss and Hassan, *ISIS: Inside the Army of Terror*, pp. 111–12.
23. Mohammad Bazzi, 'Little Known Jihadist Inspired Latest Wave of "Lone Wolf" Attacks', Reuters, 28 July 2016, http://www.reuters.com/article/us-lone-wolf-attacks-commentary-idUSKCN1071OS
24. William Harris, *Lebanon: A History, 600–2011* (New York: Oxford University Press, 2015), p. 321.
25. Interview with Bashar al-Assad, *Wall Street Journal*, 31 January 2011, https://www.wsj.com/articles/SB10001424052748703833204576114712441122894
26. Phil Sands, Justin Vela, and Suha Maayeh, 'The Man who Ignited the Syrian Revolution', *The National*, 17 March 2014, http://www.thenational.ae/world/syria/the-man-who-ignited-the-syrian-revolution
27. For full Arabic text see http://www.voltairenet.org/article173297.html; for an English version see http://www.voltairenet.org/article169245.html
28. Also see *al-Safir*, 31 March 2012: 'wa idha furadat alayna al-ma'araka al-yawm fa ahlan wa sahlan biha', http://www.assafir.com/Windows/ArticlePrintFriendly.aspx?EditionId=1810&ChannelId=42550&Articl eld=3320)
29. Human Rights Watch, *We've Never Seen Such Horror: Crimes against Humanity by Syrian Security Forces*, June 2011, https://www.hrw.org/report/2011/06/01/weve-never-seen-such-horror/crimes-against-humanity-syrian-security-forces
30. Charles Lister, *The Syrian Jihad: al-Qaeda, the Islamic State and the Evolution of an Insurgency* (London: Hurst & Co., 2015), pp. 53–5.
31. *Al-Hayat*, 31 May 2011.
32. For full Arabic text see http://www.voltairenet.org/article173298.html; for English version see http://www.voltairenet.org/article170602.html
33. In June 2013 comments to Russian television network RT, Vladimir Putin observed: 'The country [Syria] was ripe for serious changes [in 2011], and the leadership should have felt that in time and started to make changes. Then what is happening would not have happened': Reuters, 11 June 2013, http://www.reuters.com/article/us-syria-crisis-russia-idUSBRE95A0RU20130611.

34. Joseph Holliday, 'Middle East Security Report 3: Syria's Armed Opposition', Institute for the Study of War, March 2012, http://www.understandingwar.org/report/syrias-armed-opposition
35. Roy Greenslade, 'Marie Colvin Killed in Syria', *The Guardian*, 22 February 2012, https://www.theguardian.com/world/2012/feb/22/sunday-times-marie-colvin-killed-syria
36. Lister, *The Syrian Jihad*, pp. 59–60.
37. Holliday, 'Middle East Security Report 3'.
38. For a highly detailed treatment of this question, see Christopher Phillips, *The Battle for Syria: International Rivalries in the New Middle East* (London: Yale University Press, 2016).
39. Aaron Stein, 'The Origins of Turkey's Buffer Zone in Syria', War on the Rocks, 11 December 2014, https://warontherocks.com/2014/12/the-origins-of-turkeys-buffer-zone-in-syria/
40. BBC Turkish, 'Türkiye Suriye'de "tampon bölge oluşturabilir"', 16 March 2012, http://www.bbc.com/turkce/haberler/2012/03/120316_syria_buffer_zone.shtml
41. Although the Syrian Ba'athist regime consistently refused any ethno-sectarian enumeration in the Syrian census, the literature has broadly agreed on estimates. See, for example, CIA, *The World Factbook: Syria*, https://www.cia.gov/library/publications/the-world-factbook/geos/sy.html
42. Budour Hassan, 'The Forgotten Revolution in Salamiyah', *Random Shelling*, 10 February 2013, https://budourhassan.wordpress.com/2013/02/10/the-forgotten-revolution-in-salamiyah/
43. Hassan, 'The Forgotten Revolution in Salamiyah'.
44. *Al-Hayat*, 12 June 2015, http://alhayat.com/Articles/9494253
45. UN Human Rights Council, *Report of the Independent International Commission of Inquiry on the Syrian Arab Republic A/HRC/21/50—Advance Edited Version*, August 15, 2012, http://www.ohchr.org/en/HRBodies/HRC/RegularSessions/Session21/Pages/ListReports.aspx
46. Arabic text of Bashar al-Assad speech to Syrian People's Assembly (3 June 2012) in *al-Safir*, 4 June 2012.
47. Weiss and Hassan, *ISIS: Inside the Army of Terror*, p. 107.
48. Also consult Reinould Leenders, 'How the Syrian Regime Outsmarted its Enemies', *Current History* 112:758 (2013), pp. 331–7.
49. Richard Spencer, 'US and Europe in "Major Airlift of Arms to Syrian Rebels through Zagreb"', *The Telegraph*, 8 March 2013, http://www.telegraph.co.uk/news/worldnews/middleeast/syria/9918785/US-and-Europe-in-major-airlift-of-arms-to-Syrian-rebels-through-Zagreb.html; C. Chivers and Eric Schmitt, 'Saudis Step up Help for Rebels in Syria with Croatian Arms', *New York Times*, 25 February 2013, http://www.

nytimes.com/2013/02/26/world/middleeast/in-shift-saudis-are-said-to-arm-rebels-in-syria.html?mcubz=2

50. Lister, *The Syrian Jihad*, p. 115.
51. For an early survey of the jihadist surge, see Aron Lund, *UIbrief No. 13: Syrian Jihadism*, Swedish Institute of International Affairs, 14 September 2012, https://www.scribd.com/document/137448880/Syrian-Jihadism-by-Aron-Lund
52. For more on the LCCs see Samer Abboud, *Syria* (Cambridge: Polity Press, 2016), pp. 66–70; Robin Yassin-Kassab and Leila al-Shami, *Burning Country: Syrians in Revolution and War* (London: Pluto Press, 2016), pp. 58–60.
53. Lister, *The Syrian Jihad*, pp. 102 (flour) and 122 (bus services).
54. Human Rights Watch, *Death from the Skies: Deliberate and Indiscriminate Air Strikes on Civilians*, April 2013, https://www.hrw.org/report/2013/04/10/death-skies/deliberate-and-indiscriminate-air-strikes-civilians
55. Lister, *The Syrian Jihad*, pp. 125–6.
56. Ghassan Charbel interview with Lakhdar Brahimi, *al-Hayat*, 25 June 2014, http://www.alhayat.com/Articles/3192747/
57. Joby Warrick, 'More than 1,400 Killed in Syrian Chemical Weapons Attack, US Says', *Washington Post*, 30 August 2013, https://www.washingtonpost.com/world/national-security/nearly-1500-killed-in-syrian-chemical-weapons-attack-us-says/2013/08/30/b2864662-1196-11e3-85b6-d27422650fd5_story.html?utm_term=.a4c9248d5fe4
58. Aaron Blake, 'Kerry: Military Action in Syria would be "Unbelievably Small"', *Washington Post*, 9 September 2013, https://www.washingtonpost.com/news/post-politics/wp/2013/09/09/kerry-military-action-in-syria-would-be-unbelievably-small/?utm_term=.c436b49239f4
59. Consult Fawaz Gerges, *ISIS: A History* (Princeton: Princeton University Press, 2016), pp. 98–128.
60. Martin Chulov, 'Baghdad Car Bombs Blamed on Syria and Islamists by Iraqi Government', *The Guardian*, 9 December 2009, https://www.theguardian.com/world/2009/dec/08/bagdad-car-bombs-iraq
61. Daniel Serwer, 'Iraq Untethered', *Current History* 111:749 (2012), p. 347.
62. Robert Tollast, 'The Civil Wars of Iraq's Sunni Tribes: Fault Lines within 8 Sunni Tribes and Sub-Tribes, 2003–2016', *Iraqi Thoughts*, 28 March 2016, http://1001iraqithoughts.com/2016/03/28/the-civil-wars-of-iraqs-sunni-tribes-fault-lines-within-8-sunni-tribes-and-sub-tribes-2003-2016/
63. Renad Mansour, *The Sunni Predicament in Iraq* (Beirut: Carnegie Middle

East Center, 2016), http://carnegie-mec.org/2016/03/03/sunni-predicament-in-iraq-pub-62924

64. See Iraq Body Count, *Monthly Documented Civilian Deaths from Violence*, https://www.iraqbodycount.org/database/

65. Consult Aki Peritz, 'The Great Iraqi Jail Break', *Foreign Policy*, 26 June 2014, http://foreignpolicy.com/2014/06/26/the-great-iraqi-jail-break/

66. For example, see Hamza Mustafa, *al-Sharq al-Awsat*, 31 December 2013, http://aawsat.com/node/15426

67. Human Rights Watch, *'You Can Still See their Blood': Executions, Unlawful Killing, and Hostage Taking by Opposition Forces in Latakia Countryside*, October 2013, http://www.hrw.org/reports/2013/10/11/you-can-still-see-their-blood

68. Stanford University, Mapping Militant Organizations, 'Jund al-Aqsa', http://web.stanford.edu/group/mappingmilitants/cgi-bin/groups/view/669

69. Aron Lund, 'The Mujahideen Army of Aleppo', *Diwan: Syria in Crisis*, 8 April 2014, Carnegie Middle East Center, http://carnegie-mec.org/diwan/55275?lang=en

70. Lister, *The Syrian Jihad*, p. 175 estimates Islamic Front numbers at 55,000.

71. Ahmed Ali, 'Iraq Update 2014#6: Sunni Tribal Dynamics in Fallujah and Ramadi', Institute for the Study of War, 9 January 2014, http://iswiraq.blogspot.co.nz/2014/01/sunni-tribal-dynamics-in-fallujah-and.html

72. The SOHR estimated total deaths in the ISIS–Syrian opposition confrontation for January–May 2014 at 4,000: *al-Sharq al-Awsat*, 11 May 2014, http://aawsat.com/node/94111

73. Matthew Levitt, 'Terrorist Financing and the Islamic State', Washington Institute for Near East Policy Congressional Testimony, 13 November 2014, http://www.washingtoninstitute.org/policy-analysis/view/terrorist-financing-and-the-islamic-state

74. For an early survey of the private financial flows, see Elizabeth Dickinson, *Playing with Fire: Why Private Gulf Financing for Syria's Extremist Rebels Risks Igniting Sectarian Conflict at Home*, Brookings Project on US Relations with the Islamic World, Analysis Paper 16, December 2013, https://www.brookings.edu/wp-content/uploads/2016/06/private-gulf-financing-syria-extremist-rebels-sectarian-conflict-dickinson.pdf

75. Nasir al-Haqbani and Muhammad al-Shafi'i in *al-Sharq al-Awsat*, 7 May 2014, http://aawsat.com/node/91626

76. Martin Chulov (citing 'Iraqi officials') in *The Guardian*, 10 June 2014, https://www.theguardian.com/world/2014/jun/10/iraq-sunni-insurgents-islamic-militants-seize-control-mosul

77. Al-Haqbani and al-Shafi'i, *al-Sharq al-Awsat*, 7 May 2014.
78. Christoph Reuter, 'Masked Army', *Spiegel online*, 20 December 2013, http://www.spiegel.de/international/world/isis-shadowy-jihadist-group-expands-rapidly-in-syria-a-939561.html
79. Richard Berger and Kevin Truitte, 'Warning Intelligence Update: The ISF Shows Signs of Weakness in Anbar', Institute for the Study of War, 15 April 2014, http://iswiraq.blogspot.co.nz/2014/04/warning-intelligence-update-isf-shows.html
80. See, for example, Hamza Mustafa in *al-Sharq al-Awsat*, 6 May 2014, http://aawsat.com/node/91071
81. Nazir Rida in *al-Sharq al-Awsat*, 15 May 2014, http://aawsat.com/node/96236; *al-Sharq al-Awsat*, 22 May 2014, http://aawsat.com/node/101081
82. Rida, *al-Sharq al-Awsat*, 15 May 2014.
83. Nazir Rida in *al-Sharq al-Awsat*, 13 May 2014, http://aawsat.com/node/95556
84. *Al-Sharq al-Awsat*, 11 May 2014, http://aawsat.com/node/94111
85. Liz Sly, 'Syrian Rebels who Received first US Missiles of War See Shipment as an Important First Step', *Washington Post*, 27 April 2014, https://www.washingtonpost.com/world/middle_east/syrian-rebels-who-received-first-us-missiles-of-war-see-shipment-as-an-important-first-step/2014/04/27/61ec84d8–0f53–4c9f-bf0a-c3395819c540_story.html?utm_term=.33cd7ae65318 (this refers to TOWs transferred to Harakat Hazm in Idlib in March 2014).
86. *Al-Sharq al-Awsat*, 5 June 2014, http://aawsat.com/node/111016
87. Hamza Mustafa in *al-Sharq al-Awsat*, 9 June 2014, http://aawsat.com/node/113021
88. *Al-Sharq al-Awsat*, 20 June 2014, refers to KRG intelligence warnings to Baghdad and Western intelligence agencies six months previously.

2. WAR IN SYRIA AND IRAQ, 2014–2017

1. Alessandria Masi, 'Assad's Government Still Kills Way More Civilians than ISIS', *International Business Times*, 2 February 2015, http://www.businessinsider.com/assads-government-still-kills-way-more-civilians-than-isis-2015–2?IR=T
2. Russian Deputy Foreign Minister Oleg Syromolotov, interview with Rossiya Segodnya news agency, MFA Russia, 9 February 2016, http://www.mid.ru/en/about/professional_holiday/news/-/asset_publisher/I5UF6lkPfgKO/content/id/2068238
3. Megan Price, Anita Ghodes, and Patrick Ball, *Updated Statistical Analysis of Documentation of Killings in the Syrian Arab Republic, Commissioned by the*

Office of the UN High Commissioner for Human Rights (San Francisco: Human Rights Data Analysis Group, 2014) integrated information from five data sources and estimated 191,000 deaths from violence for March 2011–April 2014: see http://www.ohchr.org/Documents/Countries/SY/HRDAGUpdatedReportAug2014.pdf

4. Iraq Body Count, *Documented Civilian Deaths*.
5. *The Daily Star* (Beirut), 10 July 2014, http://www.dailystar.com.lb/news/middle-east/2014/jul-10/263416-syria-war-toll-tops-170000-one-third-civilians.ashx; Price, Ghodes, and Ball, *Updated Statistical Analysis of Documentation of Killings*, p. 14.
6. *Daily Star*, 10 July 2014.
7. Kyle Orton, 'How Many Alawis Have Been Killed in Syria?' 20 May 2015, https://kyleorton1991.wordpress.com/2015/05/20/how-many-alawis-have-been-killed-in-syria/
8. See McCants, *The ISIS Apocalypse*, on the ISIS slogan of 'Enduring and Expanding', pp. 139–40.
9. *Al-Hayat*, 4 March 2015, http://www.alhayat.com/Articles/7810911
10. Alice Fordham on National Public Radio, 4 November 2014, http://www.npr.org/sections/parallels/2014/11/04/361422673/we-are-not-slaughterers-an-iraqi-village-rejects-islamic-militants
11. Joyce Karam in *al-Hayat*, 12 March 2015, http://www.alhayat.com/Articles/7979158
12. *Al-Hayat*, 11 March 2015, http://www.alhayat.com/Articles/7956248
13. Eric Schmitt and Helene Cooper in the *New York Times*, 18 May 2015, https://www.nytimes.com/2015/05/19/world/middleeast/isis-fighters-seized-advantage-in-iraq-attack-by-striking-during-sandstorm.html?_r=0
14. Daveed Gartenstein-Ross, 'How Many Fighters does the Islamic State Really Have', *War on the Rocks*, 9 February 2015, https://warontherocks.com/2015/02/how-many-fighters-does-the-islamic-state-really-have/
15. Peshmerga officers in discussion with the author, Mosul Dam, 15 November 2014.
16. For notes on ISIS administration, see Aymenn Al-Tamimi, 'Observations on the New Islamic State Video "Structure of the Caliphate"', Aymenn Jawad Al-Tamimi's Blog, 6 July 2016, http://www.aymennjawad.org/2016/07/observations-on-the-new-islamic-state-video
17. Erika Solomon, 'The ISIS Economy: Meet the New Boss', *Financial Times*, 6 January 2015, https://www.ft.com/content/b2c6b5ca-9427-11e4-82c7-00144feabdc0
18. In February 2015, a senior Iraqi official commented regarding Mosul: 'We send 20 billion Iraqi dinars [$16 million] for civil servants

monthly, some of it through transfer, some through bank cards': *Rudaw*, 15 February 2015, http://www.rudaw.net/english/kurdistan/150220151

19. Solomon, 'The ISIS Economy'.
20. Aymenn Al-Tamimi, 'Repentance: Financial Income for the Islamic State', Aymenn Jawad Al-Tamimi's Blog, 28 September 2015, http://www.aymennjawad.org/2015/09/repentance-financial-income-for-the-islamic-state
21. Abu Mohammed, 'ISIS Emptied Raqqa from Teachers and High Studies Graduates', *Raqqa is Being Slaughtered Silently*, 3 April 2015, http://www.raqqa-sl.com/en/?p=905
22. Aymenn Al-Tamimi, 'Aspects of Islamic State (IS) Administration in Ninawa Province: Part I', Aymenn Jawad Al-Tamimi's Blog, 16 January 2015, http://www.aymennjawad.org/15946/aspects-of-islamic-state-is-administration-in
23. Solomon, 'The ISIS Economy'.
24. Tony Badran, 'Minority Report', *Now Lebanon*, 5 September 2014, https://now.mmedia.me/lb/en/commentary/562681-minority-report
25. Stefan Heißner, Peter Neumann, John Holland-McCowan, and Rajan Basra, *Caliphate in Decline: An Estimate of Islamic State's Financial Fortunes*, International Centre for the Study of Radicalisation and Political Violence, King's College London, 2017, http://icsr.info/wp-content/uploads/2017/02/ICSR-Report-Caliphate-in-Decline-An-Estimate-of-Islamic-States-Financial-Fortunes.pdf
26. Tobias Schneider, 'The Decay of the Syrian Regime is Much Worse than you Think', *War on the Rocks*, 31 August 2016, https://warontherocks.com/2016/08/the-decay-of-the-syrian-regime-is-much-worse-than-you-think/
27. Aaron David Miller, 'A Defense of Obama's Middle East "Balancing Act"', *Foreign Policy*, 15 August 2016, http://foreignpolicy.com/2016/08/15/a-defense-of-obamas-middle-east-balancing-act-syria-russia-iran-nsc/
28. Kheder Khaddour, *The Assad Regime's Hold on the Syrian State* (Beirut: Carnegie Middle East Center, 2015), http://carnegie-mec.org/2015/07/08/assad-regime-s-hold-on-syrian-state-pub-60608
29. Lakhdar Brahimi, talk at Chatham House, London: *al-Hayat*, 15 October 2014.
30. Schneider, 'The Decay of the Syrian Regime'.
31. Kheder Khaddour, 'Assad's Officer Ghetto: Why the Syrian Army Remains Loyal', *Regional Insight*, 4 November 2015, Carnegie Middle

East Center, http://carnegie-mec.org/2015/11/04/assad-s-officer-ghetto-why-syrian-army-remains-loyal-pub-61449

32. Scott Wilson in the *Washington Post*, 25 March 2014, https://www.washingtonpost.com/world/national-security/obama-dismisses-russia-as-regional-power-acting-out-of-weakness/2014/03/25/1e5a678e-b439-11e3-b899-20667de76985_story.html?utm_term=.918161186913

33. Consult Jennifer Cafarella, 'Middle East Security Report 25: Jabhat al-Nusra in Syria', Institute for the Study of War, December 2014, http://www.understandingwar.org/report/jabhat-al-nusra-syria

34. Lister, *The Syrian Jihad*, pp. 301–2.

35. Lister, *The Syrian Jihad*, pp. 310–12.

36. Cafarella, 'Jabhat al-Nusra', p. 31.

37. Ibrahim Hamidi in *al-Hayat*, 31 March 2015, http://www.alhayat.com/Articles/8325123

38. Hamidi, *al-Hayat*, 31 March 2015.

39. *Al-Hayat*, 30 March 2015, http://www.alhayat.com/Articles/8309925

40. Counter Extremism Project, *Nusra Front (Jabhat Fateh al-Sham)*, p. 2, https://www.counterextremism.com/threat/nusra-front-jabhat-fateh-al-sham

41. Mapping Militant Organizations Group (Stanford University), Hay'at Tahrir al-Sham (Formerly Jabhat al-Nusra), March 2017—citing Jabhat al-Nusra leader Jawlani, http://web.stanford.edu/group/mappingmilitants/cgi-bin/groups/view/493

42. Labib al-Nahhas (head of foreign political relations for Ahrar al-Sham), 'The Deadly Consequences of Mislabeling Syria's Revolutionaries', *Washington Post*, 10 July 2015, https://www.washingtonpost.com/opinions/the-deadly-consequences-of-mislabeling-syrias-revolutionaries/2015/07/10/6dec139e-266e-11e5-aae2-6c4f59b050aa_story.html?utm_term=.ef6c061606d5

43. Ra'id Jabar in *al-Hayat* (citing an opposition coalition communiqué referring to bombing of the Idlib hospital and governorate offices), 8 April 2015, http://www.alhayat.com/Articles/8446124

44. *Al-Hayat*, 4 August 2015, http://www.alhayat.com/Articles/10381801

45. *Al-Hayat*, 27 July 2015, http://www.alhayat.com/Articles/10226220

46. Lister, *The Syrian Jihad*, p. 33.

47. 'Damascus Threatened with Isolation', *al-Sharq al-Awsat*, 13 September 2015, http://aawsat.com/node/452036

48. English translation of 26 August 2015 'Agreement between the Russian Federation and the Syrian Arab Republic on deployment of an aviation group of the Russian Armed Forces' in Michael Birnbaum, 'The Secret Pact between Russia and Syria that Gives Moscow Carte

Blanche', *Washington Post*, 15 January 2016, https://www.washington-post.com/news/worldviews/wp/2016/01/15/the-secret-pact-between-russia-and-syria-that-gives-moscow-carte-blanche/?utm_term=.2cba84eb3e2b

49. *Al-Hayat*, 23 September 2015, http://www.alhayat.com/Articles/113 13041
50. Reuters, 22 September 2015, http://www.reuters.com/article/syria-crisis-kerry-idUSL1N11S1OI20150922
51. *The Telegraph*, 30 September 2015, http://www.telegraph.co.uk/news/worldnews/europe/russia/11903681/Russia-launches-airstrikes-in-Syria-as-it-happened-on-Wednesday-30-September.html
52. *Al-Hayat*, 17 November 2015, http://www.alhayat.com/Articles/121 86993
53. *Le Monde*, 27 November 2015, http://www.lemonde.fr/attaques-a-paris/article/2015/11/27/fabius-envisage-d-associer-l-armee-d-assad-a-la-lutte-contre-l-ei-en-syrie_4818717_4809495.html
54. UN Security Council, S/RES/2254 (2015), Resolution 2254 (2015), 18 December 2015, http://www.securitycouncilreport.org/atf/cf/%7B65BFCF9B-6D27-4E9C-8CD3-CF6E4FF96FF9%7D/s_res_2254.pdf
55. Ra'id Jabar in *al-Hayat*, 16 and 18 December 2015, http://www.alhayat.com/Articles/12811628 and http://www.alhayat.com/Articles/12855884
56. Taha Abdul Wahid in *al-Sharq al-Awsat*, 31 January 2016, http://aawsat.com/node/556531
57. Ibrahim Hamidi in *al-Hayat*, 29 January 2016, http://www.alhayat.com/Articles/13683499
58. Dania Akkad in *Middle East Eye*, 6 February 2016, http://www.middleeasteye.net/news/opposition-blame-syrian-bombing-kerry-tells-aid-workers-1808021537
59. Interview with President Vladimir Putin, *Bild*, 12 January 2016, http://www.bild.de/politik/ausland/wladimir-putin/russian-president-vladimir-putin-the-interview-44096428.bild.html
60. Amnesty International, *'Civilian Objects were Undamaged': Russia's Statements in its Attacks in Syria Unmasked*, December 2015, https://www.amnesty.org/en/documents/mde24/3113/2015/en/
61. *Al-Hayat*, 20 January 2016, http://www.alhayat.com/Articles/13546625
62. See comments by Bashir Abdul Fattah in *al-Hayat*, 12 January 2016, http://www.alhayat.com/Articles/13373399
63. *Al-Nahar* (Beirut), 3 November 2015, citing Islamic Revolutionary Guard commander Mohammad Ali Jafari: 'Our northern neighbour [Russia] also helps in Syria, but it is not happy with the Islamic

Resistance [Hezbollah] … and it is not clear that Russian positions correspond with Iran as regards President Bashar al-Assad': http://www.annahar.com/article/280909

64. *Al-Sharq al-Awsat*, 19 May 2015, http://aawsat.com/node/364546
65. *Al-Hayat*, 5 October 2015, http://www.alhayat.com/Articles/11467916
66. *Al-Sharq al-Awsat*, 25 August 2015, http://aawsat.com/node/437421
67. *Al-Hayat*, 22 October 2015, http://www.alhayat.com/Articles/11664991
68. *Al-Hayat*, 3 December 2015, http://www.alhayat.com/Articles/12520 590
69. *Al-Sharq al-Awsat*, 27 October 2015, http://aawsat.com/node/483306
70. *Al-Hayat*, 27 October 2015, http://www.alhayat.com/Articles/11750918
71. *Al-Sharq al-Awsat*, 21 December 2015, http://aawsat.com/node/524976
72. *Al-Hayat*, 22 September 2015, http://www.alhayat.com/Articles/1129 4012
73. *Al-Sharq al-Awsat*, 16 October 2015, citing US-led coalition spokesman Steve Warren as estimating the number of ISIS fighters in Ramadi at 600–1,000: aawsat.com/home/article/474966
74. *Al-Sharq al-Awsat*, 22 July 2015, http://aawsat.com/node/413041
75. This was certainly the impression given by the Russians. Kremlin spokesman Dmitry Peskov observed that President Putin 'telephoned the Syrian president to inform him of the decision': Denis Dyomkin and Suleiman Al-Khalidi, Reuters, 15 March 2016, http://www.reuters.com/article/us-mideast-crisis-syria-russia-pullout-idUSK CN0WG23C
76. Adil Salimi and Paula Astih in *al-Sharq al-Awsat*, 20 March 2016, http://aawsat.com/node/596021
77. Joyce Karam in *al-Hayat*, 1 July 2016, http://www.alhayat.com/Articles/16377398
78. See commentary by Josh Rogan, *Washington Post*, 30 June 2016, https://www.washingtonpost.com/opinions/global-opinions/obama-proposes-new-military-partnership-with-russia-in-syria/2016/06/29/8e8b2e2a-3e3f-11e6-80bc-d06711fd2125_story.html?utm_term=.4027192a53b4
79. Reuters, 1 July 2016, http://www.reuters.com/article/us-mideast-crisis-syria-assad-idUSKCN0ZG28G
80. For the situation in late 2016, see the Syria Institute/PAX, *Siege Watch: Fifth Quarterly Report on Besieged Areas in Syria, November 2016–January 2017*, 23 March 2017, http://reliefweb.int/report/syrian-arab-republic/siege-watch-fifth-quarterly-report-besieged-areas-syria-november-2016
81. Amir Toumaj and Caleb Weiss, 'Iraqi Militia Parades in Southern Aleppo', *Threat Matrix: A Blog of the Long War Journal*, 12 August 2016,

http://www.longwarjournal.org/archives/2016/08/iraqi-militia-parades-in-southern-aleppo.php

82. See advance US draft in Ibrahim Hamidi report, *al-Hayat*, 5 September 2016, http://www.alhayat.com/Articles/17213332

83. Hamidi in *al-Hayat*, 5 September 2016.

84. Nick Cumming-Price and Anne Barnard, 'UN Investigators Say Syria Bombed Convoy and Did So Deliberately', *New York Times*, 1 March 2017, https://www.nytimes.com/2017/03/01/world/middleeast/united-nations-war-crimes-syria.html?_r=0

85. Atlantic Council, *Breaking Aleppo*, February 2017, p. 8, http://www.atlanticcouncil.org/publications/reports/breaking-aleppo

86. Atlantic Council, *Breaking Aleppo*, p. 9.

87. Atlantic Council, *Breaking Aleppo*, p. 2.

88. UN Human Rights Council, *Report of the Independent International Commission of Inquiry on the Syrian Arab Republic, A/HRC/34/64—Special Inquiry into the Events in Aleppo*, 2 February 2017, p. 13, http://ap.ohchr.org/documents/dpage_e.aspx?si=A/HRC/34/64

89. For an example of Jabhat al-Nusra revenue-raising by kidnappings, including the Qatari role, see Mohammad Ballout, 'How the Maaloula Nuns Were Freed', *al-Monitor*, 11 March 2014, http://www.al-monitor.com/pulse/security/2014/03/syria-nuns-maaloula-released.html

90. UN Human Rights Council, *Report A/HRC/34/64*, pp. 8–9.

91. UN Human Rights Council, *Report A/HRC/34/64*, pp. 11–13.

92. Author's discussion with Turkish Syria analyst, Ankara, April 2017.

93. Heißner et al., *Caliphate in Decline*, pp. 7–9.

94. *Al-Hayat*, 30 June 2016, http://www.alhayat.com/Articles/16350179

95. Renad Mansour and Faleh Jabar, *The Popular Mobilization Forces and Iraq's Future* (Beirut: Carnegie Middle East Center, 28 April 2017), http://carnegie-mec.org/2017/04/28/popular-mobilization-forces-and-iraq-s-future-pub-68810

96. See translated text of 'Office Order 91' in Bill Roggio and Amir Toumaj, 'Iraq's Prime Minister Establishes Popular Mobilization Forces as a Permanent "Independent Military Formation"', *The Long War Journal*, 28 July 2016, http://www.longwarjournal.org/archives/2016/07/iraqs-prime-minister-establishes-popular-mobilization-front-as-a-permanent-independent-military-formation.php

97. Nazir Rida in *al-Sharq al-Awsat*, 13 October 2015, citing an estimate by an 'Iraqi military source', who described them as 'volunteers' travelling to Beirut as 'tourists', then on to Syria: http://aawsat.com/node/473721

98. *Al-Hayat*, 9 June 2016, http://www.alhayat.com/Articles/15981904

99. Joe Stork, 'Arm's Length is Still Too Close for US Troops and Abusive

Iraqi Militias', *Human Rights Watch News*, 9 July 2016, https://www.hrw.org/news/2016/07/09/arms-length-still-too-close-us-troops-and-abusive-iraqi-militias

100. Peter Schwartzstein, 'The Islamic State's Scorched-Earth Strategy', *Foreign Policy*, 6 April 2016, http://foreignpolicy.com/2016/04/06/the-islamic-states-scorched-earth-strategy/; NASA, 'Sulfur Dioxide Spreads over Iraq', *Earth Observatory*, 26 October 2016, https://earthobservatory.nasa.gov/IOTD/view.php?id=88994

101. Reuters, 19 October 2016, citing Iraqi Special Forces commander: http://www.reuters.com/article/us-mideast-crisis-iraq-mosul-idUSKCN12J0XG

102. Amnesty International, *At Any Cost: The Civilian Catastrophe in West Mosul, Iraq*, July 2017, p. 11, https://www.amnesty.org/en/latest/campaigns/2017/07/at-any-cost-civilian-catastrophe-in-west-mosul-iraq/

103. Amnesty International, *At Any Cost*, pp. 11–13.

104. Samuel Oakford, 'Mosul's Capture Sees ISIS Vanquished, but at a Terrible Cost', *Airwars*, 1 July 2017, https://airwars.org/news/mosuls-capture-sees-isil-vanquished-but-at-a-terrible-cost/

105. Stephanie Nebehay, '100,000 Civilians behind Islamic State Lines in Iraqi City of Mosul', Reuters, 17 June 2017, http://www.reuters.com/article/us-mideast-crisis-iraq-mosul-idUSKBN1971YZ

106. Amnesty International, *At Any Cost*, p. 6, citing the Airwars group.

107. *Al-Hayat*, 10 March 2017, reports a commitment of 900 US troops to deploy with the SDF in Syria (400 to be added to 500 already there): http://www.alhayat.com/Articles/20622925

108. Murat Yetkin wrote in *Hürriyet Daily News*, 3 August 2017, that 'the main issue is the US's strategy in Syria to defeat ISIL [ISIS] not by sending GI Joes but by using the PKK [YPG] militia as a ground force through the US central Command (CENTCOM) and coordinated by [US envoy] McGurk. ... The PKK sees a golden opportunity in the Syria civil war to establish the first autonomous Kurdish region under its own control': http://www.hurriyetdailynews.com/can-the-us-provide-autonomy-for-kurds-in-syria.aspx?pageID=449&nID=116275&NewsCatID=409

109. Turkish official in discussion with the author, Ankara, April 2017.

110. Turkish official to author.

111. Ibrahim Hamidi in *al-Hayat*, 1 January 2017, http://www.alhayat.com/Articles/19363334

112. Turkish Syria analyst to author, Ankara, April 2017.

113. Turkish official to author.

114. Turkish Syria analyst to author.

115. *Al-Hayat*, 30 May 2017, http://www.alhayat.com/Articles/22113591
116. *Al-Hayat*, 30 May 2017, http://www.alhayat.com/Articles/22113589

3. KURDS AT WAR, 2014–2017

1. KRG data on Syrian refugees up to May 2014. The commentary observes that 97 per cent of Syrian refugees in Iraq came to Kurdistan: http://cabinet.gov.krd/p/page.aspx?l=12&s=000000&r=401&p=401&h=1&t=407
2. David Commins and David W. Lesch, *Historical Dictionary of Syria*, 3rd edn (Lanham, MD: Rowman & Littlefield, 2013), p. 206.
3. For interpretation of the Syrian Kurdish situation up to PYD predominance, see Harriet Allsopp, *The Kurds of Syria: Political Parties and Identity in the Middle* East (London: I. B. Tauris, 2015), and Michael Gunter, *Out of Nowhere: The Kurds of Syria in Peace and War* (London: Hurst, 2014).
4. Ghassan Charbel interview with Salih Muslim, *al-Hayat*, 25 July 2015, http://www.alhayat.com/Articles/10184624. When asked if he aspired to an autonomous region on the KRG model, Muslim responded with a firm negative and noted: 'When we talk about Rojava we are not talking about specific geographical borders. ... We mean a geographical area with a particular name; there is no intention to draw official boundaries.'
5. Peter van Buren, Reuters, 2 June 2015, http://blogs.reuters.com/great-debate/2015/06/02/dude-wheres-my-humvee-iraqi-equipment-losses-to-islamic-state-are-out-of-control/. Van Buren cites Iraqi prime minister Haydar al-Abadi on the Humvees, and also lists 40 Abrams main battle tanks, 74,000 machine guns, and 52 M198 155mm mobile howitzers.
6. Christoph Reuter, 'The Drama of Sinjar: Escaping the Islamic State in Iraq', *Spiegel online*, 18 August 2014, http://www.spiegel.de/international/world/pkk-assistance-for-yazidis-escaping-the-jihadists-of-the-islamic-state-a-986648.html
7. Peter Beaumont, 'How Effective is ISIS Compared with the Iraqi Army and Kurdish Peshmerga?', *The Guardian*, 12 June 2014, https://www.theguardian.com/world/2014/jun/12/how-battle-ready-isis-iraqi-army-peshmerga
8. Robin Mills, *Under the Mountains: Kurdish Oil and Regional Politics*, Oxford Institute for Energy Studies Paper: WPM 63, 2016, pp. 36–7, https://www.oxfordenergy.org/publications/under-the-mountains-kurdish-oil-and-regional-politics/
9. For a perspective on KRG oil prospects in late 2014, see 'The Rise of

Kurdish Oil', *Petroleum Economist*, London, 2014, http://www.petro-leum-economist.com/resources/reports/the-rise-of-kurdish-oil

10. Keith Johnson, 'A Mysterious Pipeline Closure is Bankrupting Iraqi Kurds', *Foreign Policy*, 2 March 2016, http://foreignpolicy.com/2016/03/02/a-mysterious-pipeline-closure-is-bankrupting-iraqi-kurds/

11. Selina Williams, 'Oil Companies' Bet on Kurdistan Turns Sour', *Wall Street Journal*, 26 April 2016, http://www.wsj.com/articles/oil-companies-bet-on-kurdistan-turns-sour-1461708524

12. Stephen Kalin and Dmitry Zhdannikov, 'Exclusive: US Helped Clinch Iraq Oil Deal to Keep Mosul Battle on Track', Reuters, 3 October 2016, http://www.reuters.com/article/us-mideast-crisis-usa-mosul-exclusive-idUSKCN12314Z

13. Nabih Bulos in the *Los Angeles Times*, 2 October 2016, http://www.latimes.com/world/middleeast/la-fg-iraq-mosul-20161002-snap-story.html

14. 'Number of Refugees in Kurdistan: 1.4m', *Rudaw*, 1 September 2014, http://rudaw.net/english/kurdistan/01092014; 'Christian Refugees in Erbil Desperate to Go Home', *Rudaw*, 20 August 2014, http://rudaw.net/english/kurdistan/01092014

15. For example, two seasoned ISIS operatives tried to enter the KRG with displaced Arab families fleeing from ISIS into Daquq, south of Kirkuk, in August 2015: Dalshad Abdullah in *al-Sharq al-Awsat*, 30 August 2015, http://aawsat.com/node/441901

16. Kurdistan Referendum Movement press release, 9 February 2005, http://www.kurdmedia.com/article.aspx?id=6235

17. Joel Wing, 'New Public Opinion Poll on Iraqi Kurdistan's Independence', EKurd Daily, 3 October 2012, http://ekurd.net/mismas/articles/misc2012/10/state6535.htm

18. Kamal Chomani, 'Gorran Leader Mustafa's Hard Choices', *Fikra Forum*, Washington Institute for Near East Policy, March 2016, http://www.washingtoninstitute.org/fikraforum/view/gorran-leader-mustafas-hard-choices

19. Dalshad Abdullah in *al-Sharq al-Awsat*, 17 September 2016, http://aawsat.com/node/455206

20. Dalshad Abdullah in *al-Sharq al-Awsat*, 12 October 2016, http://aawsat.com/node/473181

21. Hushnak Ausi in *al-Hayat*, 11 October 2016, http://www.alhayat.com/Articles/11533948/

22. Bassam Francis in *al-Hayat*, 6 September 2016, http://www.alhayat.com/Articles/17226202/

23. Alessandria Masi, 'After Liberation of Kobane, Kurdish Battle with ISIS is not Over,' *International Business Times*, 26 January 2015, http://www.

ibtimes.com/after-liberation-kobane-kurdish-battle-isis-not-over-1795310; Aaron Stein and Michelle Foley, 'The YPG–PKK Connection', *Atlantic Council blogs*, 26 January 2016, http://www.atlanticcouncil.org/blogs/menasource/the-ypg-pkk-connection

24. Reuters, 8 October 2014, http://www.reuters.com/article/us-mideast-crisis-usa-kerry-idUSKCN0HX1TG20141008

25. Ayla Albarak and Joe Parkinson in the *Wall Street Journal*, 1 February 2015, http://www.wsj.com/articles/city-of-ruin-remains-after-islamic-state-defeat-in-kobani-1422843673

26. Reuters, 26 September 2015, http://www.reuters.com/article/us-mideast-crisis-usa-equipment-idUSKCN0RP2HO20150926

27. According to *al-Sharq al-Awsat*, 22 July 2017, a US general required a new name for a new force, and the YPG came up with Syrian Democratic Forces a day later: https//aawsat.com/node/980021

28. 'Syrian Democratic Forces', *Global Security*, 5 June 2016, http://www.globalsecurity.org/military/world/para/sdf.htm

29. Ghassan Charbel interview with Salih Muslim, *al-Hayat*, 25 July 2015, http://www.alhayat.com/Articles/10184624

30. Ahmed Yousef, chairman of Afrin University, quoted in EKurd Daily: 'Will Syrian Kurdistan Succeed at Self-Sufficiency?' 4 May 2016, http://ekurd.net/syrian-kurdistan-self-sufficiency-2016–05–04

31. For a more detailed survey, see Abboud, *Syria*, pp. 164–71.

32. Si Sheppard, 'What the Syrian Kurds Have Wrought', *The Atlantic*, 25 October 2016, http://www.theatlantic.com/international/archive/2016/10/kurds-rojava-syria-isis-iraq-assad/505037/

33. Karen DeYoung, 'Biden Warns Kurds Not to Seek Separate Enclave on Turkish–Syrian Border', *Washington Post*, 24 August 2016, https://www.washingtonpost.com/world/biden-visits-turkey-on-mission-to-repair-strained-relations/2016/08/24/bc684904–6a04–11e6–99bf-f0cf3a6449a6_story.html?utm_term=.1dd16d8c0752

34. *Al-Hayat*, 19 August 2016, http://www.alhayat.com/Articles/16930104/

35. *Aksalser*, 23 August 2016, http://www.aksalser.com/news/2016/08/23

36. All4syria, 23 August 2016, http://all4syria.info/Archive/337720

37. *Syrian Civil War Map* website gives a 2017 estimate of 50,000 for the YPG alone: http://syriancivilwarmap.com/syrian-democratic-forces/

38. Rudaw, 19 April 2016, http://rudaw.net/english/kurdistan/190420165

39. In a 2009 Iraqi National Media Center survey of 4,500 Iraqis, 72 per cent rejected federalism: *Promedia: Iraqi PM Wants Constitution Amendment to Strengthen Central Government*, 21 January 2009, http://www.aliraqi.org/forums/archive/index.php/t-91449.html

40. For discussion of the issues, see Brendan O'Leary, 'Power-Sharing,

Pluralist Federation, and Federacy', in Brendan O'Leary, John McGarry, and Khalid Salih (eds.), *The Future of Kurdistan in Iraq* (Philadelphia: University of Pennsylvania Press, 2005), pp. 47–91.

41. Mohammed Salih, 'Kurds Concerned about Baghdad's Increasing Military Prowess', *al-Monitor*, 18 August 2016, http://www.al-monitor.com/pulse/originals/2016/08/kurds-concerns-baghdad-weapons-iraq.html

42. Mira Rojkan, *Basnews*, 2 December 2016,. http://basnews.com/index.php/en/news/kurdistan/315228http://basnews.com/index.php/en/news/kurdistan/315228

43. Bassam Francis in *al-Hayat*, 25 June 2016, http://www.alhayat.com/Articles/16270872/

44. See, for example, KRG national security chief Masrour Barzani in EKurd Daily, 6 October 2016, http://ekurd.net/iraq-land-grabbed-kurdish-2016-10-06

45. Human Rights Watch, *Marked With an 'X'*, November 2016, https://www.hrw.org/report/2016/11/13/marked-x/iraqi-kurdish-forces-destruction-villages-homes-conflict-isis

46. Glen Field, 'Kurdistan Denies Allegations its Forces Destroyed Homes in Areas Captured from ISIS', *Rudaw*, 13 November 2016, http://rudaw.net/english/kurdistan/131120162

47. Inspector General, US Department of Defense, *Assessment of US and Coalition Efforts to Train, Advise, Assist, and Equip the Kurdish Security Forces in Iraq*, 14 December 2016, p. 15: http://www.dodig.mil/pubs/documents/DODIG-2017-033.pdf

48. For comment on a confederal path, see Brendan O'Leary interview with *Kurdistan 24*, 25 November 2015, http://www.kurdistan24.net/en/interview/c0b16021-4ef6-484f-bcd7-574b5af208fa; Gareth Stansfield, 'The Islamic State, the Kurdistan Region and the Future of Iraq', *International Affairs* 90:6 (2014), p. 1348.

49. Hazal Ateş, 'Esad'in "Kürt kartı" Barzani'ye geçti', *Sabah*, 13 July 2012, http://www.sabah.com.tr/gundem/2012/07/13/esadin-kurt-karti-barzaniye-gecti

50. *Al-Monitor*, 21 May 2013, http://www.al-monitor.com/pulse/security/2013/05/tensions-iraqi-kurdistan-syria-barzani.html

51. Hisham Arafat in *Kurdistan24*, 7 June 2016, http://www.kurdistan24.net/en/news/6de7cb99-442d-4a60-95de-3b591cc7c514/Kurdistan-Region%E2%80%93Rojava-border-opened-after-three-month-closure

52. Amberin Zaman interview with Masoud Barzani, *al-Monitor*, 22 March 2016, http://www.al-monitor.com/pulse/originals/2016/03/turkey-iraq-syria-kurds-massoud-barzani-interview.html

53. Ghassan Charbel interview with Salih Muslim, *al-Hayat*, 28 July 2015, http://alhayat.com/Articles/10246856

54. Ekurd Daily, 16 September 2015, http://ekurd.net/barzani-meets-muslim-in-erbil-2015–09–16

55. Dalshad Abdullah, *al-Sharq al-Awsat*, 17 November 2016, http://aawsat.com/node/786431

56. *Al-Hayat*, 17 December 2016, http://www.alhayat.com/Articles/19116532/

57. *Al-Hayat*, 17 December 2016.

58. Sevil Ercuş in *Hürriyet Daily News*, 26 February 2017, http://www.hurriyetdailynews.com/turkish-leaders-meet-for-second-time-in-week-with-iraqi-kurdish-leader-barzani-.aspx?pageID=238&NID=110207&NewsCatID=352

59. Wladimir van Wilgenburg, 'Kurds, Baghdad Scuffle for Control of Oil-Rich Kirkuk', *Middle East Eye*, 17 September 2015, http://www.middleeasteye.net/news/kurds-baghdad-scuffle-control-oil-rich-kirkuk-550887657

60. Umar Sitar in *al-Hayat*, 5 April 2017, http://www.alhayat.com/Articles/21126197/

61. Umar Sitar in *al-Hayat*, 5 April 2017.

62. *Al-Hayat*, 7 April 2017, http://www.alhayat.com/Articles/21163368/

63. Reuters, 26 July 2017, https://www.reuters.com/article/us-russia-iraq-tanks-idUSKBN1AA2A8

64. EKurd Daily, 18 July 2017, http://ekurd.net/irans-referendum-isolation-kurds-2017–07–18

4. TURKEY AND THE WAR ZONE

1. For discussion of Davutoğlu's outlook, see Cenk Saraçoğlu and Özhan Demirkol, 'Nationalism and Foreign Policy Discourse in Turkey under the AKP Rule: Geography, History and National Identity', *British Journal of Middle Eastern Studies* 42:3 (2015), pp. 301–19.

2. Pinar Tremblay in *al-Monitor*, 7 October 2013, http://www.al-monitor.com/pulse/originals/2013/10/personal-enmity-between-assad-and-erdogan.html

3. Anthony King, 'Two Kinds of Social Theory: The Myth and Reality of Social Existence', in Peter Martin and Alex Dennis (eds.), *Human Agents and Social Structures* (Manchester: Manchester University Press, 2010), p. 164.

4. Aylin Ş. Görener and Meltem Ş. Ucal, 'The Personality and Leadership Style of Recep Tayyip Erdoğan: Implications for Turkish Foreign Policy', *Turkish Studies* 12:3 (2011), p. 375.

5. Phillips, *The Battle for Syria*; Henri J. Barkey, 'Turkey's Syria Predicament', *Survival* 56:6 (2014–15), pp. 113–34; Özlem Demirtaş-Bagdonis,

'Reading Turkish Foreign Policy on Syria: The AKP's Construction of a Great Power Identity and the Politics of Grandeur', *Turkish Studies* 15:1 (2014), pp. 139–55.

6. Yahya al-Antaki, *Ta'rikh al-Antaki*, ed. Umar Abd al-Salam Tadmuri (Tripoli [Lebanon]: Jarrus Bris, 1990), pp. 413–18 and 421–2.

7. Meliha Altunışık, 'Turkey at a Crossroads: The Inflexibility of Turkey's Policy in Syria', *IEMed Mediterranean Yearbook 2016* (Barcelona: IEMed Publications, 2016), p. 42.

8. See, for example, Ghassan Charbel interview with Salih Muslim, *al-Hayat*, 27 July 2015, http://www.alhayat.com/Articles/10224248

9. Cengiz Çandar in *al-Monitor*, 29 July 2013, http://www.al-monitor. com/pulse/en/originals/2013/07/turkey-changes-position-on-syrian-kurds.html

10. Mustafa Akyol interview with Ahmet Davutoğlu, *Hürriyet Daily News*, 10 April 2013, http://www.hurriyetdailynews.com/the-world-according-to-ahmet-davutoglu.aspx?pageID=449&nID=44578&NewsCatID=411

11. Turkey demanded the corridors, which automatically meant no-fly zones, from the beginning of 2012: Colum Lynch, 'France, Turkey Call for Humanitarian Corridors in Syria', *Foreign Policy*, 15 February 2012, http://foreignpolicy.com/2012/02/15/france-turkey-call-for-humanitarian-corridors-in-syria/

12. Erdoğan had in mind 'something like the example of Kosovo, the Syrian regime won't be able to continue': Reuters, 30 August 2013, http://www.reuters.com/article/us-syria-crisis-turkey-erdogan-idUSBRE97T0VZ20130830

13. Merve Tahiroğlu and Jonathan Schanzer, *Islamic State Networks in Turkey*, Foundation for Defense of Democracies, March 2017, http://www. defenddemocracy.org/media-hit/islamic-state-networks-in-turkey/; Aaron Stein, *Islamic State Networks in Turkey*, Atlantic Council, October 2016, http://www.publications.atlanticcouncil.org/islamic-state-networks-in-turkey/; 'Looking for ISIL [ISIS]: How Jihadists Operate among Turks', *Hürriyet Daily News*, 22 September 2014, http://www. hurriyetdailynews.com/looking-for-isil-how-turks-become-jihadists.asp x?pageID=238&nID=72054&NewsCatID=352

14. International Crisis Group, 'Turkey and Iran: Bitter Friends, Bosom Rivals', *Crisis Group Middle East Briefing No. 51*, p. 8, https://www.crisisgroup.org/middle-east-north-africa/gulf-and-arabian-peninsula/iran/b051-turkey-and-iran-bitter-friends-bosom-rivals

15. Can Dündar, chief editor of *Cumhuriyet*, in *The Guardian*, 28 December 2015, https://www.theguardian.com/commentisfree/2015/dec/28/truth-president-erdogan-jailed-turkey-regime-state-security-crime;

Ahmet Şık in *Cumhuriyet*, 12 February 2015, http://www.cumhuriyet.com.tr/haber/turkiye/213011/Cihatcilara_TSK_dan__topcu__destegi..._iste_o_telefon_konusmalari.html

16. Soner Çağaptay and Tyler Evans, 'Turkey's Changing Relations with Iraq: Kurdistan Up, Baghdad Down', *Policy Focus 122*, Washington Institute for Near East Policy, October 2012, http://www.washingtoninstitute.org/policy-analysis/view/turkeys-changing-relations-with-iraq-kurdistan-up-baghdad-down

17. Bilgay Duman, 'Turkey's Iraq Policy after 2003 in the Light of the Recent Visit of Prime Minister Erdoğan to Iraq', *Ortadoğu Analiz* 3:28 (2011), pp. 19–25.

18. Semih Idiz in *al-Monitor*, 29 October 2013, http://www.al-monitor.com/pulse/originals/2013/10/erdogan-maliki-ties-rebuild-turkey-iraq-rapprochement.html

19. Soner Çağaptay, Christina Fidan, and Ege Sacikara, 'Turkey and the KRG: An Undeclared Economic Commonwealth', *Policy Watch 2387*, Washington Institute for Near East Policy, 16 March 2016, http://www.washingtoninstitute.org/policy-analysis/view/turkey-and-the-krg-an-undeclared-economic-commonwealth

20. For analysis of KRG–Turkey relations in 2014–15, see Natali, 'The Kurdish Quasi-State'.

21. Author's discussion with Peshmerga officers, Mosul dam, November 2014.

22. Deniz Zeyrek in *Hürriyet Daily News*, 23 September 2014, http://www.hurriyetdailynews.com/syrian-rebels-freed-isil-militants-for-the-release-of-turkish-hostages-.aspx?pageID=517&nID=72049&NewsCatID=510

23. Jenna Krajeski, 'What Kobani Means for Turkey's Kurds', *New Yorker*, 8 November 2014, http://www.newyorker.com/news/news-desk/kobani-means-turkeys-kurds

24. Alessandria Masi in *International Business Times*, 9 October 2014, http://www.ibtimes.com/isis-threatens-conquer-turkey-new-isis-video-message-erdogan-1702654

25. Anadolu Agency, 2 March 2015, http://aa.com.tr/en/politics/turkey-saudi-arabia-to-boost-support-for-syrian-opposition/70529

26. Quoted by Randa Taqi al-Din and Joyce Karam in *al-Hayat*, 28 April 2015, http://alhayat.com/Articles/8836892/

27. Bashar al-Assad televised speech to union and professional association leaders, 26 July 2015: *al-Hayat*, 27 July 2015, http://alhayat.com/Articles/10226220/

28. Anne Barnard, Michael Gordon, and Eric Schmitt, 'Turkey and US Plan to Create Syria "Safe Zone" Free of ISIS', *New York Times*, 27 July

2015, http://www.nytimes.com/2015/07/28/world/middleeast/tur-key-and-us-agree-on-plan-to-clear-isis-from-strip-of-northern-syria. html?_r=0

29. Serkan Demirtaş in *Hürriyet Daily News*, 25 July 2015, http://www. hurriyetdailynews.com/turkey-us-to-create-isil-free-zone-inside-syria. aspx?pageID=238&nID=85906&NewsCatID=510

30. Laila Bassam and Tom Perry, Reuters, 6 October 2015, http://www. reuters.com/article/us-mideast-crisis-syria-soleimani-insigh-idUS KCN0S02BV20151006

31. Bassam and Perry, Reuters, 6 October 2015.

32. Mikhail Barabanov, 'Why Russia Needs an Exit Strategy in Syria', *The National Interest*, 9 October 2015, http://nationalinterest.org/feature/ why-russia-needs-exit-strategy-syria-14044

33. Russian deputy foreign minister Sergei Ryabkov put federalism on the table in public comments on 29 February 2016, clearly part of the punitive Russian posture towards Turkey. See Maria Tsvetkova, 'Russia Says Federal Model is Possible for Syria in Future', Reuters, 1 March 2016, http://in.reuters.com/article/mideast-crisis-russia-syria-idIN KCN0W21TP

34. Mountaha al-Ramahi interview with Recep Tayyip Erdoğan, al-Arabiya, 27 December 2015, https://english.alarabiya.net/en/webtv/pro-grams/special-interview/2015/12/28/Erdogan-warns-against-Mideast-sectarian-divisions.html

35. Murat Yetkin, 'Story of Secret Diplomacy that Ended Russia–Turkey Jet Crisis', *Hürriyet Daily News*, 9 August 2016, http://www.hurri-yetdailynews.com/story-of-secret-diplomacy-that-ended-russia-turkey-jet-crisis.aspx?pageID=238&nID=102629&NewsCatID=409

36. *Cumhuriyet*, 11 August 2016, reported an apparent softening in Turkey's position, http://www.cumhuriyet.com.tr/haber/dunya/582785/ Turkiye_den_Esad_a_yesil_isik.html. In a 19 August 2016 interview with *al-Sharq al-Awsat*, Foreign Minister Çavuşoğlu denied any change, http://aawsat.com/home/article/717801/

37. Erika Solomon, 'Outside Help behind Rebel Advances in Aleppo', *Financial Times*, 8 August 2016, https://www.ft.com/content/da076 830-5d77-11e6-a72a-bd4bf1198c63

38. See, for example, Barçın Yinanç interview with Nihat Özcan, 'Post-Coup Attempt Restructuring Means Turkish Army May No Longer be Functional', *Hürriyet Daily News*, 7 November 2016, http://www.hur-riyetdailynews.com/post-coup-attempt-restructuring-means-turk-ish-army-may-no-longer-be-functional-ozcan.aspx?PageID=238&NID= 105805&NewsCatID=338

39. *Yeni Şafak*, 20 September 2016, http://www.yenisafak.com/gundem/el-baba-kadar-temizleyecegiz-2533996
40. Yusuf al-Sharif and Salih Sidqiyan in *al-Hayat*, 1 September 2016, http://www.alhayat.com/Articles/17152088
41. *t24* news channel, 21 September 2016, http://t24.com.tr/haber/erdoganin-el-nusra-sozleri-itiraf-gibi-turkiyeyle-rusya-arasinda-verhalepi-al-babi-mutabakati-mi-yapildi,366349; Sa'id Abd al-Razzaq and Caroline Akoum in *al-Sharq al-Awsat*, 2 November 2016, http://aawsat.com/home/article/775236/
42. Al-Antaki, *Ta'rikh*, p. 324; Wesam Farag, 'The Aleppo Question: A Byzantine–Fatimid Conflict of Interests in Northern Syria in the Later Tenth Century AD', *Byzantine and Modern Greek Studies* 14 (1990), pp. 44–60.
43. Tom Perry and Laila Bassam, Reuters, 7 June 2016, http://www.reuters.com/article/us-mideast-crisis-syria-assad-idUSKCN0YT18Z
44. Sa'id Abd al-Razzaq in *al-Sharq al-Awsat*, 28 November 2016, http://aawsat.com/node/794511
45. *Hürriyet Daily News*, 27 Oct. 2016, http://www.hurriyetdailynews.com/turkey-to-us-drop-pyd-lets-free-raqqa-together.aspx?PageID=238&NID=105423&NewsCatID=352
46. Sam Heller, 'Turkey's "Turkey First" Syria Policy', Century Foundation, 12 April 2017, p. 9, https://tcf.org/content/report/turkeys-turkey-first-syria-policy/
47. *Milliyet*, 30 March 2017, http://www.milliyet.com.tr/firat-kalkani-harekatinin-216-gundem-2423279/
48. *Milliyet*, 30 March 2017.
49. Heller, 'Turkey's "Turkey First" Syria Policy', p. 9.
50. Catherine Holmes, *Basil II and the Governance of Empire (976–1025)* (Oxford: Oxford University Press, 2005), p. 321.
51. Dashad Abdullah in *al-Sharq al-Awsat*, 5 and 19 August 2016, http://aawsat.com/node/433766 and http://aawsat.com/node/423386
52. Hamza Moustafa in *al-Sharq al-Awsat*, 14 October 2015, http://aawsat.com/node/474761
53. Tulay Karadeniz and Ercan Gurses, Reuters, 13 October 2016, http://www.reuters.com/article/us-mideast-crisis-iraq-turkey-idUSKCN12C0KF
54. *Hürriyet Daily News*, 11 October 2016, http://www.hurriyetdailynews.com/erdogan-slams-isolation-of-turkey-from-iraq-operation.aspx?PageID=238&NID=104861&NewsCatID=510; *Cumhuriyet*, 11 October 2016, http://www.cumhuriyet.com.tr/haber/dunya/614277/Irak_tan__Sen_benim_kalitemde_degilsin__diyen_Erdogan_a_yanit__Atese_benzin_doktu.html

55. *Al-Hayat*, 13 October 2016, http://alhayat.com/Articles/17884716/
56. Natali, 'The Kurdish Quasi-State', p. 157, comments on Erdoğan's preference to stress religious over ethnic identity.
57. Sa'id Abdul Razzaq in *al-Sharq al-Awsat*, 22 November 2016, http://aawsat.com/node/790021
58. *Cumhuriyet*, 29 November 2016, http://www.cumhuriyet.com.tr/haber/siyaset/637587/Erdogan_dan_cok_tartisilacak_sozler__Suriye_ye_Esed_in_hukumdarligina_son_vermek_icin_girdik.html
59. Andrew Osborne, Reuters, 30 November 2016, http://www.reuters.com/article/us-mideast-crisis-syria-russia-erdogan-idUSKBN13P136
60. *Novorossia Today*, 2 December 2016, http://novorossia.today/151649-2/
61. Humeyra Pamuk and Nick Tattersall, Reuters, 29 November 2016, http://www.reuters.com/article/us-mideast-crisis-syria-turkey-idUSKBN13O29M?il=0
62. *Cumhuriyet*, 21 December 2016, http://www.cumhuriyet.com.tr/haber/dunya/648479/Turkiye_nin_Suriye_politikasi_Moskova_da_coktu..._Birinci_maddeye_dikkat_.html
63. Rod Nordland in the *New York Times*, 20 January 2017, https://www.nytimes.com/2017/01/20/world/middleeast/russia-turkey-syria-deal.html?mcubz=2
64. Maxim Suchkov in *al-Monitor*, 27 January 2017, http://www.al-monitor.com/pulse/originals/2017/01/russia-meeting-syria-opposition-moscow-constitution.html
65. Mahmut Bozarslan in *al-Monitor*, 24 October 2016, http://www.al-monitor.com/pulse/originals/2016/10/turkey-russia-mediates-between-kurds-and-assad.html
66. Turkish official in discussion with the author, Ankara, April 2017.
67. Orhan Coskun and Ellen Francis, Reuters, citing Munir al-Sayal of Ahrar al-Sham, 28 December 2016, http://www.reuters.com/article/us-mideast-crisis-syria-idUSKBN14H0WE
68. *Al-Hayat*, 25 June 2017, http://alhayat.com/Articles/22544729/
69. *Hürriyet Daily News*, 22 February 2017, http://www.hurriyetdailynews.com/turkey-to-us-act-over-syrias-manbij-or-well-reconsider-.aspx?pageID=238&nID=110057&NewsCatID=352; *al-Hayat*, 6 March 2017, http://www.alhayat.com/Articles/20543264/
70. *Cumhuriyet*, 8 January 2017, http://www.cumhuriyet.com.tr/haber/siyaset/657276/Basbakan_Yildirim__Irak_Turkiye_iliskilerinde_yeni_donem_basladi.html
71. Turkish official in discussion with author, Ankara, April 2017.
72. Interview with Anadolu Agency, reported in *al-Monitor*, 19 April 2017,

http://www.al-monitor.com/pulse/originals/2017/04/iraq-turkey-iran-sinjar-pkk-kurdistan.html

73. Bilgay Duman, 'The Situation of Turkmen and the Turkmen Areas', *ORSAM Report 203*, August 2016, p. 19, http://www.orsam.org.tr/files/Raporlar/203/203eng.pdf

74. Interview with al-Jazeera, reported in *Rudaw*, 20 April 2017, http://www.rudaw.net/english/middleeast/20042017

75. Turkish official to author, Ankara, April 2017.

EPILOGUE

1. See, for example, Jonathan Spyer, 'Who Will Dominate the Post-Islamic State Landscape in Iraq and Syria?', *Jerusalem Post*, 10 March 2017, http://www.jpost.com/International/Behind-the-lines-After-ISIS-483789; Michael Young, 'Developments in Eastern Syria Indicate we are Entering a New Phase in the Country's Conflict', *Diwan: Syria in Crisis*, 1 June 2017, Carnegie Middle East Center, http://carnegie-mec.org/diwan/70124?lang=en

2. *Al-Sharq al-Awsat*, 23 August 2017, https//aawsat.com/node/1006036

3. Asa'ad Talhami in *al-Hayat*, 8 September 2017, http://www.alhayat.com/Articles/23924074/; Roi Kais and Yoav Zitun, *Ynet*, 7 September 2017, https://www.ynetnews.com/articles/0,7340,L-5013284,00.html

4. *Al-Sharq al-Awsat*, 22 August 2017, https//aawsat.com/node/1004981

5. *Al-Hayat*, 27 July 2017, http://www.alhayat.com/Articles/23108572/

6. *Al-Hayat*, 27 July 2017.

7. *Al-Hayat*, 5 September 2017, http://www.alhayat.com/Articles/2386 1815/

8. Judith Kazim, *al-Hayat*, 1 August 2017, http://www.alhayat.com/Articles/23189338/

9. *Al-Sharq al-Awsat*, 5 August 2017, https//aawsat.com/node/991031

10. Al-Nusra itself apparently seeks an arrangement with Turkey and perhaps even with Russia. See Charles Lister, 'Turkey's Idlib Incursion and the HTS Question', *War on the Rocks*, 31 October 2017, https://warontherocks.com/2017/10/turkeys-idlib-incursion-and-the-hts-question-understanding-the-long-game-in-syria/; For data on Turkey's enhanced involvement in October 2017, including to restrict the Afrin Kurds, also see *al-Hayat*, 14 October 2017, http://www.alhayat.com/Articles/24655657/

11. Nabih Bulos, 'Humanitarian Groups Fear Aid is being Diverted to Terrorist Group', *Los Angeles Times*, 16 August 2017, http://www.latimes.com/world/middleeast/la-fg-syria-idlib-aid-20170816-story.html

12. *Al-Hayat*, 26 August 2017, http://www.alhayat.com/Articles/236706 78/
13. *Al-Hayat*, 28 September 2017, http://www.alhayat.com/Articles/24317708/
14. Colum Lynch and Robbie Gramer, 'Tillerson Ready to Let Russia Decide Assad's Fate', *Foreign Policy*, 3 July 2017, http://foreignpolicy.com/2017/07/03/tillerson-ready-to-let-russia-decide-assads-fate/
15. Yunus Paksoy in *Daily Sabah*, 15 August 2017, https://www.dailysabah.com/diplomacy/2017/08/15/iranian-chief-of-staff-visits-ankara-as-common-stance-sought-in-idlib-afrin
16. Ghassan Charbel interview with Masoud Barzani, *al-Sharq al-Awsat*, 30 August 2017, https//aawsat.com/node/1011886
17. *Al-Hayat*, 17 October 2017, citing Tasnim news agency, http://www.alhayat.com/Articles/24722708/
18. Amnesty International, *Human Slaughterhouse: Mass Hangings and Extermination at Saydnaya Prison, Syria*, February 2017, https://www.amnesty.org/en/documents/mde24/5415/2017/en/
19. Amnesty International, *Human Slaughterhouse*, p. 13.

SELECT BIBLIOGRAPHY

Some useful sources in the literature

Abboud, Samer. *Syria*. Cambridge: Polity Press, 2016.

Ajami, Fouad. *The Syrian Rebellion*. Stanford: Hoover Institution Press, 2012.

Allsopp, Harriet. *The Kurds of Syria: Political Parties and Identity in the Middle East*. London: I. B. Tauris, 2015.

Altunışık, Meliha. 'Turkey at a Crossroads: The Inflexibility of Turkey's Policy in Syria'. In *IEMed Mediterranean Yearbook 2016*, pp. 39–44. Barcelona: IEMed Publications, 2016.

Barkey, Henri. 'Turkey's Syria Predicament'. *Survival* 56 no. 6 (2014–15), pp. 113–34.

De Châtel, Francesca. 'The Role of Drought and Climate Change in the Syrian Uprising: Untangling the Triggers of the Revolution'. *Middle Eastern Studies* 50 no. 4 (2014), pp. 521–35.

Gerges, Fawaz. *ISIS: A History*. Princeton: Princeton University Press, 2016.

Demirtaş-Bagdonis, Özlem. 'Reading Foreign Policy on Syria: The AKP's Construction of a Great Power Identity and the Politics of Grandeur'. *Turkish Studies* 15 no. 1 (2014), pp. 139–55.

Goldsmith, Leon. *Cycle of Fear: Syria's Alawites in Peace and War*. London: Hurst & Company, 2015

Gunter, Michael. *Out of Nowhere: The Kurds of Syria in Peace and War*. London: Hurst & Company, 2014.

Haddad, Bassam. *Business Networks in Syria: The Political Economy of Authoritarian Resilience*. Stanford: Stanford University Press, 2011.

Kerr, Michael, and Craig Larkin (eds). *The Alawis of Syria: War, Faith and Politics in the Levant*. London: Hurst & Company, 2015.

Leenders, Reinould. 'How the Syrian Regime Outsmarted its Enemies'. *Current History* 112 no. 758 (2013), pp. 331–7.

Lesch, David. *Syria: The Fall of the House of Assad*. London: Yale University Press, 2012.

SELECT BIBLIOGRAPHY

Lister, Charles. *The Syrian Jihad: al-Qaeda, the Islamic State and the Evolution of an Insurgency*. London: Hurst & Company, 2015.

McCants, William. *The ISIS Apocalypse: The History, Strategy, and Doomsday Vision of the Islamic State*. New York: St. Martin's Press, 2015.

Natali, Denise. 'The Kurdish Quasi-State: Leveraging Political Limbo'. *Washington Quarterly* 38 no. 2 (2015), pp. 145–64.

O'Leary, Brendan. 'Power-Sharing, Pluralist Federation, and Federacy'. In *The Future of Kurdistan in Iraq*, edited by Brendan O'Leary, John McGarry, and Khalid Salih, pp. 47–91. Philadelphia: University of Pennsylvania Press, 2005.

Phillips, Christopher. *The Battle for Syria: International Rivalries in the New Middle East*. London: Yale University Press, 2016.

Stansfield, Gareth. 'The Islamic State, the Kurdistan Region and the Future of Iraq'. *International Affairs* 90 no. 6 (2014), pp. 1329–1350.

Stern, Jessica, and J. M. Berger. *ISIS: The State of Terror*. New York: HarperCollins Publishers, 2015.

Weiss, Michael, and Hassan Hassan. *ISIS: Inside the Army of Terror*. New York: Regan Arts, 2015.

Wieland, Carsten. *Syria—A Decade of Lost Chances: Repression and Revolution from Damascus Spring to Arab Spring*. Seattle: Cune Press, 2012.

Yassin-Kassab, Robin and Leila Al-Shami. *Burning Country: Syrians in Revolution and War*. London: Pluto Press, 2016.

A selection of internet sources

Military affairs

Barabanov, Mikhail. 'Why Russia Needs an Exit Strategy in Syria', *The National Interest*, 9 October 2015. http://nationalinterest.org/feature/why-russia-needs-exit-strategy-syria-14044

Cafarella, Jennifer. 'Middle East Security Report 25: Jabhat al-Nusra in Syria', Institute for the Study of War, December 2014. http://www.understandingwar.org/report/jabhat-al-nusra-syria

Gartenstein-Ross, Daveed. 'How Many Fighters does the Islamic State Really Have', *War on the Rocks*, 9 February 2015. https://warontherocks.com/2015/02/how-many-fighters-does-the-islamic-state-really-have/

Holliday, Joseph. 'Middle East Security Report 3: Syria's Armed Opposition', Institute for the Study of War, March 2012. http://www.understandingwar.org/report/syrias-armed-opposition

Khaddour, Kheder. 'Assad's Officer Ghetto: Why the Syrian Army Remains Loyal', *Regional Insight*, 4 November 2015, Carnegie Middle East Center. http://carnegie-mec.org/2015/11/04/assad-s-officer-ghetto-why-syrian-army-remains-loyal-pub-61449

SELECT BIBLIOGRAPHY

Mansour, Renad, and Faleh Jabar. *The Popular Mobilization Forces and Iraq's Future* (Beirut: Carnegie Middle East Center, 28 April 2017). http://carnegie-mec.org/2017/04/28/popular-mobilization-forces-and-iraq-s-future-pub-68810

Schwartzstein, Peter. 'The Islamic State's Scorched-Earth Strategy', *Foreign Policy*, 6 April 2016. http://foreignpolicy.com/2016/04/06/the-islamic-states-scorched-earth-strategy/

Spyer, Jonathan. 'After ISIS', *Jerusalem Post*, 10 March 2017. https://jonathanspyer.com/2017/03/11/after-isis/

See Jonathan Spyer's website (jonathanspyer.com) for six years of first-hand reporting and analysis across the Syria–Iraq war zone.

Stanford University. *Mapping Militant Organizations*. http://web.stanford.edu/group/mappingmilitants/cgi-bin/

Stein, Aaron. 'The Origins of Turkey's Buffer Zone in Syria', *War on the Rocks*, 11 December 2014. https://warontherocks.com/2014/12/the-origins-of-turkeys-buffer-zone-in-syria/

Syria Institute/PAX. *Siege Watch Quarterly Reports on Besieged Areas in Syria*. https://siegewatch.org/reports/

Political and economic aspects

Al-Tamimi, Aymenn. 'Observations on the New Islamic State Video "Structure of the Caliphate"', Aymenn Jawad Al-Tamimi's Blog, 6 July 2016. http://www.aymennjawad.org/2016/07/observations-on-the-new-islamic-state-video

Also see Al-Tamimi's Blog (aymennjawad.org) for a wide range of commentary on the Syria–Iraq war zone.

Çağaptay, Soner and Tyler Evans. 'Turkey's Changing Relations with Iraq: Kurdistan Up, Baghdad Down', *Policy Focus 122*, Washington Institute for Near East Policy, October 2012. http://www.washingtoninstitute.org/policy-analysis/view/turkeys-changing-relations-with-iraq-kurdistan-up-baghdad-down

Heißner, Stefan, Peter Neumann, John Holland-McCowan, and Rajan Basra. *Caliphate in Decline: An Estimate of Islamic State's Financial Fortunes*, International Centre for the Study of Radicalisation and Political Violence, King's College London, 2017. http://icsr.info/wp-content/uploads/2017/02/ICSR-Report-Caliphate-in-Decline-An-Estimate-of-Islamic-States-Financial-Fortunes.pdf

Heller, Sam. 'Turkey's "Turkey First" Syria Policy', Century Foundation, 12 April 2017. https://tcf.org/content/report/turkeys-turkey-first-syria-policy/

Khaddour, Kheder. *The Assad Regime's Hold on the Syrian State* (Beirut: Carnegie Middle East Center, 2015). http://carnegie-mec.org/2015/07/08/assad-regime-s-hold-on-syrian-state-pub-60608

SELECT BIBLIOGRAPHY

Krajeski, Jenna. 'What Kobani Means for Turkey's Kurds', *New Yorker*, 8 November 2014. http://www.newyorker.com/news/news-desk/kobani-means-turkeys-kurds

Lund, Aron. *Ulbrief No. 13: Syrian Jihadism*, Swedish Institute of International Affairs, 14 September 2012. https://www.scribd.com/document/137448880/Syrian-Jihadism-by-Aron-Lund

Mansour, Renad. 'The Sunni Predicament in Iraq', Carnegie Middle East Center, 3 March 2016. http://carnegie-mec.org/2016/03/03/sunni-predicament-in-iraq-pub-62924)

Mills, Robin. *Under the Mountains: Kurdish Oil and Regional Politics*, Oxford Institute for Energy Studies Paper: WPM 63, 2016. https://www.oxfordenergy.org/publications/under-the-mountains-kurdish-oil-and-regional-politics/

Peritz, Aki. 'The Great Iraqi Jail Break', *Foreign Policy*, 26 June 2014. http://foreignpolicy.com/2014/06/26/the-great-iraqi-jail-break/

Petroleum Economist special supplement. *The Rise of Kurdish Oil*, London, 2014. http://www.petroleum-economist.com/resources/reports/the-rise-of-kurdish-oil

Schneider, Tobias. 'The Decay of the Syrian Regime is Much Worse Than you Think', *War on the Rocks*, 31 August 2016. https://warontherocks.com/2016/08/the-decay-of-the-syrian-regime-is-much-worse-than-you-think/

Sheppard, Si. 'What the Syrian Kurds Have Wrought', *The Atlantic*, 25 October 2016. http://www.theatlantic.com/international/archive/2016/10/kurds-rojava-syria-isis-iraq-assad/505037/

Tahiroğlu, Merve, and Jonathan Schanzer, *Islamic State Networks in Turkey*, Foundation for Defense of Democracies, March 2017. http://www.defenddemocracy.org/media-hit/islamic-state-networks-in-turkey/

Tollast, Robert. 'The Civil Wars of Iraq's Sunni Tribes: Fault Lines within 8 Sunni Tribes and Sub-Tribes, 2003–2016', *Iraqi Thoughts*, 28 March 2016. http://1001iraqithoughts.com/2016/03/28/the-civil-wars-of-iraqs-sunni-tribes-fault-lines-within-8-sunni-tribes-and-sub-tribes-2003-2016/

Human rights issues

Amnesty International. *At Any Cost: The Civilian Catastrophe in West Mosul, Iraq*, July 2017. https://www.amnesty.org/en/latest/campaigns/2017/07/at-any-cost-civilian-catastrophe-in-west-mosul-iraq/

Amnesty International. *Human Slaughterhouse: Mass Hangings and Extermination at Saydnaya Prison, Syria*, February 2017. https://www.amnesty.org/en/documents/mde24/5415/2017/en/

Atlantic Council. *Breaking Aleppo*, February 2017. http://www.atlanticcouncil.org/publications/reports/breaking-aleppo

SELECT BIBLIOGRAPHY

Human Rights Watch. *Death from the Skies: Deliberate and Indiscriminate Air Strikes on Civilians*, April 2013. https://www.hrw.org/report/2013/04/10/death-skies/deliberate-and-indiscriminate-air-strikes-civilians

Human Rights Watch. *We've Never Seen Such Horror: Crimes against Humanity by Syrian Security Forces*, June 2011. https://www.hrw.org/report/2011/06/01/weve-never-seen-such-horror/crimes-against-humanity-syrian-security-forces

Human Rights Watch. *'You Can Still See Their Blood': Executions, Unlawful Killing, and Hostage Taking by Opposition Forces in Latakia Countryside*, October 2013. http://www.hrw.org/reports/2013/10/11/you-can-still-see-their-blood

Iraq Body Count. *Monthly Documented Civilian Deaths from Violence*. https://www.iraqbodycount.org/

Orton, Kyle. 'How Many Alawis Have Been Killed In Syria?' 20 May 2015. https://kyleorton1991.wordpress.com/2015/05/20/how-many-alawis-have-been-killed-in-syria/

Price, Megan, Anita Ghodes, and Patrick Ball. *Updated Statistical Analysis of Documentation of Killings in the Syrian Arab Republic, Commissioned by the Office of the UN High Commissioner for Human Rights* (San Francisco: Human Rights Data Analysis Group, 2014). http://www.ohchr.org/Documents/Countries/SY/HRDAGUpdatedReportAug2014.pdf

UN Human Rights Council. *Report of the Independent International Commission of Inquiry on the Syrian Arab Republic A/HRC/21/50: Advance Edited Version*, 15 August 2012. http://www.ohchr.org/en/HRBodies/HRC/RegularSessions/Session21/Pages/ListReports.aspx

UN Human Rights Council. *Report of the Independent International Commission of Inquiry on the Syrian Arab Republic, A/HRC/34/64: Special Inquiry into the Events in Aleppo*, 2 February 2017. http://ap.ohchr.org/documents/dpage_e.aspx?si=A/HRC/34/64

War-zone mapping

Institute for the Study of War maps in Syria and Iraq reports. http://www.understandingwar.org/

Syria Live constantly updating maps with events display, for Syria and ISIS presence in Iraq. http://syria.liveuamap.com/

Wikimedia Commons constantly updating map series for Syria and Iraq. https://commons.wikimedia.org/wiki/File:Syrian,_Iraqi,_and_Lebanese_insurgencies.png

INDEX

INDEX

219

INDEX

INDEX

in Turkey, 64–5, 104, 109, 119,
133, 144, 147
Kurds in Syria, 6, 30, 33, 59, 75,
78, 103–9, 117–24, 173
under Ba'athist rule, 5, 106
and ISIS, 50, 60, 64, 66, 96,
118–20, 122
and KRG, 103, 107, 129
and Turkey, 64–5, 89, 96–7,
107, 119–22, 129–30,
139–40, 145–8, 152, 158–9,
169
and United States, 96–7,
107–9, 119–23, 158–9, 169,
198n108
see also Rojava
Kuwaiti financiers, 37
Kuwayris air base, 83

Lahoud, Émile, 24
Latakia, 47, 69–70, 71, 74–5, 78,
79, 146, 148
Lavrov, Sergei, 87
League of Arab States, 31
Lebanon, 4–5, 15, 20, 22, 24–5,
26, 40, 73, 163
militias in Syria, 33, 49, 58, 76,
139; see also Hezbollah
Libya, 50
Liwa al-Tawhid, 48, 139, 143, 179
local coordinating committees
(LCCs) in Syria, 30, 38, 179

Ma'an, 48
Ma'arouf, Jamal, 48, 73, 182
Ma'arrat al-Nu'man, 29, 36, 74, 76
Mahdi army, 45, 179–80
Makhlouf family, 27
Makhlouf, Rami, 23
Makhmur, 132
al-Maliki, Nouri, 2, 4, 43–7, 51,
53–4, 62–3, 82, 90, 109, 112,
125, 131, 134, 142

al-Malikiyah, 97
Malley, Robert, 69
Mamlouk, Ali, 123
Manbij, 96, 122, 148–9, 150, 151,
158
Marwanids, 145, 153
Masoum, Fouad, 63
Mastouma military camp, 75
Masyaf, 34
Mattis, James, 159
McGurk, Brett, 114, 129
Mezze air base, 86
Milli İstihbarat Teşkilatı (MİT),
140, 141, 145, 152, 180
Minnigh air base, 41
al-Mishraq, 92
Mohammad bin Salman, 166
Morek, 74, 78
Mosul, 1, 8, 126, 143, 160
ISIS occupation, 43, 53–4,
59–60, 68–9, 109
liberation from ISIS, 84, 90–4,
95, 113–14, 154
Mosul dam, 1, 111, 112, 143
Mu'adhamiyat al-Sham
[Mu'adhamiya], 86
Mubarak, Husni, 18, 26
Mughniya, Imad, 76
Mughniya, Jihad, 76
Muhammad al-Dawla, 153
al-Muhandis, Abu Mahdi, 90–1
Muslim Brotherhood, 30, 37, 139,
180
Muslim, Salih, 107, 120, 129,
139–40, 199n4
Mustafa, Nawishirwan, 115

Nahr al-Barid refugee camp, 26
Najaf, 96, 142, 166
Najib, Atef, 27
Naqshbandi order, 46, 51, 180

224

INDEX

INDEX

INDEX

INDEX